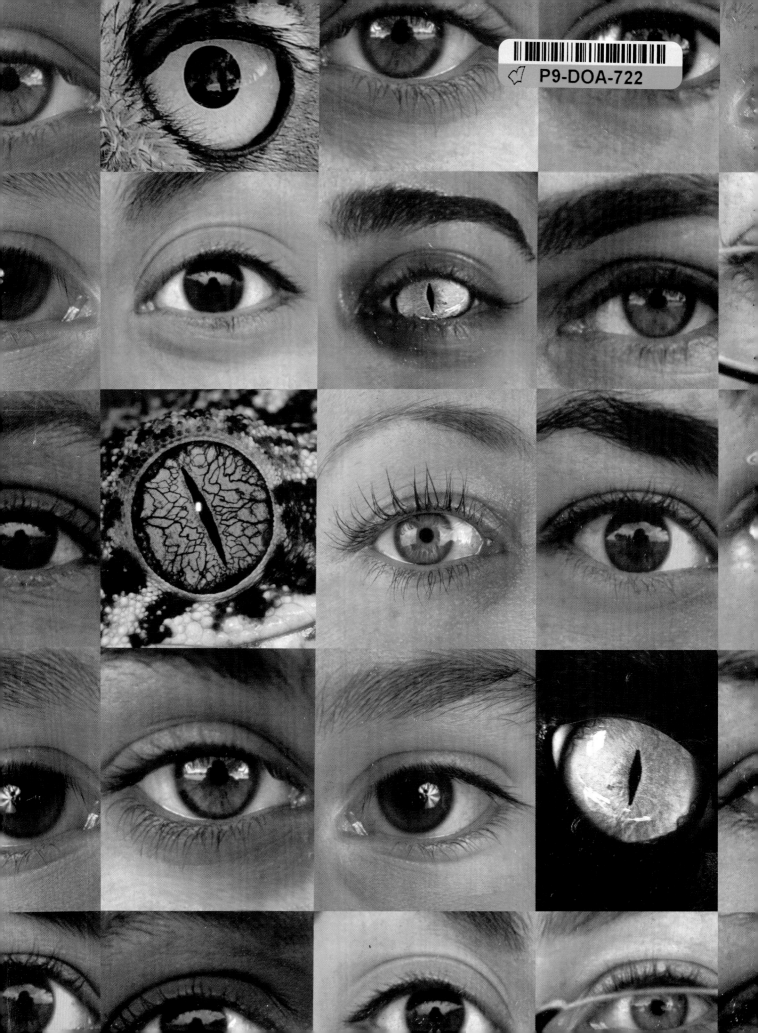

Exploratopia

by Pat Murphy, Ellen Macaulay, and the staff of the Exploratorium

Illustrated by Jason Gorski

This girl's eyes see just fine—
but they look a little odd.
Can you explain why? Turn
to page 6 to find out.

explO**ratorium**

LᴵB
1837

LITTLE, BROWN AND COMPANY
New York ⁓ Boston ⁓ London

**This book is dedicated to
the spirit of curiosity
that brings out the natural
explorer in everyone.**

Little, Brown and Company
1271 Avenue of the Americas, New York, NY 10020
Visit our Web site at www.lb-kids.com
First Edition: October 2006

Cover Photography Credits
dog with money glasses (see page 246), apple cross section (see page 129), frog wrangler
(see page 34), blue-tongued girl (see page 41): Amy Snyder; big eye (see page 8): Lily Rodriguez;
water strider (see page 107): David Hu, Brian Chan, John Bush; googly-eyed monster (see page
290): Amy Snyder; boy with meringue (see page 84): Lily Rodriguez; earth (see page 184): NASA;
butterfly (see page 123): Larvalbug.com; astronaut (see page 309): NASA

Library of Congress Cataloging-in-Publication Data

Murphy, Pat, 1955-
    Exploratopia / by Pat Murphy, Ellen Macaulay, and the staff of the Exploratorium ;
illustrated by Jason Gorski.
        p. cm.
    Includes bibliographical references and index.
    ISBN-13: 978-0-316-61281-4 (alk. paper)
    ISBN-10: 0-316-61281-2 (alk. paper)
      1. Science—Methodology—Juvenile literature. 2. Science—Experiments—Juvenile literature.
      I. Macaulay, Ellen. II. Gorski, Jason, ill. III. Exploratorium (Organization) IV. Title.

Q175.2.M87 2006
507.8—dc22   2006040942
10 9 8 7 6 5 4 3 2 1

Wals

Printed in the United States of America

Cover & interior layout by YAY! Design

Contents

Introduction

The Exploratorium is a museum where people make discoveries for themselves. The museum has created more than six hundred exhibits, and all of them run on curiosity.

You don't just look at the Exploratorium's exhibits—you play with them. At the Exploratorium, you can play with a captive tornado, freeze your shadow, make the world's biggest bubble, take white light apart to make colors, and put the colors back together to make white light. People from all over the world come to San Francisco, California, to experiment with the Exploratorium's exhibits and figure out how the world works.

I've been working at the Exploratorium for the past twenty years. Some of the things I've done over the years may not look a lot like work. I've spent time figuring out how to make lenses out of Jell-O (page 298), listening to sounds no one else can hear (page 22), singing in tune with my car (page 29), and learning how to mummify a hot dog (page 97). It's all part of the job.

Working at the Exploratorium has changed the way I see the world. Before I worked at the Exploratorium, I liked spending the day at the beach—a fine excuse to go for a swim and relax in the sun. I still like to visit the beach, but now I pay attention to all sorts of things I used to ignore. I search the sand grains for tiny jewels (page 174). I gather black sand with a magnet (page 172). I watch the clouds and try to predict the weather (page 182). The world is a much grander place than I ever knew before I worked at the Exploratorium.

Along with a team of writers, scientists, illustrators, photographers, educators, and explorers from the Exploratorium, I put together this book to help you see the world as a place to explore and experiment. Everywhere you look, everywhere you go, you can make discoveries, figure out how the world works, notice secrets that everyone else ignores. *Exploratopia* shows you how. This book shares many of the Exploratorium's favorite experiments and shows you how to explore on your own.

Scattered throughout this book, you'll find Tools for Exploration. These aren't tools you use with your hands—like hammers and screwdrivers. These are tools you use with your head—thinking tools. When you are trying to figure out how something works, these thinking tools can help you figure out how to think differently about a problem, how to look at a situation in a new way.

Maybe you are trying to figure out whether coffee grounds repel garden snails or wondering whether it will rain tomorrow. The Tools for Exploration can help. Anytime you get stuck while you are exploring, take another look at the list of Tools for Exploration on the next page. Try the tools one by one, until you find one that helps get you unstuck.

The experiments in *Exploratopia* help you start experimenting. But your experimenting doesn't end when you read the last instruction. This book is just the beginning. After you've tried our experiments, make up experiments of your own. Use the Tools for Exploration to help you take your explorations further. Who knows what discoveries you'll make!

—Pat Murphy

Tools for Exploration

1. Paying attention to stuff a lot of people ignore

Most people are so busy that they don't pay much attention to the world around them. True explorers take the time to stop and look and listen—and they notice things that most people don't. When you're experimenting, the things you notice will help you figure out other things you'd like to explore.

2. Comparing two things

One way to make sure you pay close attention is to compare two things. Ask yourself: How are these things different from each other? How are they the same? Sometimes, you make interesting discoveries when you start comparing two things that you think are the same. For instance, would you know if a dollar bill was real or fake? How would you know? (See page 242.)

3. Asking questions

Thinking of questions (and trying to figure out the answers) is part of trying to figure out how the world works. Think of some questions that you could answer by experimenting. A great way to begin a question is with the words: What would happen if . . . ? What would happen if I added more tail fins to my rocket? (See page 146.) What would happen if my ears were twice as big? (See page 19.)

4. Experimenting to test your ideas

Once you have a question, you can experiment to find out the answer. You think about what you want to do, then you make one change at a time and notice what happens. (If you make a lot of changes at the same time, you won't know which change made a difference.) For instance, you could add more tail fins to your rocket and launch it again. Does it fly higher? Does it fly farther? Or you could make ears that are twice the size of your ears. Do things sound the same?

5. Making predictions

When you make a prediction, you try to guess what's going to happen next. You guess—but your guess is what people call an "educated guess." That means you make your guess after experimenting and thinking about what has happened before. You have an idea about how something works. Making a prediction (and then experimenting to see what happens) will help you know if your idea is right.

6. Measuring and counting

Sometimes, when you do an experiment, you get results you can measure. You can measure how tall a tower you can make with whipped egg whites (page 90). You can count the number of wiggles you see in a rubber band that's wiggling back and forth really fast (page 343). The numbers you gather when you measure and count can help you figure out new questions to ask. (Like: How can I make a taller tower of egg whites?)

7. Keeping track of your discoveries

If you do a lot of experimenting (and we think you will!), you'll need a way to keep track of all the different things you notice along the way. Your memory just isn't good enough to hold all the information you collect. You can draw pictures of what you see, write down all the measurements you collect, and keep notes on what you notice. Then you can look at all the information you've gathered and see whether it all adds up to a big discovery!

8. Explaining what you see

You had a question—and you did an experiment. You paid attention to what happened. Now it's time to do some thinking. Can you explain what happened? Here's where your experimenting has a lot in common with detective work. A detective and a scientist both look at evidence. What evidence makes you think that your explanation is right? Can you think of other experiments that would give you more evidence? Can you think of other ways to explain what happened? Can you connect what you noticed to something else you know about?

9. Sharing your experience

Scientists don't just figure out how the world works. They figure something out—and then they tell other people about what they've discovered. They talk with other scientists and describe what they did, what happened, and how they explain what happened. Sometimes the other scientists don't agree with the explanation, and then they discuss the results and propose different explanations and suggest different experiments.

Tell other people about your experiments. Maybe they'll want to try the same experiment. Maybe they'll suggest ideas for more experiments. Or maybe they'll just be glad to know such an interesting young scientist!

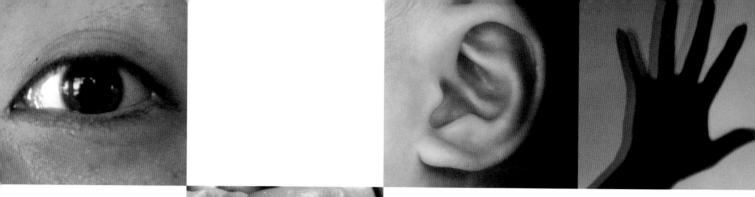

Part 1
Exploring Yourself

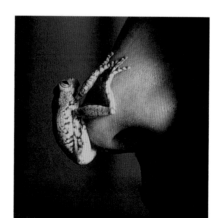

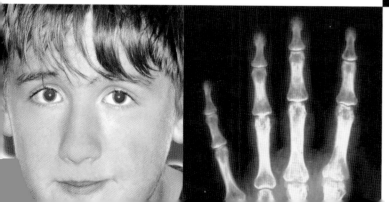

Your Eyes

Something seems terribly wrong with this person. Can you figure out what the problem is? One nose, one mouth, two eyes . . . That's it! Look closely at those eyes. How are the eyes in the photo different from your (we hope!) human eyes? Have you ever seen eyes like the ones in the photo before?

Looking at Eyes

Would you like to know more about your eyes? One of the best ways to get to know something better is to take a really close look at it and pay attention to what you see. You're in luck. What better way to take a close look than with your eyes?

Drawing Your Eye

You can start your scientific study of eyes with the ones you've got in your very own head. You can see an amazing number of things just by taking a close look at your own eyes.

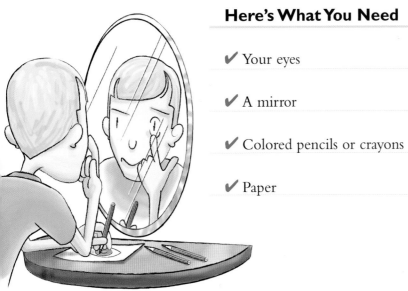

Here's What You Need

✔ Your eyes

✔ A mirror

✔ Colored pencils or crayons

✔ Paper

Here's What You Do

1. Take a close look at one of your eyes in the mirror.

2. Draw a picture of your eye. Make it larger than life-size and put in as many details as possible.

3. Try to include all the different colors in and around your eye.

4. Draw someone else's eye (if the person will sit still). Or let her draw yours.

What's Going On?

The part of your eye that you probably notice first is the colored circle known as the *iris*. Irises come in lots of colors, including brown, blue, green, hazel (a greenish brown combo), gray, or even violet. But no matter what color your eyes are, you'll see when you look closely that your iris isn't all one color. It's really many different colors. If you look hard, you'll see that even dark brown eyes contain different shades of brown.

The iris expands and contracts to change the size of the *pupil*, the round, black spot in the center of your eye. The pupil is an opening in the iris that lets light into your eye. People have round, black pupils. But while you were drawing, you may have noticed that your pupil isn't always the same size. In bright light, your pupil gets smaller. In dim light, it gets bigger. More about that in a bit.

Did you notice the tiny holes in your top and bottom eyelids? Look closely — they're in the corner near your nose. These are your *tear ducts*. Your eyes are always producing tears to keep the surface of your eyes moist, and to wash away dust and other bits of stuff. Your tear ducts drain these tears so that your eyes don't overflow. When you cry, you produce so many tears that your tear ducts can't drain them all. Did you include tear ducts in your eye drawing? (Psst . . . no one's looking — go ahead and add them in.)

Take a close look at the whites of your eyes. Do you see any red lines? Those are swollen blood vessels. Anything that irritates your eyes — like smoke or lack of sleep — will cause the blood vessels to swell. When that happens, the whites of your eyes will become the "reds" of your eyes. Got a lot of red lines? Go take a nap and rest your weary eyes!

You probably didn't draw in the *cornea* of your eye. Maybe you didn't even know you had one. The cornea is the clear protective layer covering the iris and pupil. It's really hard to see, which makes it even harder to draw. But you can feel your cornea. (See "Feeling Your Cornea," page 4.)

Your drawing of the outer eye is now complete. Or is it? Have you left anything out? What about your eyelashes? They help keep dust out of the important parts of your eye. Put your eyelashes in the drawing, too.

Tools for Exploration

Paying attention to stuff a lot of people ignore
To draw a picture of something, you have to look at it very carefully. Label the pupil, the iris, and the other parts of the eye in your drawing. This will help you remember the names of the various parts of your eye.

Parts of the Eye

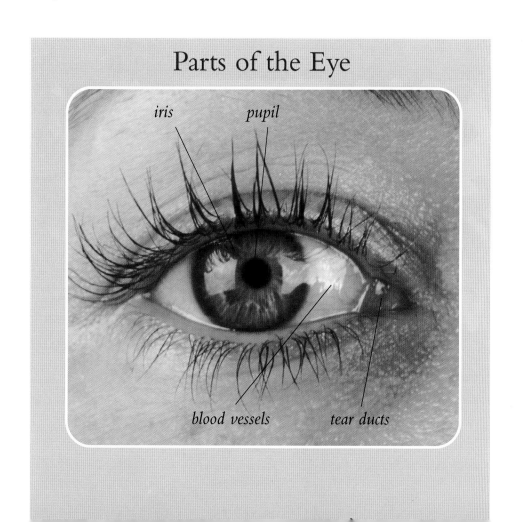

iris

pupil

blood vessels

tear ducts

Feeling Your Cornea

As mentioned before, the cornea is the thin, clear covering that protects your eye. It's hard to see, but you can feel it through your closed eyelid.

Here's What You Do

1. Close your eyes.

2. Gently and carefully press down on your eyelid with your fingertip, and slowly move your eye from left to right. You'll feel the round front of your eye moving under your finger. That's your cornea.

What's Going On?

The cornea is extremely tough, which is good because it protects your eye. The cornea also bends light that comes into your eye, working with the lens of your eye to let you see the world in focus. (For more on bending light, see page 11.)

Whose Eye Is That?

Do any of these eyes look familiar? Can you tell what creatures they belong to?
Turn to page 6 to find out.

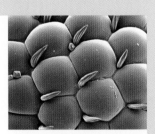

Tools for Exploration

Comparing two things

In what ways are these eyes the same as your eyes? In what ways are they different? Can you find other eyes to compare with yours?

Letting in the Light

Have you ever seen those sunglasses that darken in the sunlight and get lighter in the dark? That's cool — but your eyes adjust automatically every time you turn out the lights.

Here's What You Need

✔ A mirror

✔ A room where you can turn off the lights

Here's What You Do

1. Turn off the lights.

2. Face the mirror and count to ten very slowly.

3. Turn the lights back on while you look at your eyes in the mirror. When the lights came on, what happened to your pupils?

What's Going On?

The pupil is a hole that lets light into your eyeball. It looks black because it's dark inside your eyeball. Your iris, the colored part of your eye, contains muscles. When the light is dim, one set of muscles in your iris contracts and the pupil gets larger to let more light into your eyeball. When the light is bright, a different set of muscles in the iris contracts and the pupil gets smaller, allowing less light into your eye.

Your pupils respond quickly to any change in lighting. In just one-fifth of a second, they can expand from their smallest size to their largest. At its smallest, your pupil is just over one-thousandth of a square inch in area. At its largest, the area of the pupil is up to fifty times that size.

Animals that are active at night, like the tarsier pictured here, have pupils that open very wide in dim light. Even at their largest size, your pupils will never be as large as those of the tarsier!

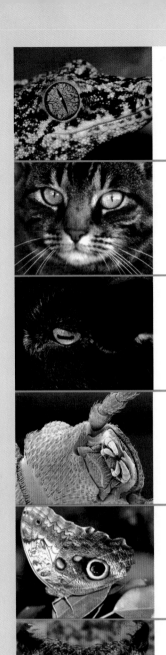

This is the eye of a gargoyle gecko. Since this lizard hunts at night, it needs good night vision. The black slit in the middle of the eye is the gecko's pupil, the hole that lets light enter the eye. Why isn't the gecko's pupil round, like yours? Round pupils are great for letting light into the eye — but not so good at keeping out bright light during the daytime. In bright light, the gecko's pupil squeezes closed to protect the gecko's eyes from too much light.

Do these eyes look familiar? We substituted cat eyes for our model's human eyes in the photograph on page 1. Like geckos, cats are active at night and have good night vision. In bright light, a cat's pupil shuts down to a slit. At night a cat's eyes reflect light and seem to glow. (See "Glowing Eyes" on page 9 for more on why a cat's eyes glow.)

The eyes of goats, kangaroos, and antelope have rectangular pupils that are horizontal to the ground. These animals have to keep close watch for predators, animals that hunt and kill other animals for food. The horizontal pupil helps these animals keep watch over a wide area.

This is the eye of a flour bug. It's called a compound eye*, and it's made of many small units that all send information to the bug's brain. The bug's brain puts together all this information to make a picture of the world.*

This isn't really an eye at all — but it looks like one. Some moths and butterflies have spots that look just like eyes on their wings. These insects use these eyespots to startle hungry animals.

This great horned owl hunts at night. Owls have very large eyes, which helps them see well in dim light. You can keep your head still and move your eyes to look around. An owl can't do that. An owl's eyes are locked in place. To look in a different direction, an owl must turn its head. Fortunately, owls are very good at that. An owl can turn its head and look directly behind itself without moving its body. Can you do that?

This is a ghost crab. It's called a ghost crab because it can disappear like a ghost, scurrying away on its tiptoes and vanishing into a burrow in the sand. (Scientists have clocked ghost crabs running at 10 miles per hour. That's one fast crab!) The ghost crab's eyes are on stalks that stick up, letting the crab see all the way around itself!

This one should look familiar.

A cat doesn't have round pupils like yours. In dim light, your cat's pupils may look round. But if you find a cat that's basking in the sun, you'll see that the cat's pupils are shaped like a slit. Why aren't a cat's pupils round? Because cats' eyes are more sensitive to light than yours are. In bright light, a cat's pupils can close down to practically nothing so that the cat isn't blinded by too much light. Round pupils can't do that.

What are those glowing spots in the Florida swamp? Those are the eyes of alligators waiting for you to come in for a swim. To find out why the alligators' eyes shine in the light of the photographer's flash, try the activity on page 9.

Sight and Light

Oh, sure, it's a breeze to see in the bright of day. You can even see when there's not much light — at night when the stars are out or there's just a sliver of a moon. But how about when there's no light at all? Can you see in the dark?

Blacker Than Black

You're going to create a world *devoid* of light. (Devoid means "without," but devoid sounds better.)

Here's What You Need

✔ A nail or a pair of scissors

✔ A shoebox with a lid

✔ Some objects to place in the shoebox

✔ A flashlight or another light source

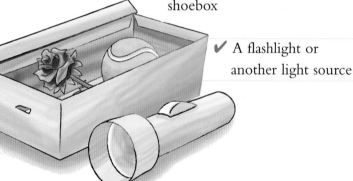

Here's What You Do

1. Using the nail or scissors, poke a small hole in one of the shorter sides of a shoebox.

2. Put some objects inside the box and put the lid on tightly. Use whatever objects you choose.

3. Look through the hole. Can you see anything?

4. Hold a flashlight or another light source near the hole. Can you see anything *now*?

5. Put a lit flashlight inside the box, put the lid back on, and look through the hole again. What do you see now?

6. Now turn off the flashlight and close the box again. Look at the hole. What color is the hole?

What's Going On?

You have to have light to see anything. Even cats can't see in total darkness. There has to be some light to get into their eyes so that they can see. At night, light comes from the moon, stars, streetlights, house lights, and car headlights. Can you think of other sources of light?

Tools for Exploration

Explaining what you notice

Can you see what's in a dark box? Why not? What do you have to do to see inside the box?

Glowing Eyes

Do a cat's eyes really glow in the dark? Do yours?

Here's What You Need

✔ A cat

✔ A flashlight

✔ A friend willing to play cat

Here's What You Do

1. Stand 6 feet away from your cat in a darkened room.

2. Hold a flashlight near your face and shine it at your cat. Do your cat's eyes look like they're glowing?

3. Ask your friend to get on all fours and pretend to be a cat. (Your friend can even meow. It won't affect the experiment one way or the other.)

4. Shine your flashlight at your friend. Do your friend's eyes glow?

What's Going On?

You probably noticed that the cat's eyes seemed to glow in the dark and your friend's didn't, no matter how much he meowed. Cats have eyes that reflect light. Their eyes take in the light and then throw it back out at you (or at whomever happens to be looking at them).

At the back of the cat's eye is a layer of tissue called the *tapetum lucidum*. That's Latin for "glowing carpet." The tapetum lucidum gives the cat better night vision. The cat's eye gets two chances to detect light: first when light enters the eye and again when light reflects *inside* the eye.

Sometimes when you take someone's picture using a flash, you get something that looks like this — a photo that makes him look like an alien from outer space! When the flash from a camera shines into the pupils, the light can bounce off the red blood vessels at the back of the eyes. This red light bounces out through the pupil and into the camera. To avoid this red-eye effect, you have to move the flash away from the camera lens. That way, the light that bounces off the back of the eyes won't get into the lens — and the eyes will keep their normal beautiful color.

Some cameras also use a preflash to eliminate red eye. The cameras flash once to make your pupils shrink, then flash again to take your photo. Because your pupils become smaller after the first flash, less light reflects back to the camera from the back of your eye.

By day, the red-eyed tree frog hunkers down on a leaf. With its eyes closed and its legs tucked under its body, this frog looks like an uninteresting green lump. When disturbed by a hungry animal looking for lunch, the frog opens its startling red eyes. Faced with that red-eyed stare, the hungry animal hesitates just long enough to let the red-eyed tree frog get away!

Dear Professor E:
Do you ever go out on a sunny day, lie down on a lush patch of cool, green grass, peacefully gaze up at the clear blue sky, and find yourself completely relaxing, maybe drifting off to sleep when... BAM! Out of nowhere a bunch of transparent, squiggly, bizarre floating things appear, ruining your view?

Signed,
Is It Just Me?

Dear Is It Just Me?:
No, it's not just you, and there's nothing wrong with your vision, either. It's common to see floating doodads in front of your eyes. Maybe you can see them right now as you're looking at this page. Maybe you even see them when you close your eyes. I bet you're wondering: *What are those things, anyway?*

They're called *floaters*. Now you may not want to hear this, so prepare yourself. Floaters are tiny bits of junk drifting in the liquid inside your eyeball. They move when the liquid in your eyes moves. Some of this junk may be extra bits of your eyeball left over from before you were born. (I tried to warn you.) Some of the junk may be what's left of red blood cells that leaked out of blood vessels. You're seeing the shadows cast in your eye by these bits of floating material.

Your floater-watching friend,
Professor E

How Do Your Eyes Work?

On a sunny day, light from the sun shines on trees, flowers, houses, cars, and everything else under the sun. Suppose you're looking out the window on a sunny day and you see a tree. You see that tree because light from the sun hit that tree. Some of that light was reflected, bouncing off the tree like a ball bouncing off a wall.

Some of that reflected light went right into your eye. That reflected light went through your eye's cornea, pupil, and *lens*, a piece of clear material shaped kind of like a magnifying glass. Along the way, your cornea and lens bent the light that reflected from that tree to make a perfect little upside-down picture of the tree on the back of your eyeball. (To find out more about lenses and how bending light makes pictures, check out page 294.)

At the back of your eyeball, there's a layer of cells that are sensitive to light. This layer is called the *retina*. When the picture of the tree shines on the retina, the light-sensitive cells send messages to your brain. The images that appear on your retina look flat and upside down, full of holes and messy blood vessels. It's up to your brain to unjumble these images and make some sense out of them. Your brain puts all these images together neatly and makes a picture of the tree in your mind.

Weird, isn't it? You think that you see the tree — but what you see is the light that bounced off the tree and went into your eye. Or if you really want to get picky, what you really see is the fixed-up picture that your brain makes from the mixed signals it gets from your eye. Amazing!

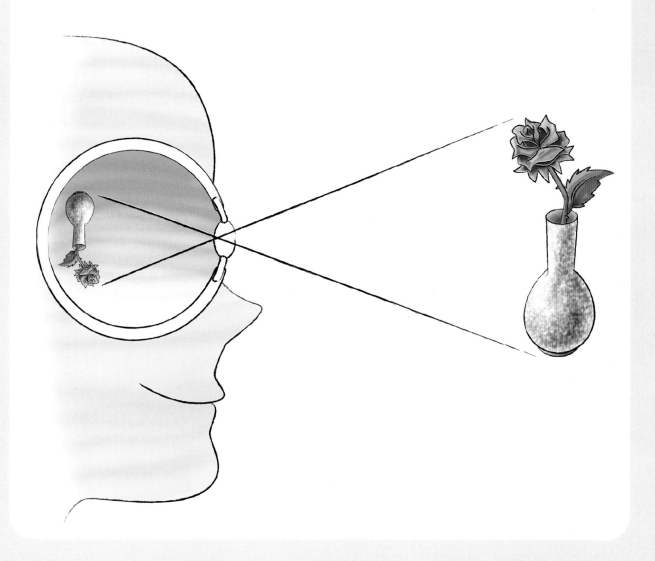

Seeing Secrets

A lot of us are afraid of the dark. But fear no more! We asked some professionals — spelunkers and astronomers — to help us out. A *spelunker* is someone who explores caves, and an *astronomer* is a scientist who studies the stars.

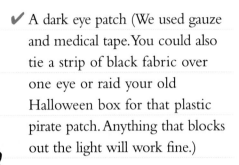

Here's What You Need

✔ A dark eye patch (We used gauze and medical tape. You could also tie a strip of black fabric over one eye or raid your old Halloween box for that plastic pirate patch. Anything that blocks out the light will work fine.)

✔ A really dark room

Here's What You Do

1. Cover one eye with your dark patch for twenty minutes. You can do another experiment (like playing one-eyed basketball — see page 13). You can watch one-eyed TV or read an excellent book (like this one!). Do whatever you like, as long as you keep the patch on.

2. Now it is time to enter your really dark room. Once you're inside, take off the patch.

3. Look around the room through the eye that was patched. (Cover your other eye with your hand.)

4. Then, switch: Cover the eye that was patched, and look around with the other eye (the one that wasn't patched).

5. Look at the room with both eyes open. Does one eye see the room better than the other?

What's Going On?

When your eyes are in the dark, they change, becoming more sensitive to light. Some of these changes happen quickly. For example, the pupils of your eyes get bigger. (See page 5 for more about that.) Other changes happen more slowly. When you're in the dark, the light-sensitive cells inside your eyes gradually become even more sensitive. It takes about half an hour in the dark for those light-sensitive cells to adjust to the dark completely. After that, your eyes may be up to a hundred thousand times more sensitive to light than they are on a sunny afternoon. You still can't see in total darkness — but you're rarely, if ever, in total darkness.

Before spelunkers enter a cave, they may use a patch to cover one eye to adapt to the dark. Having one eye that's already used to the dark really improves your vision in the dark. If you stay in the dark for a while, the other eye has time to adjust, too.

Tools for Exploration

Comparing two things

When you take off your patch in a dark room, do each of your eyes see the room differently? How is the image one eye sees different from what the other eye sees? Write down what you notice.

Seeing Double

Your eyes work as a team, giving your brain slightly different pictures of the same world. Your brain puts these pictures together to make one picture. That combined picture gives you more information than the picture from either eye alone.

One-Eyed Basketball

Who's up for a game of one-eyed basketball? Let's go!

Here's What You Need

✔ Your sporty self

✔ Your dark patch
(For suggestions on making one, see page 12.)

✔ A basketball

✔ A basketball hoop or another target to shoot the basketball at

✔ Some sporty friends (optional)

Here's What You Do

1. Cover one eye with your dark patch.

2. Play basketball!

3. If you play with friends whose eyes are uncovered, every basket you make counts double.

What's Going On?

Did you find that having only one eye made playing basketball harder? Were you the one we heard yelling: "I've got the ball! Hey, where'd it go?"

Your *peripheral vision* lets you see something to the side while you're looking straight ahead. Patching your eye reduces your peripheral vision on the patched side. If the ball bounces past you on that side, you won't see it until it's almost in front of you.

Covering one eye also affects your *depth perception*, your brain's ability to tell how far away something is. Did you miss the ball when you tried to grab it? Did you miss the hoop when you tried to make a basket? Blame that miss on the patch and be glad you have two eyes!

Tools for Exploration

Experimenting to test your ideas

Can you think of ways to improve your one-eyed basketball game? Will you get better with practice? Experiment and see.

What's with the Hole in My Hand?

If you're still not convinced that two eyes are better than one, this next activity ought to do it!

Here's What You Need

✔ A piece of notebook paper

Here's What You Do

1. Roll up the paper to make a tube.

2. With both eyes open, hold the tube up to one eye, and look through the tube.

3. Position your hand, palm side facing you, beside the tube, and look at your palm with your other eye.

4. Slowly bring your palm closer to your eye. Do you have a hole in your hand? Maybe you should have a doctor take a look at that.

What's Going On?

Because your eyes are a few inches apart, each eye sees a slightly different view of the world. With both eyes open, your brain combines the two different views, giving you one three-dimensional picture of the world. The image you see has length, width, and depth — three dimensions.

But if each eye is seeing something *very* different, those different views become rivals for your brain's attention. Your brain settles the disagreement by deciding which parts of the conflicting images are important, combining parts of what one eye sees with parts from the other eye's view. So your brain puts the hole that one eye sees right in the middle of the hand that the other eye sees. Ugh! Thank you, Brain!

Eye Wars

Because each eye sees the world from a different point of view, your eyes compete with each other all the time. You just aren't usually aware of their competition. Until now!

Here's What You Do

1. Stretch one arm in front of you and look at a distant object. Focus on the distant object and not your finger.

2. Point your finger at the distant object. This may not be easy. If you're like most people, you'll see two fingers when you look at the distant object, but do your best.

3. Without moving your finger, close your right eye. (If, like many of us, you can't wink, hold the non-pointing hand over the eye.) Did your finger seem to move or jump as you closed your eye?

4. Open both eyes and point again at the same object.

5. Close your left eye. Did your finger jump this time?

What's Going On?

Are you right-handed or left-handed? You probably know the answer to that question, but how about this one: Are you right-eyed or left-eyed? That is, do you think your brain favors the information from one of your eyes over the other? Or are your eyes equal partners?

In different situations, one of your eyes is probably *dominant*. Dominant means that your brain pays more attention to information from that eye. Did your pointing finger appear to jump when you closed one eye? If it did, then the eye you closed is your dominant eye when it comes to aiming or pointing.

Here's how it works:
- If you close your left eye and see a finger jump, you are *left eye dominant*.
- If you close your right eye and see a finger jump, you are *right eye dominant*.
- If neither is true, you probably don't have the tendency towards a dominant eye.

If you do have a dominant eye, use it. If you are baseball player, target shooter, archer, stargazer, or anything else that requires good aim, use your dominant eye when aiming or focusing.

To learn more about eyes, visit Exploratopia *online at* www.exploratopia.com.

Your Ears

Take a look at all these interesting ears we collected.

The top ear probably looks familiar. (If it doesn't, go look in the mirror!)

A cat's ear looks different from yours. But like you, a cat has an outer ear that scoops up sounds. Cats also use their ears to tell other cats (and smart humans) how they're feeling. The position of a cat's ears can tell you whether the cat is frightened, angry, or interested.

You might think that an eagle doesn't have any ears at all! A bird's ear is an opening just behind the bird's eye. You can't see the eagle's ear, but it's there — hidden by special feathers that protect the ear from wind when the bird is flying. Even though birds don't have an outer ear like yours, they can hear just fine.

What's that corn doing here? That's an ear of corn, of course!

These are interesting ears to look at. But there's more to ears than meets the eyes — as you'll learn when you start experimenting.

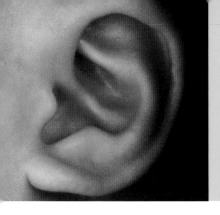

Flaps on Your Head

Feel your ear. It feels pretty weird, doesn't it? Take a look at your ear in a mirror. Yep, it looks weird, too. What's with all those folds and grooves and tucks and squishy parts anyway? Those flaps on the sides of your head are your outer ears.

Your Outer Ear

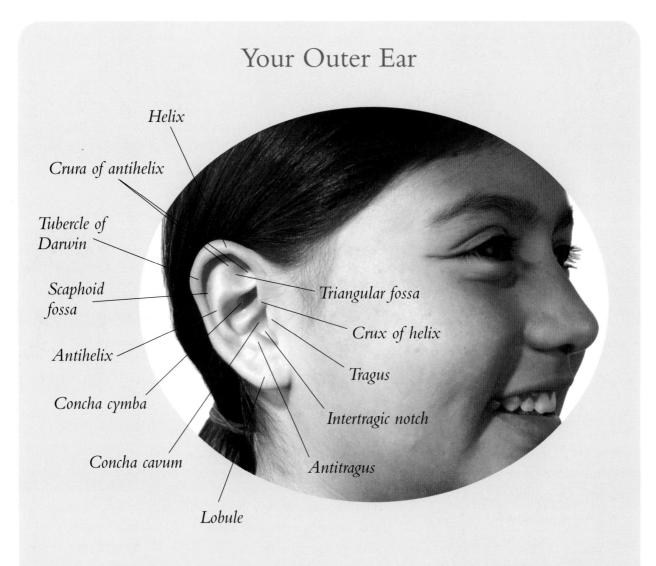

Helix
Crura of antihelix
Tubercle of Darwin
Scaphoid fossa
Antihelix
Concha cymba
Concha cavum
Lobule
Triangular fossa
Crux of helix
Tragus
Intertragic notch
Antitragus

Every fold and wrinkle of your outer ear has a name. And it turns out they have a use, too — as you'll find out if you try "Jingling Keys" on page 21. Some people believe that no two people have identical ears. In 1906, a doctor in Prague studied several hundred ears and concluded that no two pairs of ears were alike. In 1960, another study looked at the ears of 200 babies and found that no two pairs of ears were alike.

Give Your Hearing a Hand

What's the first thing you do when you can't hear someone? "WHAT??" Okay, what's the second thing? You make your own hearing aid, that's what.

Here's What You Need

✔ A sound source — a radio, TV, a friend who never stops talking

✔ Your hand

✔ A sheet of paper

✔ Tape

Here's What You Do

1. Turn on your sound source. (If you're using a friend for your sound source, simply ask, "How are you doing today?" to start him talking!)

2. Listen to the sound for a minute.

3. Now cup your hand around the back of your ear. Does the sound change?

4. Roll the sheet of paper into a cone. Make one end small enough to rest inside your outer ear *without* going into your *ear canal*. (The opening of the ear canal is that hole in your head surrounded by your outer ear.) Make the other end of the cone as large as possible. Tape the cone so it stays together. You've just made yourself an ear trumpet!

5. Rest the small end of the cone just inside your outer ear. Turn the cone so that the big end faces away from the sound source. What happens to the sound?

6. Turn the cone so that the big end faces toward the sound source. What happens to the sound?

What's Going On?

Your outer ear scoops up sounds and directs them into your ear canal. When you cup your hand behind your ear, you are making a bigger sound scoop. This simple action brings more sound into your ear.

That cone-shaped piece of paper is an even bigger sound scoop than your hand. The paper cone is basically an ear trumpet, an old-fashioned hearing aid. By scooping up more sound, an ear trumpet helps people with hearing problems catch sounds that they would otherwise miss.

Tools for Exploration

Making predictions
When you make a prediction, you try to figure out what will happen next. What do you think you will hear if you make elephant ears out of paper? How about rabbit ears? Try it and see.

Where's That Sound Coming From?

Two ears are better than one. Having two ears helps you figure out where a sound is coming from.

Here's What You Need

✔ A friend or two

✔ A blindfold for each friend

Here's What You Do

1. Have your friends sit in chairs.

2. Blindfold each friend.

3. Quietly walk around your friend. Stop and clap, or make another sound near each friend. Tell your friend to point to where he thinks the sound is coming from. If you have more than one friend participating, notice if they all point in the same direction.

4. Mix up your locations. Does your friend move his head to try to locate the sounds?

5. Switch places with one of your friends, and see how well you do blindfolded.

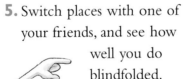

What's Going On?

Your two ears are separated by the width of your head. When you clap your hands, the sound travels through the air, from your hands to your friend's ears. (For more on how sound travels, see page 347.)

The sound of your clap will arrive at the closest ear first. A fraction of a second later, the sound will arrive at your friend's other ear. If you are standing to your friend's left, his left ear hears the clap first. The clap will also sound a little louder to the left ear.

The differences are slight. The sound could arrive in one ear a mere $1/2000$ of a second before it reaches the other ear. The difference in loudness is also tiny, but these tiny differences help the brain figure out where the sound came from.

When you made sounds directly in front of or behind your friend, the sounds reached both ears at exactly the same time. Fortunately, those flaps on the sides of your friend's head helped him out. Because his outer ears are open to the front, hand claps that come from behind sound very different from those coming from the front.

Jingling Keys

The wrinkles and folds of your outer ears help you pinpoint the exact location of a sound.

Here's What You Need

✔ One friend

✔ A blindfold

✔ A set of keys or something else that jingles when you shake it

Here's What You Do

1. Stand about 5 feet away from your friend. Face each other.

2. Blindfold your friend or have her close her eyes.

3. Shake the set of keys above her head, in front of her head, and then below her waist.

4. After each shake of the keys, ask her to identify where the keys were.

5. Mix up the locations and shake again several more times. Is your friend pretty good at locating the keys? No peeking!

6. Now try this. Have your friend, keeping her eyes closed, carefully fold over the tops of her ears so that they face the floor. (Don't tell her how funny she looks.) Have her hold her ears in this position.

7. Shake the keys in their various locations. Did folding her ears over make any difference in her hearing?

8. Switch places. You try it!

When you fold down your earflaps, it's harder to figure out where sounds are coming from.

What's Going On?

Before sounds get into your ear, they bounce off your outer ear. When sounds bounce off the folds and ridges of your outer ear, they change just a little bit. The jingling of keys that are above you end up sounding a little bit different from the same keys jingling from below you. Your brain knows the difference and figures out where the sound is coming from.

When you folded your earflaps over, you changed the way the sound bounced off your earflaps — and your brain couldn't tell where those jingling keys really were.

Inside Your Ears

Every sound begins with something that's vibrating—*moving back and forth quickly. Vibrations create waves of air called* sound waves. *Your outer ear scoops up those sound waves, which travel into the inner ear where they're turned into nerve impulses and sent to the brain.*

Secret Sounds

Experiment with sounds that only you can hear.

Here's What You Need

✔ Scissors

✔ Various kinds of string: nylon twine, fishing line, kite string, cotton thread, elastic, wire

✔ A table, desk, or other piece of heavy furniture

✔ A pen or pencil

✔ A piece of paper

Here's What You Do

1. Cut each kind of string into a 1-meter (3-foot) long piece.

2. Chose one string, and tie it to a piece of heavy furniture (maybe the leg of a table or desk).

3. Pull the string tight with one hand.

4. Pluck the string with the other hand. What does it sound like? Probably not much. But you're going to change that.

5. Wrap the string around your index finger.

6. Use that finger to plug one of your ears.

7. Pull the string tight and pluck again. Now what does it sound like?

8. Write down what you heard. Describe the sound. Was it loud or soft, high or low?

9. Repeat the experiment with each different kind of string and try using strings of different lengths. Write down what you hear.

What's Going On?

Before you plugged your ear with your finger, chances are you didn't hear much of a sound when you plucked the string. But once you plugged your ear, you probably heard a loud twanging. Why? Because the vibration of the string could take a more direct route into your ears. The vibration travels from the string into your finger, from your finger into the bones of your head, and from the bones of your head into your middle ear. Rather than traveling through the air, the vibration moved from one solid (the string) to another (your finger) to another (the bones of your head). It's easier for sound to travel this route — so you hear a louder sound.

Some people have ear damage that prevents their ears from picking up vibrations from the air. But even those people can hear sound through their bones. When famous composer Ludwig van Beethoven went deaf, he continued to write music. How? He could hear his music by resting one end of a stick on the piano and holding the other end in his teeth. As he played the piano, the sound traveled through the stick into the bones in his head to his inner ear. (If you have a piano and a stick, try it yourself!)

When you experimented with different strings, you probably noticed that some strings made high sounds and others made low sounds. When you pluck a string and let it go, the string starts wiggling back and forth, or vibrating. The sound you hear depends on how many times the string vibrates in a second — the quicker the string vibrates, the higher the note, or the *pitch*.

You can change the sound you hear by using a different string, because different kinds of strings may vibrate more quickly or more slowly.

Tools for Exploration
Asking questions
What happens to the sound if you pull the string tighter? What happens if you make the string shorter? Can you think of other questions you can answer by experimenting?

The round spot just behind the bullfrog's eye is its eardrum. Frogs don't have outer ears, like you do, but they hear quite well. After all, frogs find their mates by listening. When you hear a bunch of noisy frogs in a pond at night, what they're saying is, "Hey, I'm over here!"

Dear Professor E:

Whenever I go up in an airplane, I chew a lot of bubble gum so my ears don't hurt. That's the good news. The bad news is that my ears hurt in the first place. Why is that?

Signed,
Chewy

Dear Chewy:

When you're on the ground, all the air that's up above you is pushing down on you — and pushing in on your eardrum. Scientists call that push *air pressure.* There's also air inside your ear, on the inside of the eardrum. As long as the air pressure is the same on both sides of your eardrum, everything's okay.

Then you go up in a plane. When you do that, you climb up above some of that air that was pushing down on you. So there's less air pressure outside your eardrum.

But the air pressure inside your ear, behind your eardrum, is the same as it was before the plane took off. The air inside your ear pushes harder on your eardrum than the air outside. Your eardrum bulges out, and your ears hurt.

When you chew some gum, your ears "pop" and stop hurting. That pop happens when air moves through your *eustachian tube,* a tube leading from the middle ear down to the back of your nose and throat. The movement of air makes the air pressure the same inside and outside your eardrum. (By the way, eustachian is pronounced yoo-STAY-shun.)

Sometimes, when you get a cold, your eustachian tube becomes infected. When this happens, its lining swells. Not enough air gets through to your eardrum, and your eardrum can't move very well.

If the infection in your eustachian tube moves into your middle ear, you get an ear infection. Kids get more ear infections than grown-ups because their eustachian tubes are shorter, making it easier for infection to spread.

Your high-flying friend,
Professor E

How Does Your Ear Work?

Ever play Mousetrap? It's the game in which you set up a bunch of connecting contraptions to make a silly machine to catch a plastic mouse. Once you have everything set up, you turn a crank, which moves a lever, which pushes on a shoe, which kicks over a bucket holding a ball. The ball rolls down the steps, through a pipe, and into a hand. The hand pushes a bowling ball, which lands on a diving board and sends a diver catapulting through the air into a washtub, knocking a cage off a post and (if you're lucky) onto a mouse!

Next time you play Mousetrap, think of your ear. What goes on in your ear is like what happens in Mousetrap! Sound sets off a chain reaction. One ear part rattles this, which nudges that, which shoves the other thing. Your ear's goal is to pass along sound messages to the brain.

To figure out how your ear works, take a look at the picture on page 25 and you'll see all the connecting contraptions that make your ear work. As the vibration of a sound travels from the *ear canal* to the *cochlea,* each connecting contraption increases the push of the sound. By the time a sound hits your inner ear, the push inside your ear is much greater than the push of the original sound!

6. The **stirrup** looks like the stirrup on a horse saddle. The tiniest bone in your whole body, it pushes on the oval window, which covers the opening to the cochlea.

2. The **ear canal** is a tube that's open at one end. Sounds whoosh down the ear canal and smack into the eardrum.

4. The **hammer**, the first of three tiny ossicle bones, moves when the eardrum moves and hammers down on the anvil, the second ossicle.

9. The **auditory nerve** carries messages from your ear to your brain. Auditory is just a fancy word for "hearing" and nerves are the communication lines that connect various parts of your body with the Head Honcho, your brain. Your brain interprets the signals from your ear, and you hear the sound!

5. The **anvil** presses down on the stirrup, the third ossicle.

bone

semicircular canal

eustachian tube

3. The **eardrum** is a tightly stretched membrane, like the skin of a drum. When a sound hits the eardrum, the eardrum wobbles and bounces, passing the sound vibrations on to three tiny bones known as the ossicles.

8. The **cochlea** is shaped like a snail and filled with liquid. Tiny hairs inside the cochlea move when waves in the liquid push on them. When the hairs move, signals go out through the auditory nerve.

1. The **outer ear** gathers traveling sounds and sends them into the ear canal.

ear wax

ear wax gland

7. The **oval window** is a thin, oval-shaped membrane. It covers the opening to the cochlea.

Learning to Listen

Sounds are all around us. Often there's too much sound going on at once, so you learn to ignore some sounds and pay attention to others. You usually pay attention to sounds that matter to you personally, like someone calling your name. You can't ever turn off your ears, but you do control what you choose to listen to.

Listen Up!

Are you a good listener? Listen carefully and you may be surprised at all the sounds you usually don't hear.

Here's What You Need

✔ Your own ears

✔ A pen or pencil

✔ A piece of paper

Here's What You Do

1. Choose a quiet spot where you can sit and listen. Write down all the sounds you hear.

2. After you've written down the obvious sounds (like the ticking of a clock), listen some more. Can you hear sounds that you usually ignore? Write those down and listen some more. How many sounds can you hear?

What's Going On?

No place on earth is ever totally without sound, not even a sound-proof room. Even if you held your breath, you could hear the sounds your body makes — blood pumping to your ears, your stomach growling . . . If you paid attention to every single sound around (and inside) you, you would end up overwhelmed and distracted. The sound of your own breathing would keep you awake at night!

But by not paying attention to some sounds, you miss out on a lot. Some sounds you're ignoring could be important. One way to make discoveries is to pay attention to *everything* in the hope that it will be of future value to you.

If you liked listening to sounds you usually tune out, you could try listening in the same place on a different day. Do you hear the same sounds, or do you hear something different? Or try listening in a different place at the same time of day. Is there a sound that makes the place that you live different from any other place? Try to find the sound that lets you know you're home.

You could try to guess the size, shape, and make of cars based on the way they sound. Or you could try to identify trees by the sounds of their leaves in the wind. Or you could learn to identify birds by their songs.

Some people have jobs that require careful listening. A doctor listens to a person's heart and lungs. A mechanic identifies what's wrong with a car by listening to the engine running.

Did you have a hard time writing down the sounds you heard? You could write down the name of the object that made the sound — "I hear a dog barking." You could describe what the sound is like — "It's like a bell, very far away." You could use words such as "buzz" or "tick tock." These words imitate the sounds they describe. That's called onomatopoeia (pronounced AHN-uh-MAHT-uh-pEE-uh).

The serval is a long-legged wild cat with big ears. The serval's ears are bigger compared to his body than the ears of any other cat. These ears give the serval such keen hearing that this cat can hear a mouse tunneling underground!

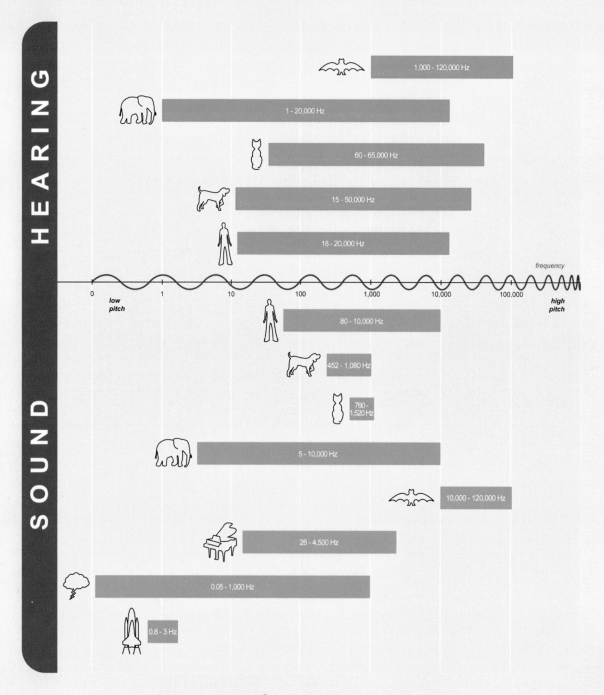

How High Can You Hear?

People sometimes talk about high-pitched sounds and low-pitched sounds. The screech of a whistling teakettle or the jingling of a tiny bell is high pitched. The pounding of a bass drum or the rumble of thunder is low pitched.

A high-pitched sound comes from something that's vibrating quickly; a low-pitched sound comes from something that's vibrating more slowly. A sound's *frequency* is the number of vibrations that happens in a single second. Scientists measure frequency in *hertz*. One hertz is equal to one vibration per second. (To learn more about frequency, see "Sound Detector," page 341.)

The top part of this chart shows the frequency of sounds that bats, elephants, cats, dogs, and people can hear. Bats, dogs, and cats can all hear higher sounds than we can — and elephants can hear much lower sounds.

The bottom part of the chart shows the frequency of different sounds, like the barking of a dog or the squeaking of a bat. A rumble of thunder includes sounds with frequencies down to just a few hertz. The rumble of thunder (indicated by a cloud with a bolt of lightning) includes sounds that you can't hear — but an elephant can!

Sing Along with Your Car

Singing along with your car can change the way you hear the machines around you.

Here's What You Do

1. Next time you're on a drive somewhere, listen to the car. Even a quiet car makes many noises.

2. Listen for the loudest noise the car makes. Then listen for the loudest note in that sound — and sing along with that note. (You might want to warn the driver first!)

3. Do the car's sounds change as it speeds up or slows down? Can you make music by singing a familiar song that blends with the car's sounds? Try it and see. How do you and your car sound? Does it sing as well as you do? Better? (Maybe you and your car should make a record. You could be stars!)

4. Listen to other machines around you. If you listen carefully, maybe you can hear the hum of fluorescent lights.

What's Going On?

When you sing along with a sound, your voice can give you clues about the frequency of the sounds that you are hearing. When women hum or sing, they tend to range from 200 to 900 hertz; men from 100 to 500 hertz.

In the United States, fluorescent lights tend to hum at a frequency of 120 hertz. That's because the standard household current in the United States changes direction 120 times a second, flowing one way and then the other. The light vibrates once each time the current changes direction, producing a hum at 120 hertz.

Singing along with machines helps you listen to them more carefully. There is music in any sound, but we don't always hear the music that's going on around us. We learn to associate certain sounds with certain objects, people, or situations. As a result, we interpret most sounds as signals of one kind or another and not as music. To hear the music of everyday sounds, you have to listen to them as if they had no associated meaning. So the next time your refrigerator starts droning away, forget that it's a refrigerator and listen to its song! Some machine sounds, taken out of context, are interesting — even pleasant. Maybe, if you're really lucky, the sounds are even easy to dance to!

I Led the Pigeons to the Flag

Have you ever thought the words of a song said one thing only to find out (much later and often with much embarrassment) that you were way, way off?

When you first learned the "ABC Song," did you think there was only one letter between *K* and *P*? *Ellemeno,* of course!

Or did you ever think the first line of "The Star-Spangled Banner," our national anthem, was "José, can you see"? And what's with the line "grapefruit through the night"? What does that have to do with our flag still being there?

We all hear the same sounds. But sometimes we each connect different meanings to the sounds. These hearing boo-boos have a name — *Mondegreens.* Writer Sylvia Wright came up with the name. As a child, she had heard the Scottish ballad "The Bonny Earl of Murray" like this:

Ye highlands and ye lowlands
Oh where hae you been?
They hae slay the Earl of Murray
And Lady Mondegreen.

Poor tragic Lady Mondegreen, Wright thought, not caring a hoot about the Earl of Murray. She found out much later that there was no Lady Mondegreen. What the poem actually says is: "slay the Earl of Murray and *laid him on the green."* Wright was so upset at losing Lady Mondegreen again that she named this hearing experience after that fair lady — thus, the Mondegreen!

You probably have some funny Mondegreens of your own. As for us, we're going to follow the example of our favorite Christmas carol and sleep in heavenly *peas.*

Big Ears

The fennec fox is the world's smallest fox. The African elephant is the world's largest land animal. These two animals are different in many ways — but they both have very big ears. These big ears help the elephant and the fox hear better by collecting sounds.

But good hearing isn't the only reason for having big ears. Both the fennec fox and the African elephant live in places where it's very hot. Their big ears help these animals keep cool. Animals lose a lot of heat through their ears (which is why wearing a hat on a cold day is a good idea).

To learn more about ears and listening, visit Exploratopia *online at* www.exploratopia.com.

Your Nose & Tongue

Congratulations, you have been just hired by some apple pie advertisers. Your job is to smell their product — an apple pie. The advertisers figure the better the pie smells, the more pies they will sell.

They have invented a new scratch-and-sniff — there's apple pie scent in the picture. So go ahead. Scratch the picture lightly.

Now take a big whiff. Can you smell the cinnamon and sugar aroma of a fresh-baked pie?

No? Try again. Think about an apple pie, fresh out of the oven. Put the picture closer to your nose. Do you smell it now?

If this scratch-and-sniff didn't work on you, don't worry about your nose. There never was any scent added to the picture. We were lying to you in the name of science!

But maybe you thought you smelled a pie. When we tried this trick on a group of kids, more than half of them smelled the pie.

Why do some people smell pie where there isn't any? Researchers have found that what you smell has a lot to do with what you *expect* to smell.

But before we tell you more about that, you might want to try a few smell experiments of your own.

Your Nose Knows

When you breathe, you inhale chemicals that are floating around in the air. Your nose detects these chemicals. It takes a whiff of the world and tells your brain whether you're in a room with baking cookies — or your brother's dirty socks! Now we're going to tell you how to test that marvelous nose of yours.

False Alarm

Fool your family and friends into smelling something that isn't there. To make this experiment work, you need to keep a straight face while telling a whopper. (But you're telling a whopper in the name of science, so it's okay.)

Here's What You Do

1. When you are with a group of your friends, think of a familiar smell. It could be popcorn or apple pie or skunk or your brother's gym shoes. Make sure the smell you choose is something that matches your location. (If you're in the middle of a forest, you probably won't convince people that they smell pizza baking. Skunk, yes. Pizza, no.) If you like, you could choose a smell that's an attention grabber. Say something like: "Do you smell something burning?"

2. Tell your friends that you smell whatever it is that you've chosen. Ask if anyone else smells it. If no one else smells it, wait a bit and then mention the smell again. It may take time and some agreement in the group (no one wants to be the only one to smell something), but keep at it.

3. After a while, a few people may say that they smell it, too. If a few agree, that's likely to convince the others.

4. When you're ready, tell your friends that they were helping you do a science experiment: There really isn't any smell. Are they surprised? Are they still your friends?

What's Going On?

If you chose the right smell, then your friends' past experiences helped you to fool them. In a kitchen, people expect to smell food, so smelling apple pie isn't unlikely. By insisting that you are smelling apple pie, you are making others *expect* to smell apple pie. And sometimes they end up thinking that they smell apple pie! Scientists call this a *false alarm*.

These false alarms happen in your brain, not in your nose. Your nose detects smells and sends a signal to your brain. The part of your brain that receives this signal is called the *limbic system*. The limbic system doesn't just receive signals about smells — it also stores old memories and controls your feelings.

When you tell your friends that you smell apple pie, they start thinking about apple pie. Their limbic system will bring up memories and emotions that are connected to apple pies. One friend might think about how good hot apple pie tastes. Another friend might be allergic to apples and have bad memories.

Good or bad, these emotional memories about apple pie will trigger smell memories stored in the limbic system, and maybe your friends will start to smell apple pie.

Researchers have found that what you expect to smell has a lot to do with what you actually smell and with how you feel about that smell. *Isovaleric acid* is a strong-smelling chemical that's found on sweaty socks and in blue cheese. When people are asked to think about blue cheese and then given a whiff of isovaleric acid, they think it smells like blue cheese. When people are asked to think of a locker room and then given a whiff of isovaleric acid, they think it smells just like dirty socks. Of all your senses, your sense of smell is the most easily influenced by what you expect.

Do you have a good nose? Most people can identify common scents — like the aroma of baking cookies or the stink of a skunk. But only one person out of four has a good enough nose to be trained to make perfumes or become a master chef, jobs that require identifying smells accurately.

Name That Smell

How's your memory for smells? Most people can recognize at least 2,000 separate odors. A perfumer knows more like 10,000!

Here's What You Need

- ✔ Masking tape

- ✔ A marker

- ✔ Five empty black film canisters with lids

- ✔ Ten cotton balls

- ✔ Five things that smell interesting (in powder, liquid, or spreadable form)

You could use spices like curry, cinnamon, or oregano, or things like perfume, liquid soap, coffee, vanilla extract, cocoa powder, dry cat food, or peanut butter.

- ✔ Notepaper and pencil for recording data

- ✔ A pushpin

- ✔ A group of friends

Here's What You Do

1. Using the masking tape and marker, label each canister with a number from 1 to 5.

2. Drop, sprinkle, dab, or smear a different ingredient on top of each cotton ball.

3. Drop one of your smelly cotton balls into each canister.

4. Place a clean cotton ball on top of the scented one to cover your mystery ingredient.

5. Write down which ingredient went into each canister (for example, canister #1 is vanilla). Put the lids back on, and let the canisters sit overnight for maximum aroma.

6. Right before your smell test, use your pushpin to make about ten holes in each lid.

7. Ask your friends to sniff each canister and guess what's inside.

8. Help your friends along with a few questions: Does the canister smell good or bad? Have you smelled this scent before? Does this smell remind you of certain people, places, or times?

9. How well did your friends do? Pretty well? You can't let them off that easy. Let's make it more of a challenge. Put two cotton balls with two different smells in one canister. (Again, write this down somewhere so you know what's in there.) How are they doing now? Can they identify both smells?

10. Create a smelly party game by making two sets of each odor. Pass out all the canisters and see if "smell buddies" can find each other.

What's Going On?

In science class, you may have learned about *atoms* and *molecules,* those tiny bits of matter that make up everything in the world. When you smell vanilla, that's because some of the molecules in the vanilla float through the air, get sucked into your nose, and bump into a *smell receptor.*

Your nose has about a thousand different types of smell receptors. Each type responds to a molecule of a particular shape. When a smell molecule bumps into a receptor that matches its shape, it locks into that receptor — and a message is sent to your brain.

There are only a thousand types of receptors in your nose — but you can detect about ten thousand different smells. That's because some smell molecules fit more than one type of receptor. Your brain combines the information from all the different types of receptors to figure out what you're smelling.

While it's figuring out what you're smelling, your brain checks your memory to figure out if you've ever smelled this scent before. If you have, your brain will send you all the other memories and feelings connected with that smell. Those memories help you name the smell.

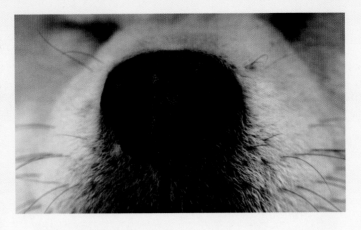

Tools for Exploration
Sharing your experience

Can you describe a smell? It's hard to do, but it's worth a try. Think about what the odor you are trying to describe smells like. Is it more like coffee or old socks? If it smells like a flower, is it more like a rose or a lilac?

Dear Professor E:
Why is my dog always smelling me? Does he want to eat me?

Signed,
Tired of Nose Prints

Dear Tired of Nose Prints:

Each of us has a unique scent. No one else smells quite like you! Your dog recognizes you more from your scent than from your good looks. (So, no, he doesn't want to eat you. He wants to greet you!) Mothers immediately recognize their own newborn babies by their smell. Babies also identify their mother's scent early on. There have been scientific experiments showing that family members can identify one another by scent alone. (Now will you please take a shower!)

Your scent changes with your body chemistry. When you start sweating because you're scared, your sweat smells different than it does if you're sweating because you're hot. When you're sick, your breath and sweat may have a different scent than when you're healthy.

Some animals communicate using chemical messages. Ants, for example, produce a range of scents that tells other ants what to do. One scent says, "Hey, there's food over this way." Another says, "Danger! Run away!" The chemicals that carry these messages are called *pheromones.*

Scientists are still studying the pheromones that human scents contain and how they affect human behavior. That's a complicated topic because people are very complicated! It's a lot easier to study pheromones in ants. (If you want to try that, check out the experiment on page 120.)

Meanwhile, try smelling your dog back. He'll like that!

Your sweet-smelling friend,
Professor E

You've Got Taste

Your nose and tongue work together to let you savor the flavor of a pizza.
Without your sense of smell, that pizza wouldn't taste nearly as good. Your
nose's smell receptors are 10,000 times more sensitive than your taste buds.
Your nose makes a big difference when you get down to some serious tasting.

You Taste With Your Nose

Okay, we admit it does sound kind of gross. But it's true.

Here's What You Need

✔ A friend who is willing to experiment

✔ An assortment of hard candies in various flavors or an assortment of jellybeans in various flavors (or even an assortment of drinks with different flavors).

The weirder the flavors, the better. Make sure to find the candies or drinks with very different tastes. Try to include some samples that are sour or salty, as well as some that are sweet.

Here's What You Do

1. Tell your friend that she will be trying to identify the flavor of a candy.

2. Have your friend close her eyes and hold her nose. Then have her suck on a piece of hard candy or a jellybean. (No chewing allowed!) Make sure she keeps her nose plugged!

3. Can your friend tell you the flavor of the candy? Can she describe its taste? Is it sweet? Sour? Salty? Bitter?

4. With her nose still plugged, have your friend chew the candy. Does that make a difference in her guess about the flavor?

5. Now let her unplug her nose and take a deep breath. Does this change what she tastes?

6. Try the same experiment yourself. (After all, you don't want your friend to eat all your candy!) How does the taste of the candy change when you chew it? How does it change when you unplug your nose?

Do you think
popcorn will taste
better with your
nose plugged or
unplugged? Next
time you have
popcorn, try it and
see. Do you think
plugging your nose
would help when
you have to eat a
food you don't like?

What's Going On?

With her nose plugged, your friend probably could tell whether the candy was sweet or sour—but that's about it. If she kept the candy in her mouth long enough, some air molecules may have reached her smell receptors and helped her figure out the flavor. If she chewed, more smell molecules reached the smell receptors, and she probably had an easier time. But only when she unplugged her nose did she taste the full flavor of the candy.

The taste buds on your tongue respond to only five basic tastes (see page 44). The rest of what we call flavor comes from what you smell. When you chew, you pump air from your mouth to the back of your throat. From there, the air drifts up into the back of your nose where your smell receptors are on the job. Your brain combines information from your smell receptors and your taste buds and tells you the candy flavor.

It's really not so weird that you taste with your nose. Did you know that rattlesnakes smell with their tongues?

What Are Those Bumps on My Tongue?

Look in a mirror and stick out your tongue. It's covered with sensory bumps called *fungiform papillae*. (How's that for a tongue twister?) Fungiform means "shaped like a fungus" and papillae is Latin for "pimple." So this is really just a fancy way of saying your tongue is covered with fungus-shaped pimples. Because that sounds really gross, we'll keep calling them fungiform papillae!

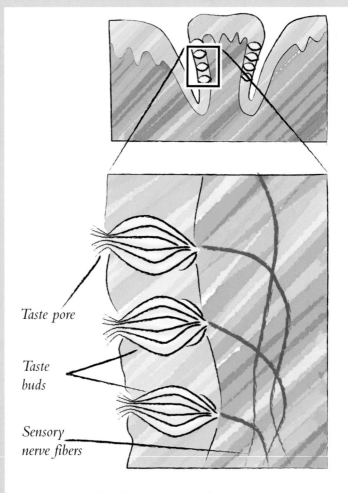

Taste pore

*Taste
buds*

*Sensory
nerve fibers*

On the sides of each fungiform papilla, you can see taste buds. Nerves that connect to your taste buds carry signals to the brain and your brain figures out what you're tasting.

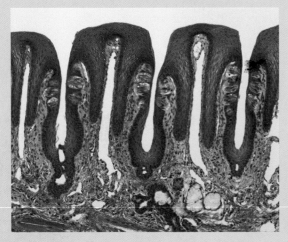

This photograph was taken through a microscope to show a magnified side view of some fungiform papillae.

The Sensitive Supertaster

Are you a supertaster? Paint your tongue blue and find out!

Here's What You Need

✔ Blue food coloring

✔ Two paper towels or napkins

✔ Two cotton swabs

✔ Two sticky reinforcement circles (those things used for fixing the holes in binder paper) or a paper coffee filter

✔ A partner

✔ A flashlight

✔ A mirror

✔ A magnifying glass

✔ A ruler (with millimeters)

✔ Notepaper and pencil

Here's What You Do

1. Put a few drops of food coloring on the cotton swab.

2. Dry your tongue thoroughly. Then, use the cotton swab to paint the tip of your tongue.

3. Move your tongue around in your mouth and swallow to distribute the food coloring evenly.

4. Dry your tongue with a paper towel or napkin. (One or two light pats should do it.)

5. If you have reinforcement circles, place one on the tip of your tongue. Looking good!

6. Have your partner shine the flashlight on your tongue. Use the mirror and the magnifying glass to examine the area inside the reinforcement circle.

7. You should see lovely pink bumps emerging from the blue background. Each of those bumps is a fungiform papilla that contains taste buds.

8. Count the number of pink bumps that you see in the circle. If there are too many to count, try to estimate (for example, count one-fourth of the bumps in the circle and then multiply that number by four).

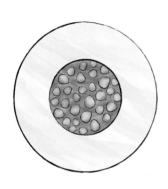

9. Switch places and repeat the activity.

10. If you don't happen to have sticky reinforcement labels hanging around the house, press the coffee filter against your blue tongue and pull it away. You should get a nice, clear print — the pink bumps will appear as white spots on the print of your blue tongue. (If you don't get a good print, just try again. You can make a lot of prints on one coffee filter.)

11. When you have a nice print of your tongue, use your ruler to draw a square that measures 10 millimeters by 10 millimeters. Count how many white spots are in the square.

12. Once you and your partner have counted your pink bumps, compare your counts. Who has the most bumps?

13. Gather more friends, neighbors, family members, pets, and check out everyone's tongues!

14. Who had the most pink bumps? The least?

15. Ask everyone to reveal their innermost, secret feelings about broccoli and brussels sprouts. Do they love these vegetables or despise them? Or do they fall somewhere in between? Does there seem to be a relationship between the number of pink bumps and whether or not a person's a broccoli hater? Hmmm . . .

What's Going On?

There are three types of people: (1) Those who do not like certain vegetables, such as broccoli or brussels sprouts. (2) Those who do. And, finally, (3) those people who refuse to even try these really-good-for-you foods. We can't help that last pathetic group, but counting the bumps on your tongue can help you figure out which of the first two categories you fall into — without actually eating broccoli or brussels sprouts!

Those pink bumps on your tongue are fungiform papillae. (See page 40.) Each bump contains between one and fifteen taste buds. When you eat, your mouth produces *saliva* (a fancy name for spit). The saliva helps break down the food and carries molecules from the food to your taste buds. The taste receptors in the taste buds send signals to your brain and let you know whether you're eating something tasty (or not).

Fungiform papillae contain taste buds that are sensitive to bitter taste. If someone has more fungiform papillae, chances are they have more taste buds. Did you find anyone with more than 30 papillae inside the reinforcement circle (or 50 papillae inside a 10 millimeter by 10 millimeter square)? A person with a tongue like that is a *supertaster.* This person is extremely sensitive to the bitter taste present in broccoli and brussels sprouts. Chances are this supertaster doesn't like those vegetables one bit! But being a supertaster isn't all bad — sugar tastes much sweeter to supertasters! About 25 percent of the people we've tested are supertasters.

A person with 10 to 30 papillae inside the reinforcement circle is most likely a *taster.* This is your average person. Average folks detect the bitterness in certain foods but are not overwhelmed by it. Tasters can enjoy the overall flavor of broccoli and brussels sprouts, or not. About 50 percent of the people we've tested are tasters.

A person with fewer than ten papillae is probably a *nontaster.*

Because they are not sensitive to bitter tastes, they can eat broccoli and brussels sprouts without complaint. About 25 percent of the people we've tested are nontasters. How do your numbers compare to ours?

If you can scientifically document that you are a supertaster, you have our permission to give all your broccoli and brussels sprouts to that kid with hardly any pink bumps — but only if you promise to eat all your spinach and carrots.

Of course, factors other than the number of bumps on your tongue also affect your tastes. Your cultural background, family background, and age all play a role. But sensitivity to one or more of the basic tastes definitely influences what you like to eat. Did you know there are people out there who do not care for sweets at all, not one little bit? It's true!

Tools for Exploration
Measuring and counting

How many supertasters are there in your family? How many nontasters? People who are related to each other are more likely to have similar numbers of bumps on their tongue. Is this true of your family?

Taste Map of the Tongue?

If you talk to people about taste buds, you're likely to hear that the taste buds on your tongue are grouped according to what taste they detect. Not so! This is a bit of misinformation that you'll find in many books. Way back in the 1800s, someone mistranslated the results of some experiments from German to English. They drew a taste map of the tongue showing that tastes were detected by certain parts of the tongue. That same map has been copied over and over again. Taste researchers have known that these maps were wrong for years, but they can't seem to get the mistake corrected in all those books!

The Fifth Taste

The taste buds on your tongue can tell whether a food is sweet, sour, bitter, or salty. They can also detect a fifth basic taste — one that scientists recognized as a basic taste in 2000, when they identified taste receptors for it.

This taste is *umami,* which is Japanese for "delicious." Umami is a more subtle taste than the other four. Some people describe it as "meaty." Back in 1907, Japanese scientist Kikunae Ikeda became interested in the umami taste. Working in a lab, he extracted a substance that tasted like umami, crystals of *glutamic acid*. From those crystals, Ikeda made *monosodium glutamate*. Monosodium glutamate (also called MSG) is used to make foods taste better.

Fooling with Flavors

If you tried the supertaster activity, you found out that broccoli alone tastes very bitter to about 25 percent of the population. But broccoli cooked in a nice cheddar cheese and hamburger meat casserole might taste fine to the same people. Good cooks know how to add seasonings to tone down a bitter flavor.

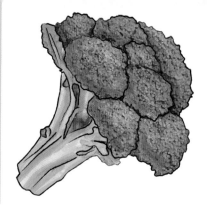

Quinine Cover-up

Playing with your food can make things taste better.

Here's What You Need

✔ A marker

✔ Masking tape

✔ Four drinking glasses

✔ Tonic water containing *quinine* (should be in soda aisle at the grocery store; check the ingredient list on the bottle)

✔ Salt

✔ Notepaper and pencil for recording data

Here's What You Do

1. Label the glasses with numbers 1 through 4. Fill each glass with 4 ounces (half a cup) of tonic water.

2. Put a pinch of salt in glass #2, $1/2$ teaspoon of salt in glass #3, and 1 teaspoon of salt in glass #4.

3. Take a couple of sips of the unsalted tonic water in glass #1. Record the taste on a bitterness scale of one to five, one being "This tastes just right, I will drink it all day" and five indicating "Gag! This is so bitter, I'll never get my lips open again!"

4. Take sips from the other glasses. Using the above one (not bitter) to five (extremely bitter) scale, record how the taste changes.

What's Going On?

Salt makes food taste less bitter. That's why many processed foods have extra salt — it's added to mask the bitter taste of the preservatives that keep the food from going bad. Salt also makes foods taste less sweet. Likewise, sugar will tone down something that tastes too salty.

What Else Can I Try?

Taste from the glasses in reverse order. How does that affect your taste experience? Find other sour or bitter foods or drinks. How about a grapefruit? This time, put sugar on the grapefruit to sweeten it. Does it work? Now try salt on the same grapefruit. Does salt take off the bitter edge? Which works better — sugar or salt?

Artificial Flavors and the Real Thing

In the spice department in your grocery store, you can buy artificial vanilla flavoring or real vanilla extract. The real vanilla extract comes from the bean of the vanilla plant. What makes vanilla extract smell like vanilla is the chemical *vanillin*. The artificial vanilla flavoring contains vanillin that was made in the laboratory. It's exactly the same chemical as the vanillin that came from a bean. Cooks prefer real vanilla extract because the artificial vanilla flavoring contains only the main ingredient of the vanilla extract, not all the other chemicals that add to the complexity and richness of the extract from the vanilla bean.

If You Can't Take the Heat . . .

If you eat something that's spicy hot, how can you cool your mouth down? Most people drink water. But water doesn't work half as well as a creamy dairy food such as milk, yogurt, or sour cream.

Welcome to the Soda Factory

Cola is made by combining many ingredients, none of which are the kola nut that gave the drink its original flavor and color.

Here's What You Need

✔ Club soda	✔ Sugar
✔ Three or four glasses	✔ Cinnamon
✔ Measuring spoons and cups	✔ Lime juice
✔ Vanilla extract or artificial vanilla flavoring	✔ Notepaper and pencil for recording data

Here's What You Do

1. Start with a cup of club soda in each glass. Add measured amounts of your other ingredients to the first glass, write down exactly what amounts you added, and then sample the result. Too sweet?

2. Move on to the next glass, and use a little less sugar. It's easiest to keep track of how your changes affect the taste if you change only one ingredient at a time.

3. After each addition, taste and adjust the flavor by adding the ingredient you think your drink needs more of. If it's a little too sweet, try adding some lime juice, which is sour. If it's too sour, add a bit more sugar.

What's Going On?

What you are doing is blending flavors. There are folks known as *flavor chemists* who do this sort of thing for a living. Food companies sometimes hire flavor chemists to concoct a flavor that matches that of a competing company's product. When you try to make a drink that tastes like cola, that's what you're doing. (So, does your soda taste like Coke or like Pepsi?)

When flavors come together, they often blend into something that may be surprisingly different from the original ingredients. On the back of some boxes of Ritz crackers, you'll find a recipe for a dessert called Mock Apple Pie, a dessert that contains no apples at all. Yet some people think this mock apple pie tastes like the real thing.

In the end, you are only one who can judge the success of your soda experiment. Who knows? You may make something you like even better than cola!

Tools for Exploration
Keeping track of your discoveries
When you're experimenting like this, it's important to keep track of what you try. If you don't keep track, you might make the perfect cola — and never be able to create it again!

To learn more about your nose, tongue, and senses of smell and taste, visit Exploratopia *online at* www.exploratopia.com.

Your Hands

No matter what people say, you are NOT a monkey's uncle. Actually, people are more closely related to gorillas, chimpanzees, and orang-utans than they are to monkeys.

You can see signs of this relationship when you take a close look at a chimpanzee's hand, which looks a lot like your hand. You and the chimp both have fingers that can curl toward the palm of the hand and grab hold of something. Like you, the chimpanzee has an *opposable thumb* — it can touch the pad at the end of its thumb to its other fingers.

Hold your hand the way the chimp in the photo is holding hers. How is your hand different from the chimp's hand? You're not as hairy as the chimp, for one thing. The chimp's thumb is short compared with yours, and her fingers are long. Because humans have shorter fingers and a longer thumb, we find it easy to pinch something between the finger and thumb. Our human hands are better at picking up and handling small objects than the hands of a chimpanzee are. Chimpanzees have long fingers that make them better at grabbing branches and swinging through the trees than we are.

Get a Grip

Human hands are something special. They can thread a needle, a job requiring great accuracy. They can grab a rope in a tug of war, an exercise in brute strength. Take a close look at your hands and discover what makes them good at so many different things.

Detective Work

"Always look at the hands first, Watson."

Who do you think said that? It was none other than that fictional detective, Sherlock Holmes.

Arthur Conan Doyle, the author who created Sherlock Holmes, based him on a doctor named Professor Joseph Bell. Doyle was dazzled by what Bell discovered about his patients by looking at their hands. For example, Bell knew that a woman with soft hands but brawny arms made a living washing clothes. The soapy water softened her hands, but the constant scrubbing strengthened her arms.

Study your own hands. Find anything interesting?

Colubus monkey   *Chimpanzee*

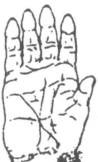 

Gorilla   *Human*

Colubus monkeys, chimpanzees, gorillas, and humans all have hands. Each animal's hand is adapted to how it lives. The colubus monkey has no thumb at all. Its hand is specialized for swinging through the trees. The chimpanzee and gorilla have thumbs — but their thumbs are much smaller than the human thumb. Our hands aren't as good for climbing trees — but the long thumb of the human hand makes us really good at picking up small objects.

If you grabbed a rope like this, your thumb would wrap all the way around to meet your fingers. This lemur's thumb doesn't reach nearly that far.

Thumbs Up!

Discover what makes your thumb so very special.

Here's What You Do

1. Find the pad of your thumb (that's the fleshy part on the side opposite your fingernail). Touch the pad of your thumb to the pad of your little finger.

2. Now try to touch the pad of your index finger (that's the finger right next to the thumb) directly to the pad of your little finger. See if you can get the pads to meet. How did you do?

What's Going On?

You could probably touch the pad of your thumb to the pad of your little finger very easily. In fact, you'll find that you can touch the thumb pad easily to all your finger pads. That's because you have *opposable* thumbs. To oppose means to place opposite or against something. Your opposable thumbs are able to reach and press up against all four finger pads.

A special joint, called the *saddle joint,* connects the thumb to the rest of your hand. The saddle joint is formed from two bones that fit together a little like a rider sitting in a saddle. This joint lets your thumb move in more ways than the rest of your fingers — and it's one of the features that makes your hand so special. You only have two saddle joints in your whole body — one for each thumb.

Did you manage to touch the pad of your index finger to the pad of your little finger? Probably not. Unlike the thumb, your other fingers aren't opposable. They can't turn to face each other.

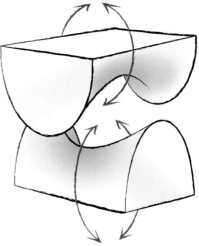

In your thumb's saddle joint, the curve of one bone fits into the curve of the other. The bones can rock back and forth or from side to side, allowing your thumb to move in more directions than your fingers.

Your Fabulous Fingers

Get a feel for those fabulous fingers of yours.

Here's What You Do

1. Try curling your fingers inward and then straightening them out again. That's easy enough.

2. Now curl up all your fingers except your index finger. Hold your finger straight and move it forward and back. Waggle it from side to side without moving the rest of your hand. No problem!

3. Now try moving just the tip of your finger from side to side without moving the rest of the finger. Hmmm . . . Not so easy. Not even possible.

4. Hold your hand out in front of you with the palm up. Watch the lower part of your arm as you make a fist. Straighten out your fingers. Can you see the muscles move under your skin?

5. Turn your hand over. Watch the top of your hand while you wiggle your fingers and thumb. Do you see any movement under your skin?

What's Going On?

Your *phalanges,* or finger bones, are connected to each another by *hinge joints.* These joints act like a hinge on a door — they let the bones move only in one direction. They can bend and straighten, but they can't waggle from side to side. But your finger is attached to your hand with a different type of joint called a *biaxial joint.* A biaxial joint can move in *two* different directions — front to back and side to side.

When you made a fist, you saw the muscles in your arm move. That's because major muscles that power your fingers are not in your hands. They're in your forearms.

When you turned your hand over and wiggled your fingers, you saw your *tendons* moving under the skin. These cords of connective tissue deliver power from the muscles in your forearm to your fingers and thumb.

Tools for Exploration

Sharing your experience

Compare your hand with a friend's hand. How are your hands alike? How are they different?

Bones of the Hand

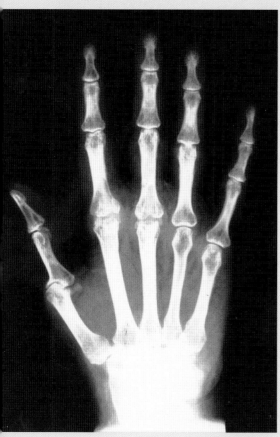

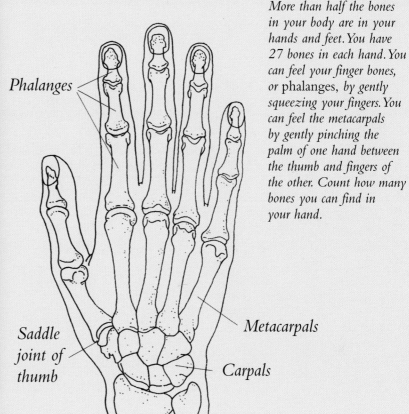

Phalanges

Saddle joint of thumb

Metacarpals

Carpals

More than half the bones in your body are in your hands and feet. You have 27 bones in each hand. You can feel your finger bones, or phalanges, *by gently squeezing your fingers.* You can feel the metacarpals by gently pinching the palm of one hand between the thumb and fingers of the other. Count how many bones you can find in your hand.

Back in the 1950s, an English physician named John Napier studied the human hand. He figured out that people usually use one of two methods to grab something. When you pick up something heavy — like a suitcase or a hammer — you use the power grip. You curl your fingers around the handle, squeezing it between your fingers and palm. Then you wrap your thumb around the top of your fingers.

When you pick up chopsticks, hold a teacup, or write with a pencil, you use the precision grip. You squeeze the object between the pad of your thumb and the pads of your fingertips. When you use the precision grip, you don't have as much power — but you have more control over the movement of the object. Try writing while holding your pencil in a power grip and you'll see why the precision grip is so useful.

Making Your Own Fingerprints

No one in the whole world has fingerprints exactly like yours.

Here's What You Need

✔ An ink pad (the kind used for rubber stamps)

✔ An index card (or a piece of stiff paper about 3-by-5 inches)

✔ A friend (to compare fingerprints with)

✔ A magnifying glass (optional)

Here's What You Do

1. Press your finger on the inkpad to get a thin, even coating of ink on your skin.

2. Roll your finger gently from one side to the other while pressing it to the index card. You may have to experiment to figure out how to do this without smearing your fingerprint.

3. Make a print of each finger. Do the prints of different fingers look different? How so?

4. Have a friend make a print of his thumb. Compare your thumbprint with his. (Use the magnifying glass to get a closer look.)

5. Have your friend make prints of all his fingers.

6. How are your fingerprints the same as your friend's? How are they different?

7. Wash your hands when you're done. (If you don't, you'll leave fingerprints all over the house!)

What's Going On?

There are about 5 billion people alive in the world today. Out of all those people, you might be able to find someone who looks enough like you to be your twin. But even your identical twin wouldn't have fingerprints that look exactly like yours. No one else has fingerprints just like yours.

Take a look at the basic fingerprint patterns. What patterns show up in your prints?

Tools for Exploration

Comparing two things

How are your fingerprints the same as the fingerprint patterns on page 55? How are they different?

What Kind of Fingerprints Do You Have?

Fingerprints can be sorted into three basic groups: arches, loops, and whorls. Each of those types can be sorted into smaller groups, making a total of eight fingerprint types. There are two kinds of loops — radial loops and ulnar loops. (Ulnar loops point toward the little finger side of the hand, while radial loops point toward the thumb side.) And there are four basic whorls — plain whorls, central pocket whorls, double loop whorls, and accidental whorls.

To figure out whether a fingerprint is an arch, a loop, or a whorl, an investigator counts how many deltas the fingerprint contains. A delta is a place where the fingerprint ridges make a little triangle, like the ones marked in red on this fingerprint.

Whorl

Delta

Delta

If a fingerprint has no deltas, it's an arch. One delta, and it's a loop. Two deltas, and it's a whorl. (If you have more than two deltas, your fingerprints are off the charts!) Compare your fingerprints with the ones here. You may have different patterns on your different fingers.

The most common fingerprint pattern of them all is the ulnar loop. Sixty-five fingerprints out of 100 have loops. Thirty out of 100 have whorls. And five out of 100 have arches.

Plain arch

Tented arch loops

Radial loop — points toward thumb

Ulnar loop — points toward little finger

Plain whorl

Central pocket whorl

Double loop whorl

Accidental whorl

How Touching!

Your brain is always sending messages to your hands. ("Hey, hands! Turn the page!") And your hands send messages back to your brain. Sensory cells in your hands send signals to your brain. Your brain figures out what your hands are touching.

Test Your Sense of Touch

Your skin isn't equally sensitive to touch all over. Find out what parts of your body are most sensitive.

Here's What You Need

✔ Seven straight pins or round toothpicks

✔ Four index cards (or four pieces of stiff paper each measuring about 3-by-5 inches)

✔ A ruler

✔ A pen or pencil

✔ A friend who likes you a lot

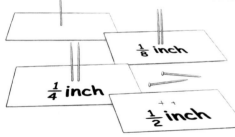

Here's What You Do

1. Both you and your friend should make charts like the one on page 58.

2. Now you need to make four measuring devices. (You and your friend can use the same measuring devices, so you only need to make one set.) To make the measuring devices, push the pins or toothpicks through the four index cards like so:

- Stick one pin or toothpick through one card.
- Label the second card $^1/_8$ INCH. Stick two pins or toothpicks $^1/_8$ INCH apart through this card.

(Use your ruler to measure the distance.)

- Label the third card $^1/_4$ INCH. Stick two pins or toothpicks $^1/_4$ INCH apart through this card.
- Label the fourth card $^1/_2$ INCH. Stick two pins or toothpicks $^1/_2$ INCH apart through the fourth card.

3. Your friend is going to be the tester, and you will be the subject. Now you're going to close your eyes while the tester keeps reading and following the instructions.

Here's What the Tester Does

1. Make sure your victim — your subject, that is — has his eyes closed.

2. Choose one of the cards without telling the subject which one it is.

3. Gently push the points of the pins (or pin if you chose the first card) onto the subject's fingertip. The key word here is *gently*! (You'll be the subject next — and too much enthusiasm with those pins could come back to haunt you.)

each part of your friend's body, try to find the card that has the smallest spacing that your friend says feels like two pins.

6. Experiment with different cards, mixing them up and repeating some so that your subject can't guess which card you are using. (Be sure to use the card with a single pin sometimes!) Keep going until you've filled out the whole chart and you know which parts of your subject's body are most sensitive.

4. If you're using a card with two pins, make sure both pins touch the subject's skin at the same time.

5. Ask your friend how many pins he or she feels. Write the answer down on the chart. Sometimes, the subject will think two pins feel like one. When that happens, go back with a card that has the pins more widely separated to see if your subject feels two pins on any of the other cards. For

7. Uh-oh! It's payback time! You become the subject and your friend becomes the tester.

Tools for Exploration

Measuring and counting

This experiment lets you measure how sensitive your sense of touch is. What part of your body is most sensitive? Is your sense of touch more sensitive than your friend's?

Body part tested	Smallest distance that feels like two points			
	1/8 inch	1/4 inch	1/2 inch	More than 1/2 inch
Back of hand				
Palm of hand				
Tip of finger				
Tip of thumb				
Wrist				
Arm				
Stomach				
Back				
Leg				
Top of foot				
Sole of foot				
Neck				
Forehead				
Cheek				
Lip				
Ear				

What's Going On?

What part of your body was best at telling two pins from one? Chances are you did the best with your thumbs. Which part was worst at telling two pins from one? Your back? Your arm?

Your whole body is covered with *pressure sensors*. When your friend touched you with the pins, the pressure sensors in your skin sent a message to your brain saying, "Hey, something's touching me."

On your fingers, the pressure sensors are very close together. On your back, they are much farther apart. In fact, you have a hundred times more pressure sensors in every square inch of your fingertip than you do in your back. That's why the skin of your fingers is so much better than the skin of your back at detecting the touch of two pins. When you measured the smallest distance between pins that your subject could detect, you were also measuring the distance between pressure sensors in the skin.

All those pressure sensors in your skin sent messages to your brain. Because there are so many pressure sensors in your hands, you use more of your brain paying attention to touch sensations from your hand than you do to touch sensations from your back.

This strange-looking little person is called a homunculus, *which means "little man." In this picture, the size of each body part is drawn in proportion to the area of the brain that receives touch signals from that body part. As you can see, your brain gets a lot more information about touch from your fingers than it does from your toes!*

Water Squeeze

There are some things your pressure sensors just don't feel.

Here's What You Need

✔ A sink or bucketful of water that's at room temperature or just a little warm (not hot and not cold)

✔ A plastic bag big enough to fit over your hand

Here's What You Do

1. Plunge your hand into a sink or bucket filled with water. Notice what your hand feels.

2. Take your hand out, dry it off, and stick it in a plastic bag. Plunge your hand (keep it inside the bag) into the water again. Does it feel different? How so?

What's Going On?

As sensitive as the pressure sensors on your hands are, there are some things they can't feel. When you didn't have the bag on your hand, you didn't feel the pressure of the water on your hand. The pressure sensors of your hand can't detect pressure if it's the same over the whole area of your skin.

That changes when you put your hand in the bag. The bag bends the hairs on your hand and pushes them against your skin. This action causes uneven pressure, which your hand can feel. When your hand is in the bag, you *feel* the water squishing your hand!

That Creepy-Crawly Feeling

The ticklish feeling you get when ants crawl on your skin has a scientific name.

Here's What You Need

✔ A friend

✔ A toothpick

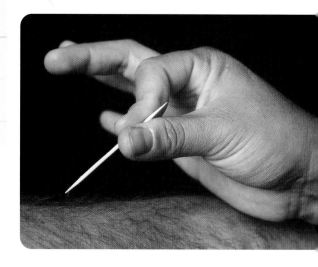

Here's What You Do

1. Find the tiny, short hairs on the back of your arm. (They're often hard to see, especially on kids.)

2. Close your eyes. While your eyes are closed, have your friend use the toothpick to gently bend one of the hairs on your arm.

3. Can you feel anything? If so, what are you feeling?

What's Going On?

The hairs on your hands and arm are *mechanoreceptors.* That means they sense mechanical distortions — someone or something messing with them.

When the hairs are bent, nerves near the base of the hair send signals to the brain. (Your ears work this way, too — you hear because hair cells in your ear bend. For more on how your ears work, see page 25.) Bending hairs can feel like insects crawling over your hands. The scientific name for this creepy, crawly feeling is *formication,* which comes from the word *formica,* which is the Latin word for "ant"!

Dear Professor E:

I've noticed that everything in my bedroom seems to be at different temperatures. The metal chair at my desk always feels freezing cold when I sit on it. But when I touch my wooden nightstand, it doesn't feel cold at all. Do you know what I mean?

Signed,
Running Hot & Cold

Dear Running Hot & Cold:

I know exactly what you mean.

In your bedroom (or any other room in your house), there are surfaces made from all kinds of different materials — like metal, wood, glass, plastic, Styrofoam, cardboard, and paper. If you touch each surface, you'll find that some (like glass or metal) feel cold when you touch them, but others (like Styrofoam or wood) feel warm.

Since all your materials are in the same room, all the materials are at about the same temperature. So why don't they *feel* that way?

Well, it's because of you and how you sense temperature. The temperature that you feel isn't necessarily the same temperature a thermometer would measure. When you touch something to decide whether it's hot or cold, the sensors in your skin tell your brain whether your skin is warming up or cooling down. If your skin warms up, you feel that the object you're touching is warm. If your skin cools down, you feel that it's cool.

Metal is a good *conductor* of heat. That means that heat flows through metal quickly and easily. When you touch a metal surface, heat flows from your hand into the metal and quickly moves away through the metal. That cools your skin down quickly, and your temperature-sensitive nerves tell you that the metal is cold.

Wood is a poor conductor of heat. That means heat does not flow through wood easily. When you touch the wood, heat flows from your hand to the wood and warms up the surface. But because the heat does not flow away quickly, the surface stays warm, and little heat leaves your hand. Your skin stays warm and your temperature-sensitive nerves tell you that the wood is warm.

Good experimenting there!

Heatedly yours,
Professor E

Fooling Your Hands

All day long, your eyes see things, your brain decides to grab them, and your hands do the work. You don't even think about it. But if everything in this hands-eyes-brain sequence doesn't go smoothly, your brain gets very confused!

Hat Trick

Will confusing your eyes confuse your hands?

Here's What You Need

✔ A baseball cap (if you have one)

✔ Masking tape or other strong tape

✔ A small mirror

✔ Paper

✔ A table

✔ Pencil, pen, or marker

✔ A maze from an activity book (if you have one)

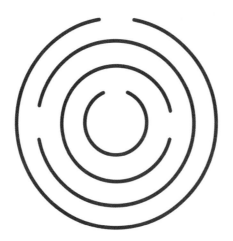

Here's What You Do

1. If you have a baseball cap, tape the mirror tightly under the visor of the cap.

2. If you don't have a baseball cap, use your left hand (if you're right-handed) to hold the edge of the mirror against your eyebrows. If you're left-handed, use your right hand.

3. Put a piece of paper on the table.

4. Look up into the mirror and try to print your name on the piece of paper. (Don't look down at the paper while you're writing; keep looking up into the mirror.)

5. Write your name a couple of times. Don't look at the paper yet!

6. Try looking in the mirror and drawing something this time — something simple like a happy face or a house.

7. Now look at what you've written and drawn. How are you doing so far?

8. There's a maze on page 62. Trace it on a piece of paper. Then put the maze on the table. Look up into the mirror and try to draw a line from the start to the finish of the maze.

What's Going On?

Drawing and writing are difficult when looking in the mirror. (You don't say!) That's because the information you get from your eyes doesn't match the messages you get from your hand. When you try to move your hand up, the mirror shows it moving down. You see your hand moving in one direction — but you feel yourself moving it in another!

Tools for Exploration
Explaining what you notice
Try writing your name over and over again while looking in the mirror. Does it get easier or harder? Why do you think that is?

It's Hot! It's Not!

Your hands always agree on what they feel — don't they?

Here's What You Need

✔ Three tall glasses

✔ Water — hot (from the faucet), iced, and room temperature

✔ A clock (so you can time yourself)

Here's What You Do

1. Fill one glass with hot water, one with ice water, and one with room-temperature water.

2. Grab the ice-cold glass with one hand, making sure the palm of your hand comes in full contact with the glass.

3. Grab the hot glass in the same way with the other hand.

4. Hold both glasses for a full minute.

5. After the minute is up, release your grip on both glasses.

6. Now grab the room-temperature glass with *both* hands, again making full contact with your palms.

7. Is the glass hot or cold?

What's Going On?

When you grasped the room-temperature glass with both hands, your hands gave you two conflicting reports. The hand that held the cold glass told you that you were holding a hot glass. The hand that held a hot glass said that you were holding a cold glass. But both hands were holding the same glass! Weird!

These mixed-up sensations show that your hands don't sense the temperature of the glass directly. The heat sensors in your skin sense the temperature change caused by heat flowing into or out of your hands.

When two objects are at different temperatures, heat flows from the hotter one to the cooler one. When you held the cold glass, your hand got cold. When this cold hand held the room-temperature glass, heat from the glass flowed into your hand to warm it up. The cold hand *gained* heat, so it sensed that the glass was hot.

When you held the hot glass, your hand got hot. When this hot hand held the room-temperature glass, heat from your hand flowed into the glass to cool your hand down. The hot hand *lost* heat, so it sensed that the glass was cold.

Confuse Yourself

Do you know which finger is which? Maybe it's all an illusion!

Here's What You Need

✔ Your own two arms

✔ A friend (to order you around)

Here's What You Do

1. Hold both arms straight out in front of you.

2. Turn your hands so that they're back to back.

3. Cross your right arm over your left arm and clasp your hands.

4. Keeping your hands clasped, swing your hands down toward the ground, up to your belly button, then all the way around until your hands end up directly in front of your chin. Try to do it in one full, circular motion.

5. Move your clasped hands out so that you can see them.

6. Ask your friend to point to one of your fingers without touching the finger.

7. Wiggle the finger that he pointed to — that finger and only that finger.

8. How did you do?

9. Try it again. But this time have your friend *touch* the finger that you're supposed to move.

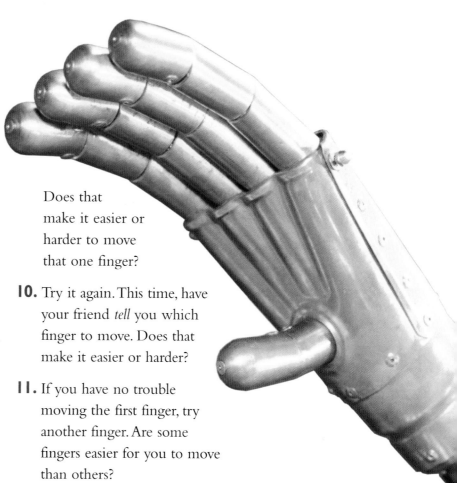

Does that make it easier or harder to move that one finger?

10. Try it again. This time, have your friend *tell* you which finger to move. Does that make it easier or harder?

11. If you have no trouble moving the first finger, try another finger. Are some fingers easier for you to move than others?

What's Going On?

If you're like most people, you'll find it hard to figure out which finger to move — even when you're looking right at it. You can see which finger you want to move. You can even feel where your fingers are. But connecting what you see and what you feel doesn't work too well when your arms are in a pretzel. The result is a *tactile* illusion. Tactile means "touch." With a tactile illusion, you have to work harder to connect what you see with your eyes with what you feel in your body.

When your friend touched your finger, you received tactile information that told you which finger to move. That provides your brain with more information to work with and makes it easier for you to figure out which finger to move. When your friend told you which finger to move, you could just close your eyes and tell your brain: "Move my right index finger."

Maybe you're one of those special people that found this whole exercise easy. Some people are just naturally good at this. The people who usually ace this activity do detailed work with their fingers — like typists and people who play the piano.

To find out more about your hands and how they sense the world, visit Exploratopia *online at* www.exploratopia.com.

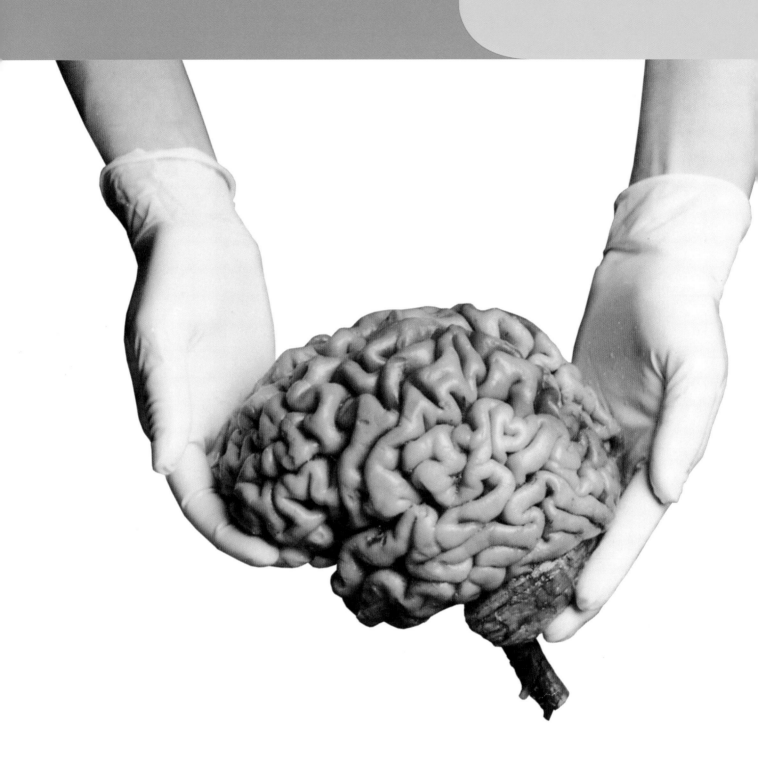

Your Brain

This is a picture of a human brain. Yes, it's a real brain. This brain belonged to a person who wanted to help others learn more about how the brain works. She donated her body to medical science when she died.

Your brain stores memories, like what you did last summer, or how to ride a bicycle. Your brain solves problems, like what to get your best friend for his birthday, or how to divide 372 by 6. Your brain makes you the person you are.

But looking at a human brain won't tell you everything. The brain is what scientists sometimes call a *black box* — something that looks simple on the outside, but does stuff that's hard to understand. We know what goes in and what comes out, but most of what goes on inside is a mystery.

Gray Matter

What's going on in that brain of yours? You can't take apart your own brain to figure out how it works. But this section will show you something about what brains look like inside—and a little bit how they work. Use your gray matter (your brain, that is) to learn about gray matter.

Take a Brain Apart

One way to learn about how something works is to take it apart, or *dissect* it. Follow along as we dissect a sheep brain.

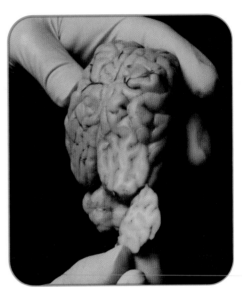

Here's What You Need

✔ Your brain

✔ This book

Here's What You Do

1. Take a look at the two brains to the left. One is a sheep brain and the other is a human brain. Can you tell which is which? (Here's a hint: your brain is bigger than a sheep's.)

2. The first step in dissecting anything is to look at the thing as a whole. So take a good look at these two brains. How are they the same? How are they different?

3. We used a small knife to slice into the sheep brain. Take a close look at the slice of sheep brain in the photo above right. What

do you see? The brain is a pale color inside, but on the outside is a layer of dark stuff. That dark stuff is called *gray matter*. (To see what gray matter looks like up close, check out page 70.)

4. The gray matter makes a thin layer on the outside of your brain. That layer is called the *cortex*. The cortex is only about a quarter of an inch thick, but that's where you think, solve problems, and decide what to do.

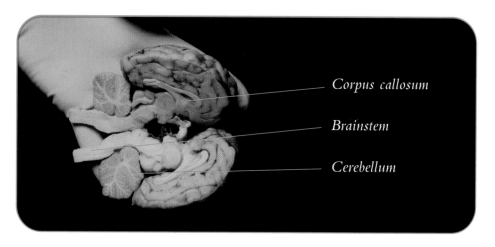

Corpus callosum

Brainstem

Cerebellum

Tools for Exploration

Paying attention to stuff a lot of people ignore

Some people think cutting up a brain is kind of icky. But taking something apart is one way to figure out how it fits together — we don't think it's icky at all!

5. See the wrinkles in the cortex? If you were able to unfold and flatten out a human cortex, it would be bigger around than an extra-large pizza! If your brain were smooth, you'd have a lot less cortex — and a lot less brainpower.

6. The photo above shows a sheep brain that we cut in half, right down the middle. We've labeled some important parts of the brain. Find the *corpus callosum*, the *cerebellum*, and the *brainstem*. The corpus callosum connects the left half of the brain to the right half of the brain. (For more about the right and left halves of your brain, see page 71.)

7. Take a look at the close-up of the cerebellum and the brainstem to the right. In your skull, the cerebellum is located at the base of your neck. Cerebellum is Latin for "little brain." Do you think it looks like a little brain? This part of your brain works hard when you learn how to do something that involves both your body and your brain— like riding a bike or playing the guitar.

8. Find the brainstem in the photo. The brainstem controls the basic body functions that keep you alive — it keeps you breathing and keeps your heart beating. The brainstem also controls blinking and sneezing (and a lot of other things as well).

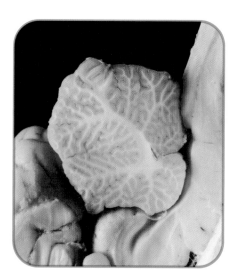

What's Going On?

When people were first trying to figure out how the human body worked, they learned by dissecting animals. The human brain is much larger than the sheep brain, but it has all the same parts. You can learn a lot about your brain by looking at the brain of a sheep.

What Is Gray Matter, Anyway?

Has anyone ever told you to use your gray matter? That means—start thinking! The gray matter of your brain is where you do all your thinking.

Your brain's gray matter is made of *cells*, the building blocks that make up all living things—from the plants in your garden to your little brother.

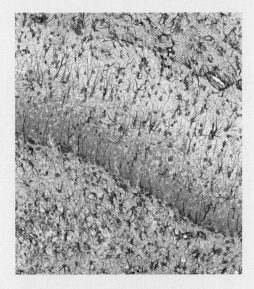

Back in 1662, a man named Robert Hooke looked through a microscope at a thin slice of cork and saw lots of little boxes. Because they reminded him of the little rooms where monks lived, he called those boxes cells, which means "little rooms." This photo shows cork cells, like the ones that Robert Hooke saw. But not all cells look like little boxes.

This picture shows a magnified view of a slice cut from a rat's hippocampus. You can see a layer of neurons in the blue. The red, tangled shapes are cells called glia, which greatly outnumber the neurons in the brain. While scientists know that glia provide support to the neurons, they are still trying to figure out all the other things glia do.

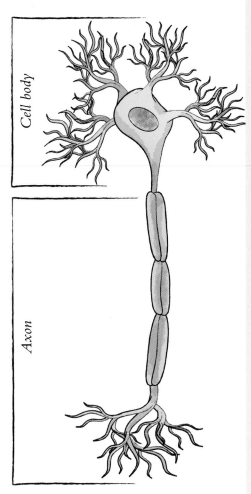

This is a sketch of a nerve cell or neuron, *the kind of cell that makes up your brain. As you can see, the cells of your brain don't look like little boxes. Neurons come in different shapes, but many neurons have dark cell bodies attached to long, stretched-out parts called axons. Your gray matter gets its color from those cell bodies. The lighter, white matter is made of those stretched-out axons. The axon of each brain cell makes connections with other brain cells. Each neuron can send information to thousands of other brain cells. This communication network makes thought possible.*

Cell body

Axon

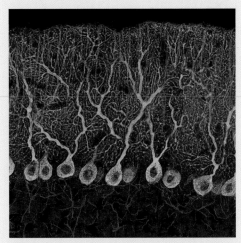

This picture shows a magnified view of a slice cut from a rat's cerebellum. In the cerebellum, there are special kinds of neurons called Purkinje neurons. In this picture, the bright green marks the Purkinje neurons. These neurons have long branches that extend out from the cell body like a tree so that they can make many connections, or synapses, with other cells. The bright red shapes are glia, another kind of cell in the brain.

Dear Professor E:
Is there really a difference
between how your right and left
brain think?

Signed,
Wondering

Dear Wondering:
As you read this sentence, the left half of your brain is probably working harder than the right side. That's because each of the two halves of the human brain specializes in doing certain kinds of thinking.

The left half of the brain usually handles stuff such as understanding language, doing math, and thinking logically (like the kind of thinking you use to solve a crossword puzzle). The right side of the brain is usually better at thinking visually — noticing patterns and judging shapes and things like that. The right brain is also thought to be more involved in creativity and emotions. When you see someone you know, your right brain recognizes her face, while your left brain remembers her name.

At least, this is what's usually true. But some people use both halves equally for all different kinds of thinking. Also, some left-handed people have their right and left brains reversed, so the left brain is more visual and the right brain handles language and math.

The two halves of your brain also split the job of controlling your body. The left half of your brain controls the right side of the body, and the right half controls the left side of your body. When you raise your left hand, the signal to your hand starts on the right side of your brain. If you stub your right toe, it's the left half of your brain that gets the message.

Brainily yours,
Professor E

Inside the Thinking Brain

Wouldn't it be cool if you could explore the inside of your brain without cutting it open? Believe it or not, scientists can do exactly that.

With a lot of high-tech equipment, scientists can create pictures of the thinking brain like the ones here. When you think about or perform an action, more blood flows to the parts of the brain involved in that thought or action. In these pictures, the areas of the brain that are getting more blood are shown as colored patches. These are the areas that are the most active during a particular activity. The fancy method that scientists use to study the active brain has a long name — *functional magnetic resonance imaging (fMRI)*.

This person is tapping his finger. The red and yellow areas show the parts of his brain that he is using to control his finger.

This person is thinking about the difference between the words "chair" and "love."

This person is trying to remember a string of letters that he just memorized.

This person is remembering an event from his past. The colored areas show the parts of his brain that are active when he tries to remember past events.

Compare Brains A human brain and a sheep brain have all the same parts.

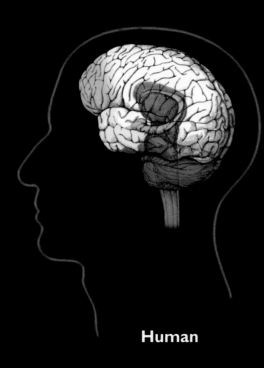

The prefrontal cortex is very important in planning and thinking ahead.

The hippocampus is the place where your brain turns things that you remember for just a few minutes into things that you remember for a long time.

The cerebellum controls movement, balance, and coordination.

The spinal cord transmits messages from the brain to the rest of the body.

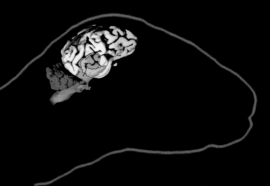

Human

Sheep

Brain Freeze!

It's a beautiful, sunny day. You dig into a refreshing dish of ice cream. "Mmm," you say, a smile on your . . . *OUCH!*

You've just been hit with the horrible headache known as *brain freeze*, or *ice-cream headache*. About one third of the population gets brain freeze, and if you're one of those people, you know how much it can hurt.

Scientists have studied brain freeze. (They want to eat their ice cream, too!) They think that brain freeze happens when the cold from the ice cream touches the nerve center on the back of your *palate*. That's the soft area at the back of the roof of your mouth.

The cold on your palate makes your body think that your brain is too cold. So your body quickly sends extra blood to the area around the brain to warm it up. This rush of blood can cause headaches in some unlucky people.

Fortunately, ice-cream headaches don't last long — usually 30 seconds to a couple of minutes, tops. And they usually only happen on really, really hot days. Here are some things people say will stop brain freeze. Do any of them help you?

- Place your tongue against the roof of your mouth to warm up the nerve center.
- Put ice against your forehead to confuse your brain.
- Slow down! Eat your ice cream in tiny bites.
- Give up ice cream, really cold soda, and other frosty things — forever. (What? Are you nuts? No one's that desperate!)

Forget About It

Draw a picture of a penny (the Lincoln side). Put in the words and the date, too. What? Can't remember the words? Don't know where the date goes? You're not alone. Experimenting with your memory can help you understand why it sometimes lets you down.

That Messy Brain

Can you list the names of all fifty states without any help? Give it a try.

Here's What You Do

1. Write down the names of as many states as you can remember.

2. If you get stuck, try picturing a map in your mind. Or think about where you have traveled, state capitals, or where your favorite sports teams come from.

3. How many states do you have on your list now?

4. Would it help to know that there are four states that start with the letter *A*, three that start with *C*, one with *D*, one with *F*, one with *G*, one with *H*, four with *I*, two with *K*, one with *L*, eight with *M*, eight with *N*, three with *O*, one with *P*, one with *R*, two with *S*, two with *T*, one with *U*, two with *V*, and four with *W*?

5. Can you fill in the blanks on your list and remember all the states now? (See page 355 to check your list.)

What's Going On?

Have you ever tried to find something in a messy drawer? You know it's in the drawer somewhere, but you just can't find it with all that other stuff in the way. Well, searching your memory can be like searching in a junk drawer. The problem with remembering isn't storing stuff in your brain — it's finding the stuff *after* you've stored it.

Tools for Exploration
Sharing your experience
Have friends try this activity — and ask what clues they used to help them remember. Some of their clues may help you out, too!

Even if you know all the states' names, you may not be able to find them in your memory when you need them. Memory researchers talk about *retrieving* memories ("retrieve" means "to bring back," like a dog bringing back a stick). To retrieve the information you need, you may have to give your brain a little hint. You need to give your brain what memory researchers call a *retrieval cue.*

A retrieval clue can be any information that connects to the name of a state. The first letter of a state's name can be a retrieval clue. So can the name of a sports team.

Improve Your Memory—Part One

You can remember a bunch of different things if you can figure out a way to connect them. Here's one way.

Here's What You Need

✔ A little imagination

✔ A piece of paper and a pencil

✔ A timer or a clock with a second hand and someone to tell you when a minute is up

Here's What You Do

1. On page 355, there are pictures of twenty different things.

2. Look at the pictures for one minute, then close the book and write down as many of the things as you can remember.

3. How did you do? Keep your list and label it MY MEMORY — WITH NO HELP.

4. Now you're going to try the same task again, using a scientifi-

cally tested trick for improving your memory. You are going to turn to page 356 and look at the pictures for one minute. While you are looking at the pictures, you're going to make up a story that has all those things in it. For instance, suppose there's a picture of an apple, a chair, a mouse, and a bowler hat. Maybe your story is about Mr. Apple, a man who always wears a bowler hat. A mouse runs into his house, so he stands on the chair. The sillier your story, the better.

5. Close the book and write down as many of the things as you can remember. How did you do? Label this list MY MEMORY — WITH A STORY.

What's Going On?

Did you do better when you made up a story? Most people do. It's hard to remember a list of things that aren't connected to one another in any way. By making up a story, you are connecting all these different things and you are picturing them in your mind. So when you remember one picture, you remember the others, too.

Improve Your Memory—Part Two

Here's a memory trick that lets you remember a list of things for a long time. It's a little harder than the last experiment, so we decided we'd start with ten items, rather than twenty.

Here's What You Need

✔ A little imagination

✔ A familiar place to walk around — like your house

✔ A timer or a clock with a second hand and someone to tell you when a minute is up

Here's What You Do

1. Walk through your house and find ten different places where you could put something — the table just inside the front door, the couch in the living room, your bed, the bathtub, and so on. Choose any ten places you like, but make sure that you can walk from one to the next easily and in the same order every time.

2. When you look at the pictures of objects you want to remember, imagine each object in one of the places in your house. Suppose the bathtub was on your list and a dog was on the list of items to remember. You could imagine a dog in the bathtub. (Hint: The sillier the picture you imagine, the more likely you are to remember it.)

3. Ready? Turn to page 356 and look at the pictures for a minute.

4. Close the book and imagine yourself walking from one place to another and seeing the things you've imagined.

5. How many pictures did you remember? Did you get all ten this time? Way to go!

What's Going On?

This memory trick is called the *loci method. Loci* is the Latin word for "place."

Imagining the place gives you the hint you need to remember the items. When you thought "bathtub," that told you to remember something else — "dog" (or whatever it was that you put in your bathtub).

Rhyming Memory

Got a long list of words to memorize? Rhyme your way through it!

Here's What You Do

1. Make a list of ten things you have to remember. It could be a grocery list, a list of errands or vocabulary words, or any other list you want to remember.

2. Now number your things on your list one through ten.

3. Assign a rhyming word to each number — one is the sun, two is a shoe, three is a tree, four is a door, and so on. (If you don't like our rhyming words, you can come up with rhyming words of your own. Maybe two is a zoo and three is a bee.)

4. Try to remember the items on your list by connecting them with the rhyming word instead of the number. Suppose your first item on a list of errands is buying chocolates for your mom. Our rhyming word for number one on the list was sun. Now imagine a big box of chocolates melting in the sun. What a mess! Chances are, every time you think of item number one, you'll think of the sun. When you think of the sun, you'll think of melting chocolate in the sun, and the memory will be triggered. ("That's it! I'm supposed to buy chocolates!")

What's Going On?

This works because you attach a mental picture to each item on your list. When you remember the picture, you remember the original item.

The beauty of this method is that you can run through the list from start to finish or from back to front, or you can start somewhere in the middle.

Chunking

Want to remember a list of numbers? Here's a trick that might help.

1 8 1 2 1 9 9 8 2 0 0 1

Here's What You Do

1. Read the numbers above. Then cover them up and write down as many numbers as you can remember. How did you do?

2. You probably read the numbers one by one. Now take a look at those numbers again and see if there's some other way you can read them.

3. Any ideas? Here's our suggestion. Instead of reading the numbers one by one, group them together to make three big numbers: 1812, 1998, and 2001. It's easier to remember three numbers than twelve numbers.

What's Going On?

Scientists who study memory call this trick "chunking." Organizing lots of little things into large chunks makes them easier to remember. Without chunking, most people can remember between 5 and 9 numbers or letters. With chunking, many people can do much better.

Tools for Exploration
Experimenting to test your ideas
We've given you four ways to remember a list. Can you think of any others? Think about other ways that you can link a list of items to something you *know* you can remember.

Don't you hate it when you can't remember someone's name? Especially when she just told you what it was a minute ago!

We've included this photo of one of the Exploratorium's photographers to teach you a way to get better at remembering names. That's Amy. She's aiming a camera, of course. Remember this picture, and the memory of Amy aiming the camera will remind you of her name. When you meet someone, make up a mental picture that connects the name with the person. By remembering the picture, you can remember the name.

It may take some thinking to come up with a picture for some names, but that extra thought is important. Often you forget someone's name because you never really paid attention to it in the first place. Thinking about a picture that goes with the name will make you pay attention. You might also want to immediately repeat the name to yourself, or say it out loud when you're talking to the person. ("It's nice to meet you, Amy.")

Brain Work

Now that you know (a little) about how your brain works, it's time to work your brain (a little) by doing some puzzles. We've included lots of different types of puzzles because we want you to use all of your brain. If you get stuck on a puzzle, read Hints and Suggestions and try our problem-solving tips.

Crossing the River

A farmer was taking his dog, a chicken, and a sack of grain to the market. He came to a river. There was a rowboat, but it would only hold him and one possession. He couldn't leave the dog alone with the chicken because the dog would eat the chicken. He couldn't leave the chicken alone with the grain because the chicken would eat the grain. How did he get all his possessions across the river?

Hints and Suggestions

This puzzle drove us crazy — until we realized that we were forgetting one important thing. (Putting it another way, we were assuming something. *Assuming* is when you take something for granted and don't think about it much.) Obviously, the first move is to take the chicken across the river first, then go back for the dog or the grain. But you can't leave the chicken alone with either the dog or the grain while you go back across the river for the last item. So you're stuck. Or are you? Are you assuming the same thing we did? (See page 356 for the answer.)

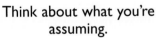
Think about what you're assuming.

Stick Squares

Get sixteen toothpicks or twigs and arrange them in five squares, as they are shown in the picture. Using all sixteen sticks, move just three sticks to make four squares. Yes, you really have to use all sixteen sticks!

Hints and Suggestions

Shuffling the sticks around isn't the quickest way to solve this puzzle. Stop for a moment and think. If you need to make five squares with no shared sides, you'd need twenty sticks. You only have sixteen sticks; so you know that some squares share a common side. To make four squares with sixteen sticks, you must arrange them so that each stick forms the side of only one square. Four squares have a total of sixteen sides. (See page 356 for the answer.)

Ask a lot of questions!

The Ping-Pong Contest

Suppose you are running a Ping-Pong contest for 205 players. When a player loses, he or she drops out of the contest. If you need one scorecard for each match, how many total scorecards will you need?

Hints and Suggestions

Start with a simpler problem. How many scorecards would you need for a tournament with three players? Five players? Solving a simple version may help you solve the more difficult problem. (See page 357 for the answer.)

Consider a simpler model!

Sacks of Gold

You have twelve sacks of gold. One of these sacks is either heavier or lighter than the others. You have a balance scale that can hold as many sacks as you like on each side of the scale. You can use the scale only four times. How can you find the odd sack of gold and figure out whether it's heavier or lighter than the others?

Break the problem into smaller pieces.

Hints and Suggestions

Putting six stacks on either side of the balance will only tell you that the two groups weigh different amounts — it won't tell you which one has the odd sack. Somehow, you need to establish that some of the sacks are the same weight, so you can figure out which one is not the same. Start with smaller groups, and proceed step by step. If you can't solve a problem, try breaking it down into smaller parts. If you still can't solve it, break it down into even smaller parts until you arrive at a problem you can manage. Be patient. This is a tough one! (See page 357 for the answer.)

Tangled Up with a Friend

You'll need a friend and two pieces of string, each about 3 feet long. Have your friend tie one end of the string around one of your wrists and the other end around your other wrist. Tie the string tightly enough so that you can't slip your hand out, but loosely enough so that there's a little bit of space between your wrist and the string. Now tie one end of the second piece of string to your friend's wrist. Put the other end of the string through the loop that's formed by your arms and the first piece of string. Then tie the other end of the string to your friend's other wrist as shown in the illustration.

Your goal is to untangle yourself from your friend without cutting the string, untying the knots, or slipping either of your wrists out of the loop that's tied around it. When you're done, you and your friend will still have the strings tied to your wrists, but you won't be tied together. Really!

Hints and Suggestions

Look closely and see if there's some way that you can put your friend's hand through the loop of string that joins you together without untying the loop, slipping your wrists out of the loop, or hurting your friend. It's tricky — if you put your friend's hand through the loop the wrong way around, you'll get an even bigger tangle! (See page 357 for the answer.)

(See page 357 for the answer.)

Tools for Exploration

Sharing your experience

If you get stuck on any of these puzzles, ask a friend for help. Sometimes another person can give you an idea that helps you get unstuck.

To find out more about your brain and how it works, visit Exploratopia *online at* www.exploratopia.com.

Part 2
Exploring Interesting Places

The Kitchen

What is this kid doing? Well, he's whipped up a bunch of egg whites to make a batch of meringue. And now he's performing a scientific test. A good meringue will stay in its bowl, even if you flip the bowl upside down. To add a bit of drama, we suggested that he hold the bowl upside down over his head! If his meringue doesn't stay in the bowl, he'll soon be wearing it!

Fortunately for him, his meringue was successful. Will you be able to say the same? If you make a good meringue, you can turn it into tasty cookies. Your kitchen is a great place to do scientific experiments, and sometimes you can even eat the results. Here's something you don't hear every day: Quit eating your food! Play with it!

Amazing Eggs

Allow us to introduce (drum roll, please) the amazing egg! You probably already know that eggs are tasty. You've got to have eggs to make birthday cake, lemon meringue pie, egg salad, and deviled eggs. But there are lots of things to do with eggs besides eat them.

Naked Eggs

We're going to strip a raw egg of its protective shell so you'll see what a raw egg looks like — naked. (Who's blushing?)

Here's What You Need

✔ A few eggs

✔ A bowl that's big enough to hold all your eggs or a coffee cup for each egg

✔ White vinegar

✔ A big spoon or ladle

Here's What You Do

1. Place your eggs in the bowl so that they are not touching. (If you can't keep the eggs from touching, put each egg in a coffee cup instead.)

2. Add enough vinegar to cover the eggs.

3. Watch. Do you see bubbles forming on the eggs' shells?

4. Cover the bowl and let it sit for 24 hours.

5. After 24 hours, *carefully* scoop the eggs out of the vinegar. At this point, the eggs' outer shells have started to dissolve.

6. Dump out the old vinegar. Put the eggs back in the container. Cover the eggs with fresh vinegar, and let them sit for another 24 hours.

7. *Carefully* scoop the eggs out again and rinse them. If any of your eggs turned into an oozing mess, throw those away.

8. The others are your naked eggs. With the shell gone, the egg is held together by a membrane, a thin skin just under the shell. You can see through the membrane.

9. *Gently* squeeze a naked egg. Don't squeeze *too* hard! Oops! We distracted you. Sorry about that!

What's Going On?

Foods, even completely natural foods such as eggs or vinegar, contain chemicals. When you put some chemicals together, they can react to make different chemicals. That's what happened when you put the eggs in the vinegar.

The egg shell is made of *calcium carbonate,* a chemical made of calcium, carbon, and oxygen. Chemists write it like this: $CaCO_3$. Ca stands for calcium; C stands for carbon, and O stands for oxygen. (The little 3 tells you that there is three times as much oxygen as there is calcium and carbon.)

Vinegar contains *acetic acid,* which is made up of carbon, hydrogen, and oxygen. When you put calcium carbonate (the egg shell) and acetic acid (the vinegar) together, the chemicals combine to make several different things — including carbon dioxide and water. The *carbon dioxide* makes the bubbles that you saw. (Chemists write carbon dioxide as

CO_2.) The vinegar dissolves the egg's shell. That means the shell becomes part of the liquid surrounding the egg. In the end, you are left with . . . a naked egg!

Put one of your naked eggs in a cup of water. The membrane that holds your naked egg together lets water leak into or out of the egg. When you put the naked egg in water, the egg swells up. That's because there's a lot of water outside the egg and not as much inside the egg. So water leaks through the membrane into the egg.

Corn syrup is a mixture of sugar and water. So when you put a naked egg in corn syrup, water and sugar surround your egg. Now there's more water inside the egg than there is outside (because there's all that sugar in the water outside the egg). So water moves out of the egg into the corn syrup, leaving your naked egg all wrinkled and flabby.

Tools for Exploration

Experimenting to test your ideas

You now know that vinegar can dissolve an eggshell. Can you find anything else vinegar will dissolve? What happens if you pour vinegar on a piece of chalk? What happens if you mix vinegar and baking soda? What happens if you pour vinegar on a seashell?

Foaming Egg Whites

Ordinary egg whites can be beaten them into a foaming frenzy. That foam becomes meringue, a baked tower of sweet bubbles. Whip up a batch of meringue and make a science experiment you can eat. Sometimes science can be mighty tasty!

Separating the Whites and Yolks

We're going to do some experiments with egg whites — no yolks allowed. But to do that, we need to separate the yolks from the whites. Here's how:

Here's What You Need

✔ Four eggs

✔ Two bowls (one for the egg whites; one for the yolks)

✔ A butter knife

✔ A grown-up helper

Here's What You Do

1. Hold an egg over one of your bowls.

2. Crack the egg's shell firmly with your butter knife.

3. Pour the raw egg yolk back and forth between the two shell halves so the whites run out into the bowl but the yolk remains in the shell. (You may have to get some help from your grown-up assistant here. This is tricky.)

4. You should end up with a bowl full of egg whites only. Throw the yolks away, or cook them up for your favorite neighborhood dog (check with the owner, not the dog).

Making Meringue

This experiment is both entertaining and tasty. You take some ordinary egg whites and beat them into a foaming frenzy. Then you make a meringue, a baked tower of sweet egg white foam.

Here's What You Need

✔ An oven

✔ Four egg whites at room temperature (See page 88 to learn how to separate egg whites and egg yolks.)

✔ A bowl made of ceramic, glass, stainless steel, or copper (anything *except* plastic)

✔ $1/2$ teaspoon white vinegar or cream of tartar

✔ An electric mixer, an egg beater, or a wire whisk

✔ $2/3$ cup sugar

✔ A tablespoon

✔ A Teflon baking/cookie sheet or an ordinary cookie sheet lined with brown paper cut from a paper bag

✔ A pot holder

✔ A grown-up helper

✔ Vanilla or almond extract (optional)

Here's What You Do

1. Set your oven to 250°F.

2. Put the egg whites in the bowl and add the vinegar or cream of tartar.

3. Put your electric mixer (or your egg beater or whisk) into the bowl of egg whites.

4. Turn your mixer up full blast (or start beating or whisking as hard as you can).

5. Keep beating the egg whites until they are foamy.

6. Slowly add the sugar to your fluffy egg whites. Keep beating until your egg whites form soft, bright white peaks.

7. Test to see if your egg whites are stiff enough by holding the bowl upside down over your head. (Who says we're kidding? See the photo on page 84.)

What's Going On?

If you try to whip plain water into a foam, you won't have much luck. Bubbles in plain water pop quickly.

But once you've made bubbles in egg whites, they don't pop! When you beat egg whites, they stretch out and make a network that holds the bubbles.

Adding a little bit of acid in the form of vinegar or cream of tartar helps egg whites hold bubbles even better. The network of bubbles — with a bit of sugar added — makes a *meringue*.

You can use your meringue to make meringue cookies. First, preheat your oven to 250°F. If you want to, you can add ¼ teaspoon almond or vanilla extract to your egg whites before you bake them into cookies.

But if you don't have any extract, don't worry about it. Drop spoonfuls of egg-white foam on your baking sheet. Put your cookies in the oven for 45 minutes. After 45 minutes, turn the heat off, but leave the meringue cookies in for at least another hour to cool. Remove the cookies from the oven when they feel cool to the touch. Use a pot holder just in case.

Be sure you *always* bake your egg whites before you eat them. Raw egg whites may make you sick!

Messing With Meringue

Now that you know how to make a meringue, experiment to see if you can make a better meringue.

Here's What You Need

✔ All the stuff you used for "Making Meringue," page 89.

Here's What You Do

1. Good cooks and scientists both like to experiment. They experiment by asking questions like: "What would happen if I put in more sugar?" or "What would happen if I added cocoa to the egg whites?" Think of some questions of your own that start with "What would happen if . . ."

2. If you need help thinking of questions, look at the chart on page 91. It shows your original meringue recipe. What would you like to try changing?

3. Choose one thing you'd like to try changing. If you change more than one thing, you don't know which change made a difference. So if you decide to add cocoa, don't add more sugar, too. Try one change at a time.

4. Think about how you'd like to test your meringue. Do you want to make a tastier meringue? Or are you looking for a meringue that can hold its shape better — one that you can use to make tall meringue towers? Decide how you will judge your finished meringue.

What's Going On?

Cookbooks provide many rules for would-be meringue makers. They say you should always use room temperature egg whites because they foam better. They say you should use a metal or glass bowl because the oils that stick to a plastic bowl will make the meringue flop. They say you should be careful to use egg whites without a drop of yolk. The fat in the yolk will get in the way and stop the egg whites from foaming.

Cookbooks also say to add the sugar after you have a nice foam. If you add sugar at first, it'll take your whites longer to foam. Adding vinegar (or any other acid) helps you make a smoother foam that holds its bubbles better.

Tools for Exploration
Keeping track of your discoveries
If you want to keep track of your experiments, copy our chart and fill in your results. As part of keeping track, you may want to figure out a way to measure your success. Can you rate your meringue's tastiness on a scale of one to ten? Can you measure how tall a meringue tower you made?

You can experiment to see if any of these rules make a difference in your meringue. And you can eat the results of your experiments. Mmmm . . . good!

Original recipe	Possible changes (Make only one change at a time)	In my experiment, I used
Four egg whites	*Fewer egg whites?* *Add a touch of yolk?*	
At room temperature	*Use cold eggs?* *Use hot eggs?*	
$1/2$ tsp. white vinegar or $1/2$ tsp. cream of tartar	*Use some other acid? Lemon juice and orange juice are acids.*	
$2/3$ cup sugar added at end	*Add sugar at beginning?* *Add less sugar? Add more sugar?*	
Nonplastic bowl	*Use a plastic bowl?*	
What happened?		**What happened?**
A great meringue! *Very fluffy and nice.* *Made some tasty cookies!*		

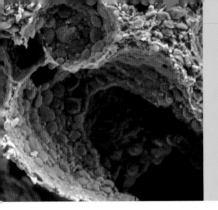

Let's Have a Bake Sale!

A loaf of bread is basically dough wrapped around a bunch of bubbles. The bubbles make the bread light and fluffy. The picture to the left shows a slice of bread magnified 100 times. You can see the holes left by all those bubbles! In this section, you'll do some experimenting with baking and bubbles.

The Fungus Among Us

Yeast creates the bubbles that make bread rise.

Here's What You Need

✔ A large balloon

✔ One packet of active dry yeast (available in grocery stores)

✔ 2 tablespoons of sugar

✔ 1 cup very warm water (105°F to 115°F). If you can't take your water's temperature, try for just under burning hot (better have a grown-up assistant test the temperature for you).

✔ A small (1 pint to 1 liter) empty bottle

Here's What You Do

1. Make sure the neck of the balloon fits over the top of the bottle. If not, you'll need a bigger balloon.

2. Blow up the balloon and then let out all the air. Do this a few times to get the balloon all stretched out.

3. Add the yeast and the sugar to the cup of very warm water and stir so that the yeast dissolves.

4. Once the yeast is dissolved, pour the yeast-sugar mixture into the bottle.

5. Is the water bubbling already? Quick! Attach the balloon to the bottle as shown at left.

6. Watch as your balloon gradually fills.

7. How long before your balloon is standing upright?

8. What do you think the balloon is filled with?

What's Going On?

Yeast is a living thing! It's a *fungus,* which means it's in the same group of living things as mushrooms and molds. That package of yeast you tore open contained billions and billions of tiny, living yeast cells. (To find out more about cells, see page 70.)

Yeast is alive, but like a lot of us, it needs food to become active. And like a lot of us, yeast likes to eat sugar. As the yeast devours sugar, it produces carbon dioxide. That's the gas that filled your balloon. When you mix yeast with bread dough, bubbles of this same gas make the bread rise.

You can buy yeast in the store, but there are other yeasts all around

you. There are different kinds of yeast scattered in the soil and in the air. There are so many different types of yeast that no one has ever counted them all. The number really wouldn't matter anyway because yeast strains change, or mutate, over time. If all the yeasts got together, they could probably take over the world! Luckily for us, they seem content just to eat their sugars and peacefully pass their gases.

Here's a close-up picture of the yeast cells like the ones that filled your balloon with carbon dioxide. Yeasts like these make bread rise. They also turn grape juice into wine. In fact, without the yeasts, we wouldn't have beer, soy sauce, hard cider, or many other foods.

Tools for Exploration

Making predictions

What will happen if you don't give the yeast any sugar? Try it and see. Part of doing science is thinking of experiments and predicting what will happen when you try the experiment.

Not-So-Nice Spice Cake

In this recipe, you change the ingredients to make something that looks like a spice cake but is really a not-so-nice cake!

Here's What You Need

✔ Six paper liners (cups) for your cupcake pan (found in baking section of grocery store)

✔ Pen or marker (to mark the bottoms of the cupcake liners)

✔ 2 cups of flour

✔ 1 1/2 cups of sugar

✔ 2 teaspoons of cinnamon

✔ 1 teaspoon powdered cloves (available in spice section of grocery stores)

✔ A large bowl

✔ Three medium bowls

✔ 2 teaspoons of margarine or softened butter

✔ One beaten egg (To beat an egg, crack it into a small bowl and swoosh it around with a fork until the yolk and white are blended.)

✔ 3 tablespoons of vanilla

✔ 4 teaspoons of Vaseline

✔ 1/2 teaspoon of liquid soap

✔ 1/4 cup of ginger ale

✔ A cupcake pan (also known as a muffin tin)

✔ An oven

✔ A pot holder

✔ Masking tape (for labeling bowls)

Here's What You Do

1. You are going to make three different kinds of cupcakes. You'll make two of each kind. Use your marker to label two cupcake liners #1. Label two liners #2. And label two liners #3.

2. Mix the flour, sugar, cinnamon, and cloves together in the large bowl. Set the mixture aside.

3. Label your three medium bowls — Bowl #1, Bowl #2, Bowl #3

4. In the three medium bowls, mix the following ingredients:
- Bowl #1: 2 teaspoons margarine, 1 tablespoon beaten egg (the egg is gloppy and difficult to measure so just do your best), and 1 tablespoon vanilla
- Bowl #2: 2 teaspoons Vaseline, 1 tablespoon beaten egg (do your best to measure), and 1 tablespoon vanilla
- Bowl #3: 2 teaspoons Vaseline, $1/2$ teaspoon liquid soap, and 1 tablespoon vanilla

5. Divide your flour mixture (in the large bowl) into three equal parts.

6. Add one-third of the flour mixture to each of the three medium bowls.

7. Add $1/4$ cup of ginger ale to each medium bowl. (It's okay, even better for what we're doing here, if you slosh over the $1/4$ cup mark a smidge. By the way, how do you like our technical cooking terms like *slosh* and *smidge*? Pretty impressive, huh?)

8. Mix the ginger ale in quickly, but gently, so you don't lose too many bubbles.

9. Pour the batter into the paper liners in your cupcake pan.

10. Put your cupcake pan into the oven and bake at 375°F for 30 minutes.

11. Compare the three varieties of your spice "cake." How does each one look?

12. Go on — take a wee nibble! You know you want to! How does each taste?

13. What's the *texture* like? That means the feel of it. Which one looks good enough to bring to school for lunch? Which one is nice and which is not-so-nice?

What's Going On?

A cook making a nice spice cake may substitute one ingredient for another. Instead of butter, a cook might use margarine, for instance. Chemically, the different ingredients react the same way. In our recipe, we replaced some tasty ingredients with ones that didn't taste so good.

Why would we do this to you? Well, we wanted to show that baking a cake involves science. (Baking a cake that actually tastes good is an art!) Take a look at the chart below; it'll help explain how substituting ingredients affected your cake.

Here's another science combination to keep in mind — a teaspoon of baking soda (a base) mixed with a cup of water will settle an upset stomach (which is filled with acid). Good luck!

Ingredient in real cake	Substitute ingredient	Chemical function of both ingredients
Margarine	Vaseline	Greasy stuff, like margarine or butter or Vaseline, helps keep certain proteins from sticking together to make long strands. This helps make your cake tender, rather than chewy.
Baking powder	Ginger ale	Both baking powder and ginger ale provide bubbles. These bubbles expand as the cake bakes, making a cake that's fluffy, rather than flat. (For more about bubbles, check out "The Fungus Among Us," page 92.)
Egg	Liquid soap	To make greasy stuff (like margarine or Vaseline) mix well with watery stuff (like ginger ale), you need to add something called an *emulsifier*. An emulsifier can stick to grease and stick to water, bringing these two things together. Egg and soap are both emulsifiers, and aren't we lucky that one of them tastes good in a cake!
Vanilla and cinnamon	Vanilla and cinnamon	We didn't change anything here! Vanilla and cinnamon make your not-so-nice cake smell like the real thing, and that's important. (For more about your sense of smell, see page 39.)

Inedible Experiments

You're about to discover two highly scientific procedures. One is from ancient Egypt and one is extremely modern. Both are inedible, *meaning, you don't get to eat anything. (We don't think you'll even be tempted, but we thought we'd warn you just in case!)*

Mind Your Mummy

Let's make a mummy! That's a preserved body. The ancient Egyptians used to mummify dead people. We hope you don't have any of *those* hanging around! You can use a hot dog instead.

Here's What You Need

✔ A plastic container that's several inches longer, wider, and deeper than your hot dog

✔ A very large box (or two smaller boxes) of baking soda (sodium bicarbonate)

✔ A small scale, like a postage scale (optional)

✔ An ordinary hot dog (could be beef, turkey, vegetarian — doesn't really matter because you're not going to eat it)

✔ Paper and pencil

✔ A ruler

✔ A piece of string at least 3 inches long

Here's What You Do

1. The ancient Egyptians mummified very important people — royalty like King Tut. Out of respect to your very important hot dog, we have named him King Oscar.

2. Fill the plastic container about two inches deep with baking soda.

3. If you have a scale, weigh King Oscar now. Record his weight.

4. Use your ruler to measure how long King Oscar is now.

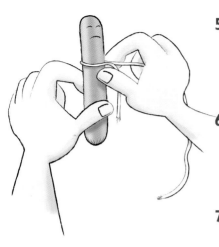

5. Use your piece of string to measure the distance around King Oscar's middle. This is his *circumference*.

6. Make notes on what King Oscar looks like now so you can compare that with what he will look like later.

7. Place King Oscar on top of the baking soda in the container and cover him with more baking soda. Make sure the baking soda is a couple of inches thick on the top and sides of dear departed King Oscar.

8. Place King Oscar in a special place (not back in the refrigerator). Leave him there for a week.

9. A week later, remove King Oscar from the baking soda. Does he look different? What does he smell like? How long is he now? What is his circumference? Write down your observations.

10. If you have a scale, weigh him again. Did he lose or gain weight?

11. Throw away the old baking soda and surround King Oscar with fresh, new baking soda and put him back in his special place for ten more days.

12. Ten days later, take King Oscar out of the baking soda again. What's he like now? He's been transformed into a stiff, leathery mummy! Now he will last a very long time. (Egyptian mummies are thousands of years old!) Put King Oscar in a place of honor.

We're ready for a picnic with a hot dog (right) and a mummified hot dog (left). Notice that the mummified dog is much shorter than the regular dog. Guess which one we plan to eat! (Not even the ants will go for the mummified hot dog!)

What's Going On?

The dramatic changes seen in King Oscar are direct results of *dehydration,* which means that water is removed from something.

If you'd left King Oscar out in the open without baking soda, he would get moldy and smelly. Food that's not refrigerated goes bad because bacteria and mold break it down, turning it into a slimy, rotten mess. To survive, bacteria and mold need water — and you've used baking soda to take the water out of King Oscar. No water . . . no rot!

King Oscar is preserved for *posterity*. (That means for future generations, infinity and beyond.) One fine day, some future archeologist will dig up your mummified hot dog . . . or maybe not!

Tools for Exploration
Measuring and counting

The numbers you gather when you measure King Oscar can help you figure out what's going on in this activity. Why do you think King Oscar gets lighter after a week in the baking soda? Why is he shorter and skinnier?

We Know Who You Are

How do we know who you are? Your DNA gives it all away — so come on, hand it over.

Here's What You Need

✔ A tablespoon

✔ Salt

✔ An 8-ounce measuring cup

✔ Water

✔ Liquid dishwashing soap

✔ A small bowl

✔ A teaspoon

✔ A ¼ teaspoon

✔ A small, clean cup

✔ A large test tube or something that looks like a test tube — something clear, narrow, and skinny. It should also have an opening that's wide enough to dip a spoon in. Possibilities include these items: juice glass, olive jar, or pill bottle.

✔ Plastic wrap or, if you have it, a rubber stopper or lid

✔ A stirrer. Possibilities include a plastic straw, a chopstick, a skewer (metal or wooden), or a Popsicle stick.

✔ Rubbing alcohol

Here's What You Do

1. Dissolve 1 tablespoon of salt in 1 cup of water to make a 6 percent solution of NaCl. (The chemical formula for salt is NaCl. Salt is made up of sodium and chloride. The Na stand for sodium and the Cl stands for chloride. This will now be called the NaCl solution.)

2. Dilute the liquid dishwashing soap by mixing one tablespoon liquid soap with 3 tablespoons of water in your small bowl. This will now be called the detergent solution.

3. Swish 1 teaspoon (not tablespoon this time) of plain (not soapy) water around in your mouth, vigorously, for at least 30 seconds. Then, spit it out into the small cup. This will now be called spit water.

4. Put $^1/4$ teaspoon of your NaCl solution into the test tube.

5. Pour your spit water from the cup into the test tube with the NaCl solution.

6. Add $^1/4$ teaspoon of the detergent solution to the test tube.

7. Cover the top of the test tube securely with the plastic wrap, rubber stopper, or lid.

8. Gently turn the tube or jar *almost* upside down several times. Avoid making any bubbles.

9. Take off the stopper and dribble about 1 teaspoon of the rubbing alcohol down the side of the tube into the mixture. Look for the rubbing alcohol to form a layer on top of the spit water/NaCl/detergent mixture.

10. Did a white, stringy layer form? Good. Now try and grab the white, stringy layer with your stirrer. (It won't be easy!) That gunk is made up of your DNA. Oh, it contains some proteins and other stuff, too. But it's mostly your DNA.

What's Going On?

Deoxyribonucleic acid, better known as DNA, is the genetic material present in all organisms, from bacteria to humans. From before you were born, your DNA provided instructions on how to build your body.

Your DNA is found in your blood, your cheek cells, your skin, and the various parts of you. There are many similarities in the DNA of different organisms — you may have more in common with a kiwi fruit than you imagine. But, with one exception, your DNA is unique and all your own. Family members have similar DNA, but no other person (or fruit or animal or potted plant) in the entire universe has the exact same DNA as you, unless you are an identical twin. If you are, you and your twin have the same DNA.

The white, stringy layer you captured from the test tube contains your personal DNA. Each string is composed of thousands of DNA molecules all stuck together.

DNA is easy to get. There are about fifty trillion cells of DNA in the human body! You got your own DNA when you swished water around in your mouth. The swishing removed cells from your cheeks. (The more swishing you do, the more cells you'll collect.)

The dishwashing detergent broke down the cells, releasing the DNA into the mixture. The salt combined with the DNA, and the DNA clumped together where the water and alcohol layers met.

The procedure you used here in your kitchen is the same basic process researchers use in their labs to isolate, analyze, and identify DNA. Scientists have figured out how to read DNA codes. They can extract DNA from in a drop of blood found at a crime scene and figure out whether it matches the DNA of a suspect.

DNA has become such a valuable tool in crime solving that it seems that criminals can't get away with anything any more. Ha! (Speaking of which, where were you on the night of . . . ?)

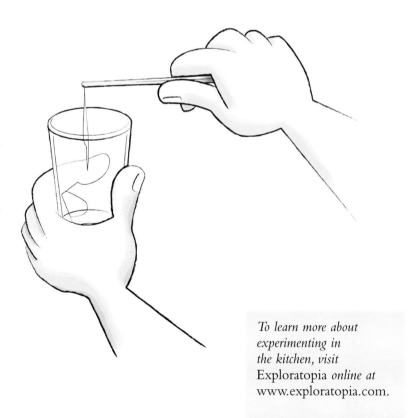

To learn more about experimenting in the kitchen, visit Exploratopia *online at* www.exploratopia.com.

The Bathroom

A raging hurricane and the water draining from a bathroom sink have a lot in common. Both form a spiraling whirlpool called a *vortex*.

Watch what happens when you drain water. Does your whirlpool spin clockwise (in the same direction that the hands move on a clock) or counterclockwise (the opposite direction)?

Some people say that the water draining from a tub spins counterclockwise if you're in the Northern Hemisphere—the northern half of the earth—and clockwise if you're in the Southern Hemisphere—the southern half of the earth.

This isn't quite true for the water going down your drain. The direction in which your bathwater spins depends on things like the position of the drain in your tub, breezes over the water surface, and any leftover water movement from you.

But the direction of a hurricane *does* depend on where it is on the earth. The earth's spin causes hurricane winds to revolve counterclockwise in the Northern Hemisphere and clockwise in the Southern Hemisphere. French physicist Gaspard de Coriolis first realized this in 1844. Today it's called the *Coriolis effect*.

Bet you never thought you'd learn about hurricanes from watching water in your tub!

Mirrors

How many candles are in this picture? Hmm . . . that's not an easy question to answer. Mirrors can be very tricky, as you'll find out when you start experimenting with them. (And for your information, there's only one candle. The rest are reflections.)

Looking into Infinity

When you bounce light between mirrors, you get a view that goes on and on and on and . . .

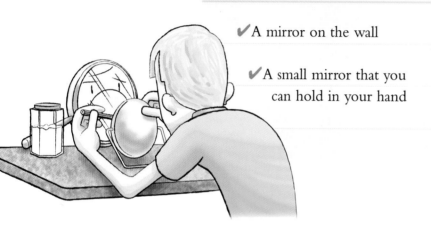

Here's What You Need

✔ A mirror on the wall

✔ A small mirror that you can hold in your hand

Here's What You Do

1. Stand about 6 inches from the mirror on the wall.

2. Hold the small mirror right under your eyes and look into the mirror on the wall.

3. Hold your finger between the two mirrors. Can you see its reflection? How many fingers do you see?

What's Going On?

When you look at yourself in a mirror, you see yourself because light bounces off you, hits the mirror, and reflects back into your eyes. (To find out how light lets you see, check out page 11.)

When light bounces off a mirror and hits another mirror, you get a reflection of a reflection. When you have two mirrors facing each other, you get a reflection of a reflection of a reflection of a . . . you get the idea.

Something that is *infinite* goes on forever and ever. *Infinity* is an endless distance or time.

The reflections in your mirrors don't really go on to infinity — even though they look as though they do. With each reflection, the mirrors absorb a little light. Each reflection is a little darker than the one before. Eventually, they fade out altogether.

Tools for Exploration

Asking questions

What happens if you tilt the mirror? What happens if you move closer to the mirror? What happens if you move farther away? Can you think of other questions that you can answer by experimenting?

Alphabet Flip

When you put a mirror above the alphabet, do all the letters look upside down?

Here's What You Need

✔ A small mirror

✔ A pen or pencil

✔ Paper

A B C D E F G H I J K L M N O P Q R S T U V W X Y Z

Here's What You Do

1. Put your mirror on the dotted line above the alphabet.

2. Look in the mirror. The letters are all upside down. Or *are* they?

3. Can you find letters that look the same in the mirror as they do in the book? Those letters look the same right side up as they do upside down. Write those letters on a piece of paper.

4. What words can you make with these letters? Can you make a sentence from these words? We used them to write about a fishing expedition. Put a mirror on the dotted line above our sentence. Can you read the words in your mirror?

What's Going On?

Most of the alphabet letters look upside down in the mirror. But some of the letters don't seem to change at all.

The *H* looks perfectly fine in the mirror. So do the *E* and the *O*. There are six other letters that look the same in the mirror as they do in the book. Did you find them all? (If not, take another look. If you're still stumped, see page 358 for all nine letters.)

What do these letters have in common? In all nine, the top half of the letter and the bottom half of the letter are mirror images of each other. Letters like this are *horizontally symmetrical*. (For more on symmetry, see page 230.)

When a letter that's horizontally symmetrical is upside down and backward, it looks the same as it did when it was right side up and facing forward.

The words that you can read in the mirror only use letters that are horizontally symmetrical.

I HOOKED COD

What Else Can I Try?

Hold this page in front of your bathroom mirror. Can you still read our fish story?

I HOOKED COD

Take a look at the alphabet on page 105 in the mirror. Some letters look backwards in the mirror — but eleven letters look just fine. Can you find all eleven? (If you're stumped, see page 358.)

When you reflect the alphabet in the mirror like this, the letters are reversed — but they aren't upside down. The letters that look perfectly fine when they are reversed in the mirror are *vertically symmetrical*. That means that the left side and the right side of the letter are mirror images of each other. Letters like *T* and *M* and *H* are vertically symmetrical. (For more on symmetry, see page 230.)

Take a look in the mirror at the restaurant name below.

OHIO HAM HUT

All the letters look fine in the mirror, but you can't read the words. The order of the letters is reversed.

Can you write a sentence that you can read when you reflect it in the mirror? Here's the best we could do. Can you do better?

TOOT OTTO TOOT

A word that you can read in the mirror must be made up of vertically symmetrical letters — and it has to read the same backward and forward. That's true of *TOOT* and *MOM*. Can you think of any other words that will work? Words (and sentences) that read the same backward and forward are called *palindromes*. But not all palindromes are made up of letters that are vertically symmetrical. One of our favorite palindromes is RATS LIVE ON NO EVIL STAR. Write the letters of the sentence from beginning to end — or from end to beginning — and you get the same sentence!

Water Tight

In this photo, blue dye in the water reveals the motion of the water caused by the legs of a water strider, an insect that walks on water.

How do water striders walk on water? That's what you'll find out with a little bit of experimenting.

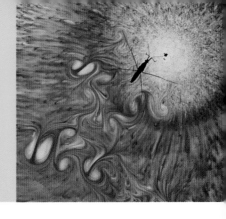

The Shape of Rain

What's the shape of your water?

Here's What You Need

✔ Three medicine droppers

✔ Water

✔ Rubbing or isopropyl alcohol (check your bathroom cabinet for this)

✔ Vegetable oil

✔ Wax paper

✔ Toothpicks

✔ Liquid soap or detergent

Here's What You Do

1. Use the medicine droppers to place a drop of water, a drop of rubbing alcohol, and a drop of vegetable oil on a piece of wax paper.

2. Take a close look at the three drops. How are they different?

3. Try poking the water drop with a clean dry toothpick. How does it react?

4. Poke the water drop again with a toothpick that has been dipped in liquid soap or detergent. Now what happens?

What's Going On?

A drop of water on a waxy surface looks kind of like there's a skin around it, holding the water in. The drop looks a little bit like a water balloon sitting on the floor. Do the drop of alcohol and the drop of oil look the same or different?

When you poked the water drop with the clean dry toothpick, nothing happened. But when you poked it with the soapy toothpick, it flattened like a popped water balloon. Weird!

We'll talk about why water acts like it has a skin — but first try a few more experiments.

Tools for Exploration

Comparing two things

You poked your water drop with a dry toothpick and a soapy one. What else can you put on a toothpick? Try poking a water drop with a toothpick dipped in salt. Or rubbing alcohol. Or lemon juice. What happens?

Next time you are out after a rainstorm (or early in the morning before the dew has dried), look for drops of water on leaves, spider webs, or newly waxed cars. Those water drops form little beads, just like your water drop did before you poked it with the soapy toothpick.

Sink or Swim

Will a paper clip float or sink? Take a guess and then try it and find out.

Here's What You Need

✔ Paper clips (must be flat and not bent out of shape)

✔ Bowl of water

✔ A fork

✔ A candle

✔ Liquid soap

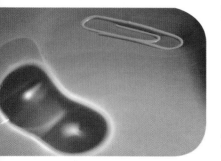

Here's What You Do

1. Drop a paper clip into the bowl of water. It sinks. That's it! The experiment is over! Now, now, not so fast . . . we're just kidding!

2. Try it again. This time, use your fork to lower the paper clip gently onto the water's surface. Does your paper clip float?

3. If it doesn't, rub your paper clip with a candle and try again. A paper clip that's rubbed with wax or oil will float better.

4. Once you get your paper clip to float, notice how it bends the surface of the water.

5. Can you see the shadow of the floating paper clip on the bottom of the bowl? Do you see anything unusual about it?

6. Add a touch of liquid soap to the water. What happens to the floating paper clip?

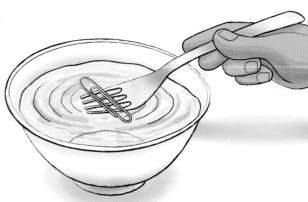

What's Going On?

Your paper clip looks like it's sitting on top of the same thin skin that held your water drop together in "The Shape of Rain" experiment. When you add soap, the stretchy skin breaks and your paper clip sinks.

Water acts like it has a stretchy skin on top because of a property known as *surface tension*. To figure out what causes surface tension, we need to take a really, really close look at water.

Water, like everything else around you, is made of tiny particles called atoms. Those tiny atoms stick together to make combinations of atoms called molecules.

Water molecules like to stick together. When something, like a paper clip, tries to push the molecules apart, they won't let it through, unless it pushes hard. When you dropped a paper clip into a bowl of water, it shoved the water molecules aside and fell to the bottom of the bowl. But when you lowered the paper clip carefully, it didn't push hard enough to shove the water molecules apart. So it stayed on the surface of the water — just like the water strider!

The paper clip and the water strider look like they are resting on a stretchy skin, but there really isn't a skin on top of the water. Surface tension results from water molecules sticking together all through the water. You see the results of all that stick-togetherness at the water's surface.

A little bit of soap decreases water's surface tension and makes the paper clip sink. That's because soap squeezes between the water molecules, pushing them apart. When the water molecules are farther away from each other, they aren't attracted to each other as much and it doesn't take as much of a push to shove them apart.

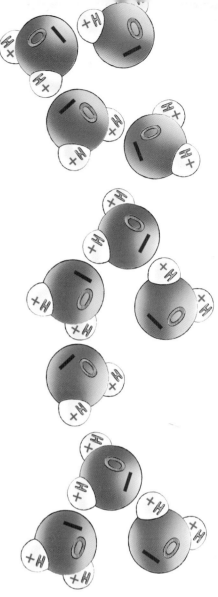

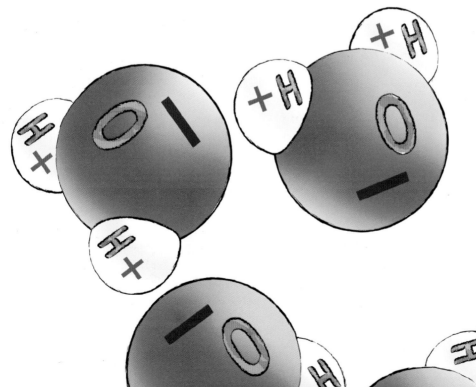

Have you ever heard someone call water H_2O? Each molecule of water is made of two atoms of hydrogen (that's the H) and one atom of oxygen (that's the O). At room temperature, hydrogen by itself is a gas — and so is oxygen. But if you put hydrogen and oxygen atoms together in just the right way, you get H_2O, or water. Water molecules stick together because the hydrogen atom in one water molecule is attracted to the oxygen atom in another water molecule.

Bubbles

The Exploratorium held its first Bubble Festival in 1983. People came from all over to show us cubical bubbles, bubble caterpillars, bubble towers, bubbles that popped right away, and bubbles that could sit on a shelf for almost a year. Some people think studying bubbles is silly. We disagree!

Handfuls of Bubbles

Here's an experiment to try the next time you take a bath!

Here's What You Need

✔ Your hands

✔ Water

✔ Some liquid or dishwashing soap

Here's What You Do

1. Get your hands completely wet.

2. Wash your hands with liquid soap but don't rinse. Make sure your hands are covered with soap and water.

3. Make a fist, then slide your fingers open to make an okay sign. Is there a soap film stretched across the O? If not, try again until there is.

4. Blow gently through the O to blow a bubble. When you have a big bubble, gently squeeze your thumb and finger together to close the O.

5. Slowly turn your palm up. Did you get a bubble on your hand?

6. Now that you have a bubble, play with it! Float it, poke it, stretch it — OOPS!

7. Can you figure out any other way to blow bubbles using your hands?

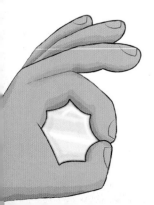

What's Going On?

A bubble is a thin skin of soap and water, stretched around a puff of air. And there's no getting around it — you need soap to make bubbles. Plain water likes to stick together. You just can't make it stretch out to wrap around a puff of air.

If you tried "The Shape of Rain" on page 107, then you already know that adding soap makes the water less sticky. Once you've added soap, the water will make a film that can stretch and make a bubble.

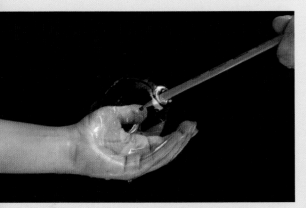

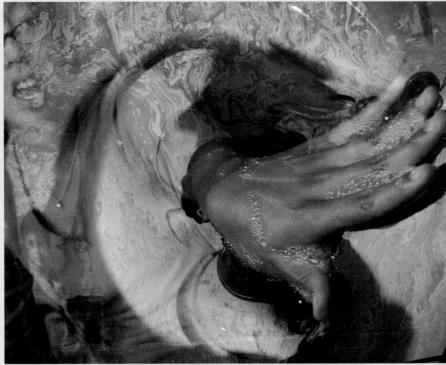

Were you able to touch your bubble without popping it? You can touch a bubble as long as your hand (or whatever touches the bubble) is wet. When your hand is wet, the water on your hand becomes part of the bubble, and the bubble doesn't pop.

Here's a bubble rule: Dry stuff pops bubbles. Wet stuff doesn't.

You can blow a bubble by making a bubble hoop using your two hands.

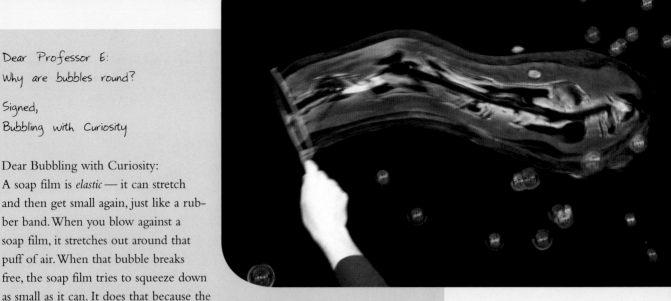

Dear Professor E:
Why are bubbles round?

Signed,
Bubbling with Curiosity

Dear Bubbling with Curiosity:
A soap film is *elastic* — it can stretch and then get small again, just like a rubber band. When you blow against a soap film, it stretches out around that puff of air. When that bubble breaks free, the soap film tries to squeeze down as small as it can. It does that because the water molecules in the film are attracted to each other. (Remember, water molecules like to stick together!) That's why most free-floating bubbles look round, or *spherical*. A *sphere* is the shape that provides the most space for the air (largest volume) with the least stretching of the soap film (smallest surface area). As a scientist, I'd say that the soap film *minimizes its surface area*. That means it makes itself as small as it possibly can.

But you know what? Not all bubbles are round. Keep experimenting and you'll find out what I mean.

Your bubbly friend,
Professor E

Bubble Juice

To do the rest of our bubble experiments, you'll need a supply of bubble juice!

Here's What You Need

✔ 1 gallon of water

✔ $2/3$ cup dishwashing liquid (Dawn or Joy works well)

✔ 1 tablespoon of glycerine (optional, available at drug stores)

Here's What You Do

1. Mix the water and dishwashing liquid.

2. Add glycerine if you have it. (This will increase the strength of your bubbles.)

3. For the best bubbles, let your bubble juice age for a day or two.

Building With Bubbles

Bubbles are round when they are floating through the air. But when you pack bubbles together, you'll make lots of different shapes.

Here's What You Need

✔ Bubble juice (see page 112)

✔ A cookie sheet (with sides) or another flat dish

✔ A plastic straw

✔ A cup of water

Here's What You Do

1. Pour enough bubble juice onto the cookie sheet to completely cover the bottom.

2. Dip the straw into the bubble juice. Hold the straw over the cookie sheet and blow through the straw to make a bubble on the cookie sheet. What shape is your bubble?

3. Blow another bubble, which touches your first bubble. Now what shapes are the bubbles?

4. Blow another bubble so that you have a cluster of three bubbles. What happens where they meet?

5. Blow a lot of bubbles. How many different shapes can you find in your mess, uh, that is, *mass* of bubbles?

6. Try blowing more bubbles on top of your layer of bubble domes. Look carefully at the shapes formed when bubbles are squashed between other bubbles.

What's Going On?

As Professor Exploratorium explained on page 112, the water molecules in a soap film want to get as close together as they can. So the water molecules squeeze together and make the smallest possible film. That need to squeeze together is what makes bubbles form the shapes they do.

Tools for Exploration

Making predictions

When the two bubbles that are the same size meet, the wall between them is flat. What do you think will happen when one bubble is bigger than the other one? Try it and see.

When a bubble is clinging to a bubble wand or floating through the air, it's round or spherical. That's the shape that lets the soap film shrink to the smallest size.

When a bubble rests on a wet cookie sheet, the water on the cookie sheet forms one wall of the bubble, and the soap film can shrink to make a bubble dome. (In this photo, you can also see the beautiful bubble colors. To learn more about those colors, see page 310.)

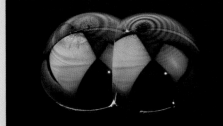

When two bubbles meet, they grab onto each other and form a common wall between the bubbles. That lets each soap film get a little bit smaller.

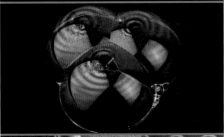

When three bubbles meet, they all form common walls. When the bubbles are about the same size, they always meet at about the same angle.

A bunch of bubbles squeezed between two panes of glass look a little like the wax honeycomb that bees build to hold their honey. The soap film shrinks to the smallest shape that will let it hold the air inside. The bees build the shape that lets them store the most honey while using as little wax as they can. So they end up with similar shapes! The cells of a honeycomb always meet in groups of three, forming equal angles of 120 degrees. Bubbles in a cluster often do the same.

Bubbles are round when floating through the air. But when packed close together, bubbles make all kinds of shapes.

You can see this with your own bottle full of bubbles. Pour two cups of bubble juice into a big plastic soda bottle. Cover the top of the bottle and shake it. Then dump the bubble juice out into a container so you can play with it later. To get the best bubbles, turn your bottle upside down and empty it so that goes glug, glug, glug, rather than pouring out smoothly. You'll end up with a bottle full of bubbles.

Use a marker to trace where the bubble walls meet the plastic bottle. When you look at the traced patterns, you can see how each bubble in a cluster makes use of neighboring bubbles to get as small as it can.

The Scoop on Poop

All right, we know you're snickering now. But if we're using the bathroom as a scientific laboratory, we can't ignore the toilet. Scientists are interested in everything in the world — including poop. They have discovered you can learn a lot from poop.

Watching Whirlpools

Watch what happens to the water as you flush the toilet or drain the bathtub.

Here's What You Do

1. Next time you take a bath, watch what happens when you drain the water. Chances are the water will make a whirlpool as it swirls down the drain.

2. Which direction does your whirlpool spin? Does it go clockwise (in the same direction that the hands move on a clock) or counterclockwise (the opposite direction)?

3. Flush the toilet. Which way does the whirlpool in the toilet swirl?

What's Going On?

As we told you at the beginning of this chapter, some people say that draining water swirls counterclockwise in the Northern Hemisphere, where North America is, and clockwise in the Southern Hemisphere, where Australia is.

What hemisphere do you live in? Which way did your water swirl?

At the Exploratorium, we asked lots of people to tell us which way the water swirled as it drained. All the people we asked lived in California, which is in the Northern Hemisphere. Some people reported that the water swirled counterclockwise, but many also reported that the water swirled clockwise!

Scientists say that the direction that the water spins depends on things like the position of the drain and the direction of any water flowing into the container. Your position on the planet really doesn't matter.

It just goes to show — you can't believe everything you hear! Sometimes, you just have to experiment for yourself.

Dear Professor E:
I just have to ask: What is poop, anyway?

Signed,
Pooped in Pasadena

Dear *Pooped in Pasadena,*

You had to ask? That's good. That's a sign that you are a real scientist, curious about everything in the world. Scientists ask lots of questions, even about things that some people would just like to flush away!

Your body *digests* the food you eat. That means it breaks down the food to obtain the nutrients you need to live and grow. Poop, also called *feces, scat, dung, manure,* or *excrement,* is what's left of food after your body absorbs all that it can. Poop also contains water, protein, fats, and salts released from the intestines and liver, as well as some of the bacteria that live in your intestine and help you digest food. These bacteria produce the gases that give poop its distinctive smell.

Poop also contains wastes produced by your body. Poop is usually brownish in color because of one of those waste products, a substance called *bilirubin.* Your body makes bilirubin when it breaks down old, worn-out red blood cells. Since your body is always breaking down and replacing red blood cells, it makes a lot of bilirubin.

But your poop can change color depending on what you eat. If you eat large amounts of green, leafy vegetables, your poop can turn green. (Well? What are you waiting for?)

If food bits appear in your poop, the food wasn't digested. Some foods that are hard to digest are corn, peanuts, peas, carrots, cereals, and beans.

So, there you have it — the whole poop and nothing but the poop!

Yours in scientific curiosity,
Professor E

This lovely beach is made of parrot fish poop. That's right. Parrot fish eat the algae that grow on coral rock, scientifically known as calcium carbonate. Naturally, a lot of this calcium carbonate gets into the digestive system of the fish. The fish can't digest it, so they poop the calcium carbonate out as they swim. The calcium carbonate poop ends up as sand, which washes up on the shore. So the next time you take a walk on a tropical coral beach, thank the parrot fish for pooping out all that beautiful sand for you! (See page 174 for more about coral sand.)

Dear Professor E:
I was wondering how a whale goes to the bathroom, where it goes to the bathroom, and how big its poop is. My friend said it's as big as a person! Now I'm scared to swim in the ocean.

Signed,
A Whale of a Tale?

Dear A Whale of a Tale?
To get your answer, I spoke with the biologists at the Bamfield Marine Sciences Centre in Canada. They said not to worry. Whale scat (that's what they called it) comes out as a cloudy liquid. It can contain little bits of shell and bone, but those get scattered in the water quickly. The whale releases its scat as it dives down from the water's surface.

Marine biologists study a whale's scat to find out what the whale ate. The solid parts of the scat are scooped up with a net or a bucket, dried out, and then analyzed.

Whalefully yours,
Professor E

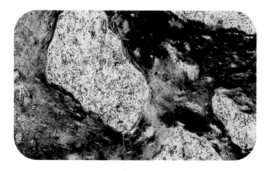

This, my friends, is the biggest piece of coprolite, *or fossilized dinosaur poop, ever found. About the size of a super-sized loaf of bread, it measures in at a whopping 44 cm (17 in) long, 13 cm (5 in) high, and 16 cm (6 in) wide.*

By looking at dinosaur poop, scientists can tell a lot about what the animal ate, which can reveal where the dinosaur lived. This photo shows a thin slice through that giant coprolite. Those light yellow chunks are pieces of bone from a young, plant-eating dinosaur, probably the last meal of the dinosaur that left this coprolite behind.

Scientists are pretty sure that this giant poop came from none other than a Tyrannosaurus rex. This particular piece of dinosaur poop is 65 million years old.

This is the fossil of a termite, captured in fossilized tree sap, or amber. Look closely and you'll see some small bubbles, also preserved in the amber. Those are fossil termite farts.

No, we aren't kidding.

Because of their diet and their digestive processes, termites fart a lot. Scientists had noticed that when they found termites fossilized in amber, there were usually bubbles in the amber, too. Some scientists analyzed the gas in the bubbles and discovered that these were no ordinary bubbles. They were fossilized termite farts, hundreds of thousands of years old.

We told you that scientists are curious about everything.

To learn more about mirrors, bubbles, and other explorations in the bathroom, visit Exploratopia *online at* www.exploratopia.com.

The Backyard

What's in your backyard? Some grass, some dirt, maybe a tree or two?

Think again! That may be all you see when you look out the door, but there's a lot going on in that patch of dirt and grass.

You share your backyard with millions of busy animals. That's right. Even if you have only a teeny, tiny backyard, you'll find ants, worms, snails, and other critters out there. With a little effort, you can get to know all these critters — and the world in which they live — a lot better.

Garden Critters

Your backyard is filled with living creatures. Hiding in the dirt, grass, and flower gardens, there are ants, snails, worms, slugs, and many other small animals all going about their lives.

The experiments here will give you a bug's-eye view of your backyard.

Ants Come Marching One by One

Have you ever noticed that ants like to play "follow the leader"? One ant finds a bit of food, and all the other ants follow the exact same path to get to the snack. Do an experiment to find out why.

Here's What You Need

- ✔ A small plate
- ✔ A sheet of paper or lightweight cardboard at least 16 inches square
- ✔ A pencil
- ✔ Scissors
- ✔ Masking tape
- ✔ Ants
- ✔ Honey

Here's What You Do

1. Center the small plate upside down on the cardboard and draw a circle around it.

2. Draw another circle about 1 inch larger around this first circle. (It doesn't have to be perfect.) Then draw another circle an inch larger around that one, and another circle an inch larger than that . . . until you have a circle surrounded by four circles.

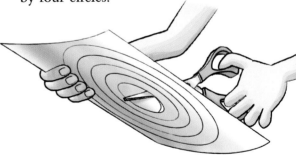

3. Cut along each line. Remove the circle in the middle. You'll have a circular hole surrounded by four rings.

4. Lightly tape the rings together.

5. Find a spot outside where there are ants — a sidewalk, a patio, or a smooth patch of dirt. Place a drop of honey near the ants.

6. Put your rings down with the honey in the center hole. Tape down the outer and inner edges of the rings, or use a rock to weigh the rings down.

7. What happens when the first ant finds the honey? The ant drinks some honey and then heads back to the anthill. Before long you'll have a trail of ants from the anthill to the honey.

8. Notice that all the ants heading for the food follow the same path. The ant returning to the ant hill with honey marked its trail with a scent that other ants can smell. The other ants follow that scent.

9. Remove the ring in the center. When you take away the ring, you take away part of the scent trail that the ants were following. How do the ants react to the break in their trail? What do they do?

10. Watch until the ants have found their way to the honey again. Then remove the next two rings, closest to the center. Do the ants take longer to find their way across the bigger gap to their trail?

11. Put an object — a small rock or a clump of dirt — in the ants' way. What do the ants do?

What's Going On?

An ant, returning to her nest from a source of food, marks her trail with a scent that other ants follow. If you want to get fancy, you can call this scent a *pheromone*. That's what biologists call chemical messages that cause animals to behave a certain way.

Every ant that returns to the anthill with food marks her trail with pheromones. When the honey is all gone, the ants stop marking the trail. The trail disappears and the ants stop returning to the spot where the honey used to be.

Ants produce many different pheromones. Each one carries a different message. All the work in the anthill, from caring for the eggs to taking dead ants out to the rubbish heap, is controlled by pheromones.

Tools for Exploration

Asking questions

Can you think of some questions that you could answer by experimenting? A great way to begin a question is with the words: What would happen if . . .

What would happen if you put something with a strong smell — such as perfume — on the ant's trail? What would happen if you tried to wipe away the trail? What would happen if _____? You fill in the blank. Once you have a question, you can experiment to find out the answer.

These fuzzy blue dots are streptomyces, a kind of bacteria that live in the dirt. Bacteria are microorganisms — micro means "tiny" and organism is a fancy word that means "living thing." These bacteria are tiny — it would take more than a thousand of them, lined up side by side, to stretch from one side of the head of a pin to the other. One teaspoon of soil can hold over five billion streptomyces bacteria. There are many different kinds of bacteria. This kind of bacteria produces the chemical that gives soil its earthy smell. Basically, these are the living things that make dirt smell like dirt.

Butterfly Garden

Plant a garden that brings butterflies into your yard.

Here's What You Need

✔ A sunny spot in your yard or some big flowerpots if you don't have the yard space

✔ A grown-up who wants to help with this project

Here's What You Do

1. First, figure out which plants butterflies like. Go to a park or a neighbor's garden and look for butterflies. Do the butterflies seem to like certain flowers? Butterflies drink nectar, a sweet liquid that flowers make. Draw pictures of the butterflies and their favorite flowers.

2. Before a butterfly becomes a butterfly, it's a caterpillar. Butterflies lay their eggs on certain plants — the plants that their caterpillars like to eat. These are called *larval* plants. (The caterpillar is the *larva* of the butterfly.) Check your library for books on butterflies and butterfly gardening.

Ask a reference librarian to help you figure out what kinds of butterflies you saw and what kinds of plants those butterflies and their caterpillars like.

3. Make a list of plants for your butterfly garden. Visit a plant nursery and look for the plants on your list. Ask the people at the nursery for help.

4. Plant your butterfly garden in a sunny place that's sheltered from the wind. In the summer, check the larval plants for eggs and caterpillars. Some kinds of caterpillars spin threads and wrap those threads around themselves to make a *cocoon*. Other kinds of caterpillars cover themselves in sticky stuff that hardens into a shell, or *chrysalis*.

If you're lucky, you may find a cocoon or chrysalis hanging on a leaf of your larval plants. If you do, leave it where it is so that the caterpillar inside can turn into a butterfly.

Tools for Exploration

Paying attention to stuff a lot of people ignore

Many people like butterflies. But how many people pay attention to what butterflies like? By watching butterflies, you can figure out what flowers they like. Is there anything else you notice that might make your butterfly garden even better?

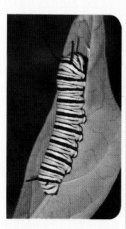

Every butterfly starts as a tiny egg laid on a twig, leaf, or bud. That egg hatches into a caterpillar, like this one. The caterpillar feeds on leaves, eating and eating and eating . . .

When the caterpillar is full grown, it attaches itself to a plant or building and sheds its skin.

Its soft green outer layer hardens into a shiny case called a chrysalis. Inside the chrysalis, the caterpillar turns into a butterfly.

When the butterfly is almost ready to leave its chrysalis, the walls of the chrysalis become clear. Can you see the wings of the butterfly through the chrysalis?

A monarch butterfly like this one hatches from a chrysalis, spreads its wings, and flies away!

Get to Know a Snail

Learn a few things from a garden snail. You can start by slowing down.

Here's What You Need

✔ Some snails or slugs

✔ A container with a lid for your snails or slugs. Punch holes in the lid so your snails and slugs can breathe.

✔ Some plants for your snails, slugs, or worms to crawl on

✔ A piece of something stiff and clear, like one side of a plastic CD case (optional)

✔ A magnifying lens (optional)

✔ Paper and crayons or colored pencils

Here's What You Do

1. Find a few snails or slugs in your yard or a neighbor's yard. The best time to look for snails is early in the morning, when the plants are still wet with dew. If you get up late (yawn!), look for snails in moist, sheltered places such as old flower pots or shady corners. Put your snails in your container with some plant leaves.

2. Watch your snails crawl around your container. (Allow a lot of time for this!) Can your snails crawl up a wall? Ours can. Can your snails crawl upside down? Can they crawl on different surfaces? If you have different containers, see if they can crawl up all of them.

3. Snails lay down a trail of slime as they crawl. Do they slime everything or just some surfaces? Does it matter whether the surface is wet? dry? smooth? rough? To get a good look at the slime trail, let your snails crawl over a piece of black paper. They'll leave a lovely trail behind.

4. What do your snails like to eat? Offer them a variety of foods and nonfood items. Do they like lettuce? grass? apples? cardboard? (Oops — there goes your container!)

5. If you have a piece of clear plastic, put a snail on it. Watch from the other side of the plastic as the snail crawls. Give the snail a snack. As the snail eats, watch it from below through the clear plastic. Can you find your snail's mouth? If you have a magnifying glass, look through that. (Don't use the magnifying glass in direct sunlight! You don't want to burn your snail.)

6. Draw a portrait of a snail. Put in all the interesting things you noticed about the snail.

7. Make a snail obstacle course or maybe a snail circus. Try to get your snails to crawl on a tightrope, up a ladder, or along a loop-the-loop.

What's Going On?

Bet you didn't know that snails could be so fascinating. (And all this time, you've been ignoring them, or worse, squishing them!)

When did your snails make the most slime? Our snails lay down trails of slime when they need some extra sticking power — when they are climbing walls, for example.

Did you find your snail's mouth? It's on the underside of its head.

Tools for Exploration

Experimenting to test your ideas

Some gardeners say that snails don't like coffee grounds or copper, the metal that pennies are made of. Gardeners use these things to try to keep snails away from their garden plants. Can you think of ways to find out whether these gardeners are right? How could you test these ideas and find out what out what might make snails leave a plant alone?

Your snail has a long tongue covered with tiny teeth. This tongue is called a radula.

A snail's radula may have as many as a quarter of a million teeth of different sizes and shapes! When the snail scrapes its radula against some food, the teeth tear the food into pieces that the snail can eat.

This picture of a snail's radula was taken through a microscope. It shows what the radula looks like magnified 75 times. The radula in this picture is from a rare deep-sea snail species that feeds on sponges. The radula of your garden snail may not be quite as spectacular as this one, but a quarter of a million teeth are impressive no matter what!

Even a small backyard probably has a few hundred worms. Some scientists say a single acre of moist dirt contains about 50,000 busily burrowing earthworms.

Next time someone is digging in the garden, keep an eye out for worms. If you find a worm, stop for a moment and watch it move. You'll see lots of little rings around the worm's body. These are called segments. A full-grown earthworm may have as many as 170 segments. (How many does your worm have?) You may also notice the worm's clitellum, a swollen band about one third of the way down the worm. The clitellum makes the stuff that forms cocoons for baby earthworms.

You may think that the worm's head looks just like its tail, but if you look closer you'll see that the head is a little darker in color than the tail. You'll see parts of the worm's body get thicker and then thinner, as the worm uses its muscles to move. When the worm's body bulges, tiny bristles (much too small to see without a microscope) extend from the worm and push against the ground, holding that part of the worm in place while the rest of the worm moves forward.

Watch the worm, then let it go. Worms are good for your garden. They burrow through the ground, eating rotting leaves and other plant matter. They help break this stuff down into the nutrients that plants need to grow.

Tail   Clitellum   Segments   Head

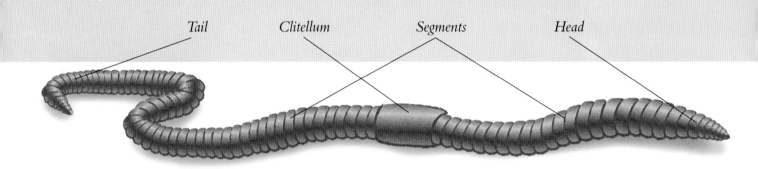

What's Under That Rock?

Look under rocks and flowerpots in your garden. Chances are you'll find some critters that look like this. When you bother one of them, it will roll up into a ball, hiding its belly and legs.

Some people call this critter a roly-poly. If your roly-poly rolls up all the way, it's a pillbug. If it rolls up halfway and has two tail-like things on its rear end, it's a sowbug. A scientist calls pillbugs and sowbugs *isopods* — that's the type of critters they are. Even though they are called bugs, they aren't insects. They are *crustaceans* — like crabs or lobsters. Pillbugs eat decaying vegetation, like rotting leaves. Mostly they hide in dark places, but at night they'll wander about. As a pillbug grows, it must shed its hard outer skin. A pillbug will do this a dozen or more times during its life. The average life of a pillbug is about two years, but some have lived as long as five years!

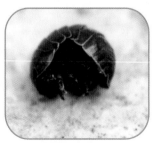

Your Friends, the Plants

Plants make the oxygen that we need to breathe. This photo shows a magnified view of a leaf. The spots that look like eyes are stomata, *openings that let air and water move in and out of the plant. When the plant has lots of water in its leaves, the stomata open and let water vapor — and some oxygen — escape.*

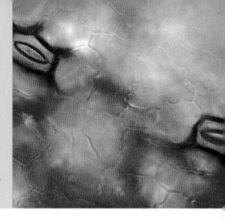

Fifteen-Bean Garden

Use beans from the grocery store to make a garden.

Here's What You Need

- ✔ A bag of fifteen-bean soup mix from the grocery store
- ✔ A bowl
- ✔ A plastic bag
- ✔ Water
- ✔ Paper towels
- ✔ A clear, plastic container at least 3 inches deep
- ✔ A sunny window

Here's What You Do

1. Dump the fifteen-bean soup mix into the bowl. Can you find all fifteen kinds of beans? Pick out three or four of each kind of bean you want to grow. Put the rest of the beans in a plastic bag (or use them to make soup).

2. Put your chosen beans in a bowl, cover them with water, and leave them to soak overnight.

3. The next day, fold a paper towel into a ring that fits inside the clear container.

4. Pour water into the bottom of the container. The paper towel will soak up most of the water. Add water until the paper towel stops soaking it up, then add a little bit more. There should be just a little water in the bottom of your container.

5. Pick out one of each kind of your soaked beans. Don't use beans that have cracked open.

Tools for Exploration

Keeping track of your discoveries

Which bean sprouts first? Last? Did all your beans sprout, or did you get a dud or two? How soon can you see leaves? Do roots grow up or down? Do leaves grow up or down? What happens to the original beans? Make a lab notebook, and write down what you notice about your beans.

6. Slide each bean about halfway down between the paper towel and the side of the container. Make sure you can see each bean through the side of the container.

7. Space the beans out all the way around the container. Don't push the beans all the way to the bottom of the container. You don't want to drown them! The paper towel will keep them wet.

8. Put your container in a safe, sunny spot. Check it every day to make sure there's some water in the bottom of the container. How do your beans change over time?

What's Going On?

The beans in the fifteen-bean soup mix are seeds, just like the seeds you plant in a vegetable garden. Beans and other seeds are nutritious because they contain food for the sprouting plant they become. When you eat a bean, you digest that food.

If you want to make a bean garden, choose the beans you like best from the ones you've sprouted. Choose identical beans from the fifteen-bean soup mix, soak them overnight, and plant them in your garden.

Bees and Flowers

Flowers need bees, and bees need flowers. Before a plant can make seeds, the flower needs to be *fertilized*. That is, some of the flower's powdery yellow pollen needs to be moved from the flower's *anthers,* where pollen forms, to the flower's *pistil.* But a flower needs help to move that pollen.

Flowers make *nectar,* a sugary liquid. Bees visit flowers to drink nectar and collect pollen. While they are drinking nectar and collecting pollen, they often, accidentally move a little pollen from the anthers of one flower to the pistil of another. This fertilizes the flower so that the plant can make seeds, which grow to make more flowers. Flowers are a plant's way to attract the attention of bees. A flower is a plant's way of saying, "Hey, bee! Come here and get some nectar."

Take a close look at the flowers in your garden. Can you find the pistil and the anthers? (On some flowers it's easy to identify them. On others, it's not!)

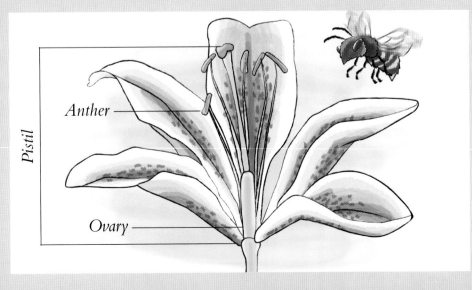

Pistil

Anther

Ovary

Take a look at the apple blossom, the flower of the apple tree. Now take a look at what you find when you cut an apple in half crosswise. See any similarities? The apple flower has five petals. When you slice the apple, you see that it has five compartments filled with seeds.

Every apple started as a flower. A bee visited one apple blossom, brushed against the flower's anther, and picked up some pollen. Then the bee visited another flower and left some pollen on that flower's pistil. (For more on this process, see page 128.) Seeds developed in the flower's ovary, and the ovary became an apple!

Just as the flower had five petals, the flower's ovary had five sections. When the ovary becomes a fruit, you can still see those five sections, the five compartments that hold the apple's seeds.

Have you ever eaten a flower? Are you sure?

Take a close look at a piece of raw broccoli. If you can, choose an older head of broccoli that's starting to yellow a bit. Using tweezers, pick off a single yellow-green or green piece from one of the clusters. Use a magnifying glass to take a really close look at the little piece of broccoli. You'll see four leaf-like things. Use your tweezers to pull those off and you'll find four little white petals. Hmm, what else has petals?

A head of broccoli is really a clump of tiny flowers that hasn't bloomed yet. When you eat broccoli, you are eating flowers!

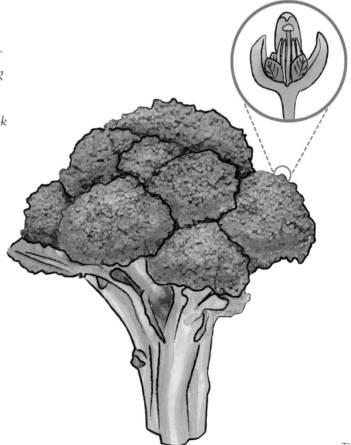

Your Kitchen-Scrap Garden

You can grow a vegetable garden starting with — what else? — vegetables!

Here's What You Need

✔ Imagination

✔ Patience

✔ An understanding cook who is willing to share vegetable scraps

✔ Toothpicks

✔ Some jars

✔ A pot and some potting soil

Here's What You Do

1. Ask the understanding cook to keep an eye out for potential plants for you. (*Potential* means full of possibilities. The stuff your cook collects may not be plants yet — but it has possibilities.) Here are some potential plants to ask the cook to look for: potatoes, onions, and garlic bulbs that are starting to sprout, left-over ginger root, avocado pits, apple seeds, a pineapple top with the pineapple sliced away. All of these things can grow into plants if you treat them right.

2. When this cook finds some potential plants for you, it's time to experiment. You could plant your potential plants in the garden — or in a pot of potting soil. Water them and see what happens. (Be patient!)

3. Plants don't always need soil to grow. They need water — but too much water will drown most plants. Can you figure out a way to keep your potential plant part-ly in and partly out of the water?

4. Try your ideas. Put your experiments in a sunny place and keep them watered. How does your garden grow?

What's Going On?

The potato that started to sprout in the cupboard was trying to grow up into a plant and make other potatoes.

A potato is a *tuber,* an underground part of a plant stem that stores food for the plant. A ginger root is a *rhizome,* a different kind of underground stem. With a little loving care, these pieces of plants will grow up and make new plants. You can probably find avocado pits, apple seeds, and other seeds among your kitchen scraps. Give them a chance and see if they'll grow.

Your Backyard at Night

Your backyard is a very different place at night. Different critters come out — moths, toads, maybe even bats. You'll hear different sounds too, frogs croaking, crickets chirping, mosquitoes buzzing. You can see stars that are hidden during the day. If you're lucky, you can see a shooting star. Go ahead, make a wish!

Moon Watch

Want to know when the next full moon is? Keep a moon journal and you'll know. (Not that you believe in werewolves; you're just interested in the moon, that's all.)

Here's What You Need

✔ Paper and a pen or pencil

✔ Today's newspaper

✔ Two weeks of reasonably clear skies (a few clouds are okay, but don't try this during a stretch of rainy weather)

Here's What You Do

1. First draw fourteen squares, one for every day you'll be watching the moon. In each square, draw a circle. Under that circle, make a line for the date. This is your moon journal. You'll use it to keep track of the shape of the moon.

2. When the moon is *new,* you can't see it at all. Look in your newspaper to find out when the moon is new. This information is usually in the section on weather. Start your moon journal a day or two after the new moon.

3. When it's time to start your moon journal, check the newspaper to find out what time the sun sets. This information is also in the section on weather. Pick a time not long after sunset when you'll be at home and can check on the shape of the moon. (No fair choosing a time that's after your bedtime.)

Making predictions

You watched the moon as it changed from a new moon to a full moon. If you start watching the moon when it's a new moon next month, do you think it will change in the same way as it did before? Why do you think that?

4. To find the moon on your first day of moon watching, look to the west right after sunset. You'll see a thin crescent moon in the western sky.

5. Draw this crescent shape in the first circle of your moon journal. Notice exactly where the moon is in the sky. Is it above your neighbor's house? Next to the telephone pole across the street?

6. Every night for the next two weeks, look for the moon at that same time. Each night, the moon will be a different shape, and it will be in a different place in the sky. Draw each night's moon shape in your journal. If clouds block the moon on some nights, draw clouds in your moon journal and look for the moon again the next day.

7. About two weeks after the new moon, the moon will be full. It will be a bright, round ball. Look for it at sunset, low in the eastern sky.

What's Going On?

If you kept your journal for two full weeks, you watched the moon grow from a little sliver of light to a bright, round circle. Every night, the moon was in a different spot when you looked at it. That's because it rose at a different time each night. (See "Finding the Moon," below.)

In 29 1/2 days, the moon goes from a new moon to a bright round circle and back to a new moon. The full moon appears in the middle of this cycle.

The moon is *waxing* when the lighted part of the moon (the part you can see) gets bigger each night. It's *waning* when the lighted part starts getting smaller again. In North America, the lighted part is on the right when the moon is waxing and on the left when it's waning. (To find out why the moon looks different each night, see page 133.)

Now anytime you see the moon, you can tell by its shape just where it is in its monthly cycle.

Finding the Moon

The moon rises at a different time each day of the month. The new moon rises at sunrise and sets at sunset. Each day the moon rises about fifty minutes later than it did the day before.

The full moon rises at sunset and sets at sunrise. As the moon rises fifty minutes later every night, a few days after the full moon, it will rise after your bedtime. That's why we only had you keep a moon journal for two weeks. We don't want the moon journal to be an excuse to stay up all night waiting for the moon to rise! But if you want to check on the shape of the moon when it's waning (that is, getting smaller), you can. Look for the moon in the morning sky. When the moon rises late, it doesn't set until after sunrise. (Remember the first day of your moon journal. The crescent moon was just about to set after being in the sky all day.)

Here's a photo of the earth and the moon, taken from Galileo spacecraft. In this photo, the moon doesn't look round, and neither does the earth! That's because light from the sun is shining on the earth and moon from the side. Only one side of each sphere is reflecting the sun's light, and that's the part we see.

The Changing Moon

The moon doesn't really change shape at all — it's always a round ball. But it sure looks as though it changes shape!

Here's What You Need

✔ A Ping-Pong ball

✔ A lamp that you can take the shade off of

✔ A grown-up helper

✔ A room you can darken

Here's What You Do

1. You see the moon because it reflects light from the sun. When sunlight shines on the side of the moon that's facing the earth, you see a bright, round full moon. As the moon orbits the earth, it always keeps the same side toward the earth. But all of that side isn't always lit by the sun. We see only the parts that are reflecting light to the earth. The parts of the moon that are in darkness seem to disappear. That's why each evening you see a moon that has a slightly different shape. You can use your Ping-Pong ball to see how this works.

When your back is to the lamp, the ball looks like a full moon—round and bright.

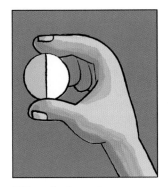

When the lamp is to one side of you, the ball looks like a half moon.

2. Ask your grown-up helper to take the shade off the lamp. Put the lamp on a low table so that it's at eye level. Turn that lamp on. Turn off all the other lights in the room.

3. Stand so that you are looking away from the light and hold the ball in front of you. If your shadow falls on the ball, hold the ball a little higher so it's in the light.

4. The light is the sun. Your head is the earth. The ball is the moon. Right now, it looks like a full moon, bright and round.

5. If the ball is the moon, it *orbits* (that means it moves in a circle around) your head. So move the ball to the left until it's a quarter of the way around its orbit of your head. Now only half the ball is reflecting light, and you see a Ping-Pong ball that looks like a half moon.

6. Keep moving the ball in a circle around your head. As you turn toward the lamp, you'll see a Ping-Pong ball that looks like a crescent moon.

7. Keep moving the ball until it is between you and the light. Now the side of the ball facing you is dark. The Ping-Pong ball looks like a new moon, so dark you can't see it.

8. As you move the Ping-Pong ball around your head, you'll see all the phases of the moon. If your head gets in the way of the light, you'll also see a lunar eclipse! That's when the earth (your head) blocks the sunlight (light from the lamp) so that it doesn't reach the moon (the Ping-Pong ball).

What's Going On?

To the right is a picture of a kid doing this activity. We are looking down at the kid from above. You can see that half of the Ping-Pong ball is always lit up by the lamp. But the kid sees only the brightly lit part of the ball. To see what the kid sees, try the experiment for yourself!

Like the Ping-Pong ball, the moon is always round. It looks as though it changes shape because you only see the part of the moon that is lit up by the sun.

Ask Professor Exploratorium

Dear Professor E:

I was stargazing the other night, and I saw a whole bunch of falling stars! What makes the stars fall anyway?

Signed,
Starry-Eyed

Dear Starry-Eyed:

Falling stars, also known as *shooting stars,* are actually not stars at all. They are *meteors,* which are chunks of space dust and rock particles that burn as they fall through the earth's atmosphere. Most meteors are tiny — about the size of a grain of sand. Most of these rock particles burn up before they reach the ground. But if a meteor is large enough, it doesn't burn up in the air. Once it reaches the ground, it is called a *meteorite.*

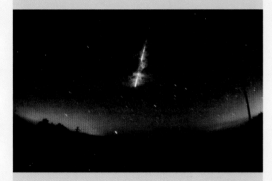

You were very lucky in your stargazing! You said you saw many falling stars. I think you witnessed a *meteor shower.* On certain nights of the year, the earth passes through space dust and streams of particles that lie in the wake of a comet. As a result, there are many meteors. On a moonless night during a meteor shower, you may see a shooting star every few minutes.

There are regular meteor showers many times during the year. Here are some dates to put on your stargazing calendar: January 1–3, April 20–22, May 4–6, August 10–13, October 8–10, October 18–23, November 8–10, and December 10–12.

Your superstar friend,
Professor E

Please Don't Feed the Mosquitoes

Mosquitoes have to eat just as anyone else does. But why does their favorite dish have to be *us*?

How can you protect yourself from these pesty bloodsuckers? You could use *diethylmetatoluamide* (that's DEET for short). The United States Army developed DEET in the 1940s. Now you'll find it in many of the sprays and goop people use to keep from getting bitten by mosquitoes.

DEET doesn't poison mosquitoes — it tricks them into flying away. Mosquitoes fly around searching for hot, humid air rich in carbon dioxide. That hot, humid air is often rising from a warm human body. The mosquito uses this air to home in on a tasty meal. (That would be you!)

DEET messes with this system. As the DEET molecules leave a person's skin, they contact the mosquito's antennae and send a signal telling the mosquito that she's flown out of the nice warm air. That mosquito was on the right track — on her way to a happy landing on someone's arm — but she turns away, fooled by the false signal.

To learn more about what's going on in your backyard, visit Exploratopia *online at* www.exploratopia.com.

The Playground

Some people think playgrounds are for kids, but folks at the Exploratorium know playgrounds are for scientists. The playground is filled with science experiments!

Take the swing, for instance. A swing is a pendulum where you are the *bob* (the weight at the end of the pendulum). Because you are a living bob, you can move around and change the way the pendulum moves. That's what swinging is all about.

How do you make yourself swing higher? When you're moving forward, you stick your feet out and lean back. When you're moving backward, you lean forward and tuck your legs under. This pushes the swing higher and higher, but only if you move at the right time. You have to move in rhythm with the swing.

After you have the swing swinging high, can you pump the swing to make it *stop* swinging? What do you do to make that happen?

Balls

Have you ever tried to play baseball with a tennis ball? Or tennis with a baseball? It just doesn't work. Different balls are designed for different games. How you play with a ball depends on how it bounces, spins, and flies through the air.

That's the Way the Ball Bounces

We need scientists ready and willing to play with water balloons. Any volunteers? (Don't all speak up at once!)

Here's What You Need

✔ Some round balloons (suitable for filling with water)

✔ A little cooking oil for making super-strong water balloons

✔ Water

Here's What You Do

1. You're going to see how a ball bounces by watching a ball that bounces in slow motion. That slow bouncing ball is a super-strong water balloon.

2. To make a super-strong water balloon, oil up the outside of one balloon with cooking oil and push this greasy balloon into a second balloon. Then fill the inner balloon with water and knot both balloons.

3. Drop one of your super-strong water balloons onto a smooth surface. Keep a close eye on what happens.

4. Try it again.

What's Going On?

Your water balloon bounces like a ball in slow motion, so you can see what's happening. Drop your water-balloon ball again. What happens?

Here's what we see happening. The balloon is round as it's falling, but it squashes when it hits the ground. Then it springs back into a round shape as it pushes itself up off the floor. Is that what you see?

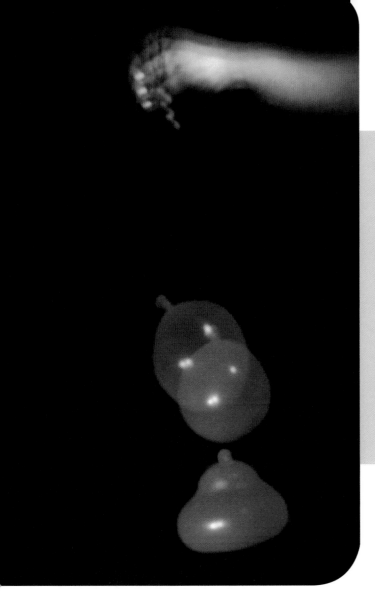

When you lift up your water balloon, you are giving it potential energy. "Potential" refers to something that could happen. (You have the potential to become an astronaut, for example.) If something has potential energy, it has energy that's stored up.

When you drop your water balloon, that potential energy becomes kinetic energy. Kinetic energy is the energy of motion. A car moving at 100 miles per hour has a lot of kinetic energy.

When the balloon hits the floor and stops, that kinetic energy has to go somewhere. (See page 143.) The kinetic energy goes into squashing the balloon flat. When the balloon squashes, the rubber stretches. And as you know if you've ever stretched out a rubber band and then let go, stretched-out rubber wants to snap back. (Ow!)

When the stretched rubber of the balloon snaps back, it pushes against the floor, and the floor pushes back. As a result, the balloon goes bouncing away.

Hot and Cold Bounce

Some sneaky baseball players have been known to freeze the baseballs before a game. You're about to find out why.

Here's What You Need

✔ One or two golf balls

✔ One or two baseballs

Here's What You Do

1. Drop two golf balls from the same height to see how high they bounce. (You want two that bounce to about the same height.)

**Experimenting to
test your ideas**

You have experimented
with baseballs and golf
balls. Do you have
any other balls around
the house that you
could experiment
with? Do you think a
Super Ball will bounce
higher when it's cold
than it does when
it's hot? How about
a basketball? Try it and
see. (But first you'll
have to find space
for a basketball in your
freezer!)

2. Put one golf ball in the freezer
for an hour and then drop them
again. Are the two balls still
equally bouncy?

3. If you don't have two golf balls,
bounce one and notice how high
it bounces. Waist high? Knee
high? Then, put the golf ball in
the freezer for an hour and try
it again. Be sure to drop it from
the same height as last time.

4. Try the same thing using
baseballs. Which one bounces
higher?

What's Going On?

Which was bouncier — the cold
ball or the ball kept at room
temperature? If your golf balls are
like ours, the cold ball bounced only
about three-quarters as high as the
one at room temperature. Cold balls
just don't bounce as well. That's
why smart golfers keep their golf
balls in their pockets on cold days.

A cold baseball is also less
bouncy, but the difference isn't as
dramatic as it is with the golf ball.
An hour in the freezer makes a
baseball 10 percent less bouncy than
one at room temperature. (A 10
percent difference means that if your
regular baseball bounced up 10
inches, the cold baseball would
bounce up 9 inches.)

This small difference in the
baseball's "bounciness" is enough to
make the big difference between a
pop fly and a home run. This is
why batting teams have frequently
accused their opponents of cooling
their baseballs!

Putting a Spin on It

How does spinning a ball change how it bounces?

Here's What You Need

✔ A Super Ball (if you have one) or another bouncy ball of your choice

Here's What You Do

1. You're going to spin the ball as you drop it. The easiest way to drop a ball with a spin is to hold it between your palms and then move one hand up and one hand down until the ball drops.

2. Okay, give it a try. How does the spin change the ball's bounce?

What's Going On?

A spinning ball always bounces in the direction that the top of the ball is spinning. When you move your right hand up, the top of the ball will spin to the left and the ball will bounce to the left. If you move your left hand up, the top of the ball will spin to the right and your ball will bounce to the right.

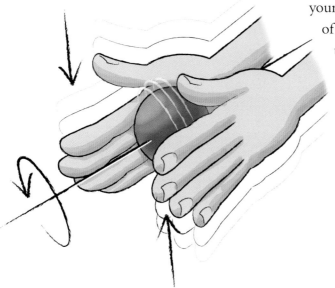

Baseball pitcher Barry Zito is known for his amazing curveball. To throw a curveball, a pitcher must be an expert in the use of spin. If a ball is spinning from top to bottom, it tends to nosedive into the dirt. If it's spinning from left to right, it will curve to the right. Spin is one of the secrets to curveballs, fastballs, screwballs, and sliders.

A Scientific Party Trick

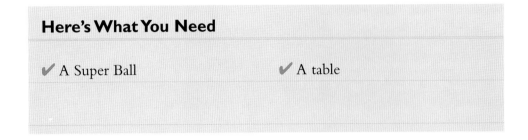

The Exploratorium scientists know how to have fun. This is one of their favorite party tricks.

Here's What You Need

✔ A Super Ball   ✔ A table

Here's What You Do

1. Throw the Super Ball under a table as shown in the picture below.

2. Can you get the ball to bounce right back into your hand?

What's Going On?

If you get the angle just right, your Super Ball bounces off the underside of the table, bounces off the floor and then ends up right back in your hand!

The ball leaves your hand with no spin to speak of (unless you snuck one in there). But when the ball hits the floor, it picks up a topspin.

When the ball hits the bottom of the table, that topspin causes it to bounce back in the direction that it came from. That bounce off the table also causes the ball to reverse the direction of its spin. That new spin means that when the ball hits the floor, it will bounce forward, right back into your hand.

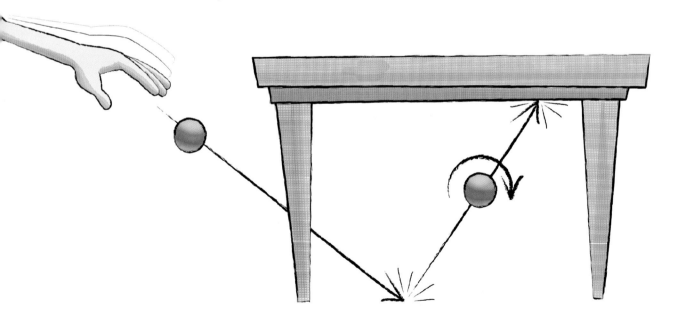

Ball Buddies

There's more than one way to bounce a ball.

Here's What You Need

✔ A baseball, a basketball, and a few other balls (we used a tennis ball, a softball, and a Super Ball).

Here's What You Do

1. Drop a baseball on the floor and notice how high it bounces.

2. Now hold the baseball on top of the basketball and drop the two balls together. What happens?

3. Try this experiment again, replacing the baseball with one of the other balls you've gathered. Which ball bounces the highest?

What's Going On?

When you drop the baseball, it bounces a little. But when you bounce a baseball and a basketball together, your baseball goes flying!

To get a feel for what's going on here, drop the basketball on its own and notice how high it bounces. Then drop the basketball and the baseball together and notice how high the basketball bounces. When you send the baseball flying, the basketball doesn't bounce as high.

How high the basketball bounces is an indication of how much *kinetic energy* it has. (Kinetic energy is the energy of motion.) When the basketball sends the baseball flying, the basketball has transferred some of its kinetic energy to the baseball. That's why the basketball didn't bounce as high.

This experiment demonstrates one of nature's important laws: *energy can't be created or destroyed*. All you can do is change energy from one form to another. In this case, the kinetic energy of the basketball becomes the kinetic energy of the baseball. (To learn more about this law of nature, see page 158.)

Tools for Exploration
Comparing two things

Drop different balls with the basketball. You could try a tennis ball, a Ping-Pong ball, a Super Ball. Which ball bounces highest when you drop it with the basketball? Which one bounces highest on its own?

Launching Rockets

You may not be ready to launch a rocket to the moon, but everyone has to start somewhere. You can start your career in rocketry by making a rocket that you launch with 100 percent stomp power. Keep reading to find out how.

Making a Rocket Launcher

Who needs NASA? Collect your materials and make your own rocket launcher.

Here's What You Need

✔ A few 2-liter plastic soda bottles (You need one for your launcher and the rest as spares, to make more launchers as needed.)

✔ 60 centimeters (about 2 feet) of PVC pipe with a $1/2$-inch inner diameter (Available at a hardware store. Ask a grown-up to help you.)

✔ 1 meter (about 3 feet) of clear, flexible vinyl tubing with a $1/2$-inch inner diameter and a $5/8$-inch outer diameter (another object you'll find at the hardware store)

✔ Duct tape

Here's What You Do

1. Remove the cap from the bottle.

2. Stick about an inch of flexible tubing into the bottle opening.

3. Tape the tubing in place with duct tape so the connection between the tubing and the bottle is airtight, which means that no air can escape.

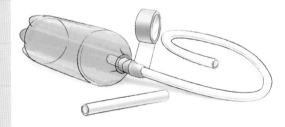

4. Push the PVC pipe up against the other end of the flexible tubing and tape the tubing and the PVC pipe together. (Don't try to get the tubing to go into the pipe, just put them together.) Again, use your tape to make an airtight connection.

5. Your launcher is complete! Now it's time to make a rocket.

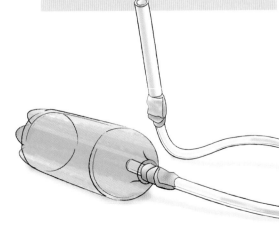

Making a Rocket

No self-respecting rocket launcher is complete without a rocket!

Here's What You Need

✔ A sheet of regular paper

✔ Cellophane tape

✔ A 3-by-5 inch index card (or stiff paper)

✔ Scissors

✔ A marker

Here's What You Do

1. Roll the sheet of paper around the PVC pipe to make a tube. The tube should be just wide enough so that it can slide off the pipe.

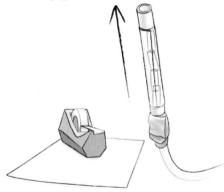

2. Tape the paper tube together and slip it off the pipe.

3. Twist the tip of the tube or fold two sides at one end of the paper tube over to make the rocket's nose. Tape it down. Mash the nose down so it's rounded.

4. Rocket fins help your rocket fly straight. Make fins by folding your index card in half to make a short rectangle. Cut the card in half along the fold line. Put one half on top of the other half of the index card. Cut from one corner to another and you will have four fins.

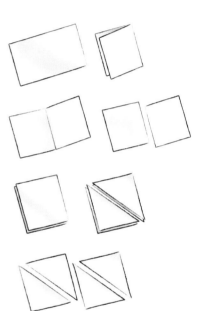

5. Attach tape to both sides of each fin. Space the four fins out equally along the base of the rocket. Tape as shown.

6. Use the marker to write your name on or decorate the side of the rocket.

7. Your rocket is complete! Now get ready to launch it!

Launching Your Rocket

You've got your launcher. You've got your rocket . . . time to blast off!

Here's What You Need

✔ Your rocket

✔ Your rocket launcher

✔ A friend (to hold the PVC pipe upright)

Here's What You Do

1. Place your rocket over the PVC pipe of your rocket launcher.

2. Place the launcher on the ground. Have your friend hold the PVC pipe off to one side, pointed away from everyone. (You want to make sure the rocket flies up in the air, *not* into someone's face.)

3. To launch your rocket, stomp down on the plastic bottle with one foot. On the count of three — 1, 2, and . . . blast off!

4. Watch your rocket fly high up into the air.

5. To blow up, or inflate, your bottle for the next launch, put your hand around the end of the PVC pipe to make a mouthpiece. Blow!

6. To get the greatest height, point the rocket launcher straight up. Suppose you wanted your rocket to fly the greatest distance? How would you hold the launcher? Experiment and find out what angle to the ground gives you the greatest distance.

Tools for Exploration

Experimenting to test your ideas

What changes might make your rocket fly farther? Can you think of some experiments that would help you answer this question? What if you added more fins? Or used fewer fins? What if you added weight to the nose of the rocket? What if you made a longer rocket? What other "What if . . ." questions do you want to answer?

How High?

How high did your rocket fly? That's hard to measure using a tape measure. Scientists approximate *these kinds of measurements. That means they guess, in a scientific way. You're about to learn how to make scientific guesses of your own.*

The Hypsometer

Make a simple tool that lets you measure the height of your rocket's flight. You can also measure the heights of buildings, bridges, basketball hoops, basketball players . . . anything you want!

Here's What You Need

- ✔ A 4-by-6-inch index card
- ✔ Pencil
- ✔ Hole puncher
- ✔ A piece of string, about 40 cm long
- ✔ A washer or a few large paper clips
- ✔ Metric ruler
- ✔ Scissors
- ✔ A plastic straw
- ✔ Tape

Here's What You Do

1. Place your index card flat in front of you, with one long side toward you.

2. The right side of the card measures about 10 cm. Write this number on the right-hand side of the card. (We are using metric measurements because it'll make the math easier when you're through.)

3. Use the hole puncher to make a hole in the upper right corner, as close to the edge as you can (and still have a hole).

4. Thread your string through the hole.

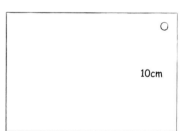

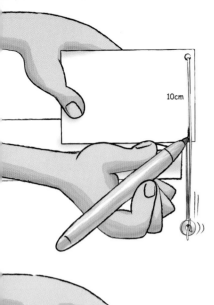

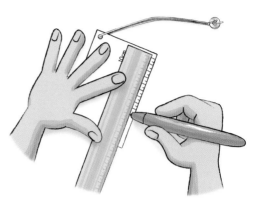

5. Thread your string through your washer or several large paper clips. The washer or paper clips are your bob.

6. Tie the two ends of the string together. The bob should be able to swing freely.

7. Rest the long side of the card on a table as shown, so that the bob hangs straight down. Mark the point where the string crosses the long side of the card with a line (near the lower right corner). Write the number zero above this line.

8. Line up your metric ruler with this zero mark in the lower right corner of the card.

9. Going from right (by the zero mark) to left, make a mark every 1 cm. Number these marks.

10. Make a smaller mark halfway between each centimeter mark to represent half centimeters. Don't bother to number these marks.

11. Cut the straw to the length of the long side of the card.

12. Tape the straw along the top edge of the card.

13. Your measuring device is complete!

What's Going On?

You just made a *hypsometer. Hyps* is from a Greek word meaning "height," and a hypsometer is a device for measuring height. Hypsometers have been used to measure tall objects for a long time, ever since the Middle Ages. Read on to find out exactly how your hypsometer works.

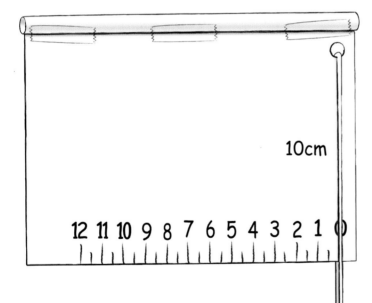

Using Your Hypsometer

Use your handy hypsometer to measure and calculate the height of something too tall to measure with a ruler.

Here's What You Need

✔ Your hypsometer

✔ A friend

✔ Metric measuring tape or meter sticks

Here's What You Do

1. You're going to use your hypsometer to measure something tall — a building, a basketball hoop, a flagpole, or the playground slide.

2. Look along the top of the straw (not through the hole) at something that's at eye level (straight ahead).

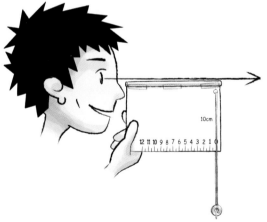

3. Ask a friend to check where the string crosses the hypsometer. If you're holding the hypsometer level, the string should hang at your zero mark.

4. Now, with the string hanging freely (and your fingers out of its way), look up to the top of your tall object. Your hypsometer tilts right along with the motion of your head.

5. Notice that the string moves when you look up. The string crossing the hypsometer marks the *angle* of your head tilt — the measurement of how far up your head moved.

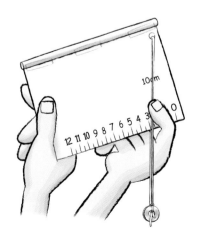

6. Have your friend read the number where the string crosses the measurement marks on the lower edge of your hypsometer. You can also pinch the string against the card to hold it in place, take the hypsometer away from your eye, and read the number yourself.

7. Now move a little closer to the object you're measuring. Look along the top of the straw at the object. How does the number on your hypsometer change? The distance to the object makes a difference. The closer you are, the more you tilt your head to look at the top of the object. The more you tilt your head, the farther the string on your hypsometer moves back. Write down the measurement from your hypsometer.

8. Measure your distance to the bottom of the tall object. If your tall object is close by, you can measure this distance with a meter stick or metric measuring tape. If it's far away, you can use the "Stride Ruler" activity on page 226 to measure the distance. If you are measuring something with a broad base, like a swing set or a building, you'll need to figure out the distance to the spot that's right underneath the tallest part of the object you are measuring.

9. To get the height of the object, you need one more measurement — the distance from the ground to your eyes. To make things easy later on, measure that in the same units you used to measure the distance to the object. (If you measured that in centimeters, measure your eye height in centimeters. If you measured the distance in feet, measure your eye height in feet.)

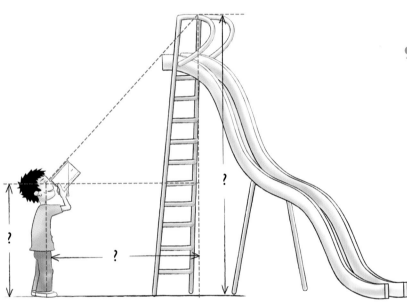

Calculating the Height

With the three numbers you collected, you can calculate the height of the object you're measuring. You just need to do a little bit of math.

First, multiply the measurement on the hypsometer by the distance to the object. Then divide your answer by the height of the card (10 centimeters). The number you get is the height of the object above your eye level. If you measured the distance to the object in feet, your answer will be in feet. If you measured the distance in meters, your answer will be in meters.

Now add your eye height to the answer, and you'll get the height of the object.

We measured the height of a basketball hoop. We stood 10 feet away from the point right below the hoop. When we looked at the hoop, the measurement on our hypsometer was 5 centimeters. So we did the math:

Tools for
Exploration
Measuring and counting
Using indirect measurements and estimating skills, you can measure a tall object, a rocket's flight, and even the distance to the moon.

$$\frac{5 \text{ centimeters} \times 10 \text{ feet}}{10 \text{ centimeters}} = 5 \text{ feet}$$

This is the height of the hoop above eye level.

Pat Murphy, who did the measuring, has an eye height of 5 feet 3 inches. So the height of the hoop is:

$$5 \text{ feet} + 5 \text{ feet } 3 \text{ inches} = 10 \text{ feet } 3 \text{ inches}$$

Our basketball hoop is a few inches higher than regulation height for basketball hoops. (Regulation height is 10 feet.) Well, our measurement could be a little bit off. Scientists talk about something they call the *margin of error*. Error is another word for mistake. The margin of error is a measurement of how far off a measurement may be.

When you use your hypsometer, it's easy to be a little bit off when figuring out where the string crossed the bottom of the card. Suppose this measurement was off by $1/4$ centimeter. In our measurement of the basketball hoop, an error of $1/4$ centimeter leads to a difference of 3 inches in our measurement. So that basketball hoop may be the right height after all!

Why Does This Work?

It all has to do with triangles.

When you tilted your head back to look at the top of the object, you were at one point of a triangle. (See the picture to figure out where the other points of the triangle are.)

Because the triangles are *similar*, mathematicians know that the lengths of the triangle's sides have to follow certain rules. Using those rules, we figured out the formula for calculating the height of the object. Thanks to similar triangles, we know the height of the basketball hoop!

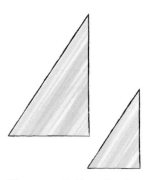

These are similar triangles.

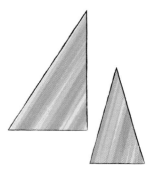

These are not similar triangles.

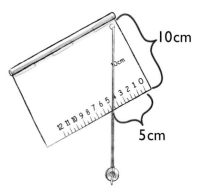

A mathematician would say that these are similar *triangles. Similar triangles are triangles that have the same basic shape but different sizes. What makes triangles similar is their angles. The length of the sides can be different, but the angles must be the same.*

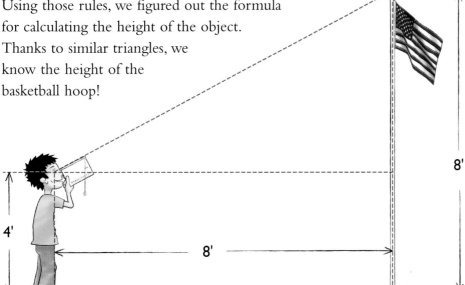

The string and the edges of your hypsometer also made a triangle.

How High Does Your Rocket Go?

Yay! It's time to play with your rocket and launcher again. But now that you're an expert hypsometrist, you'll want to calculate the height of your rocket's flight too.

Here's What You Need

✔ One or two friends

✔ Chalk or sticks to mark the ground

✔ A metric measuring tape or meter sticks

✔ Your hypsometer

10 m

Here's What You Do

1. You're going to get a friend to launch your rocket while you track its height using your hypsometer.

2. Mark a launch pad — the place where your friend will launch the rocket. Mark a spot that's 10 meters (that's 1,000 cm, or approximately 33 ft) away from the launch pad. That's where you'll stand. (If you are on blacktop, you can use chalk to mark these spots. If you are standing on grass, you can use sticks or rocks.)

3. Now, with the string hanging freely (and your fingers out of its way), lift the hypsometer to your eye. Now give your friend a signal to launch the rocket.

4. Hypsometer in place, look up as your rocket is launched. Your hypsometer tilts right along with the motion of your head. Follow the rocket with your hypsometer as it flies up and then . . .

5. Freeze at the rocket's highest point. (It may take a few launches to get the timing just right.)

6. Have a friend read the number where the string crosses the measurement marks on the lower edge of your hypsometer. You could also pinch the string against the card to hold it in place, take the hypsometer away from your eye, and read the number yourself.

7. Write down the measurement from your hypsometer. Go back to the Calculating the Height section of "Using Your Hypsometer," page 150, to do the math that will give you the height of your rocket's flight.

8. How high did your rocket fly? Whoa! They could use you at NASA!

Dear Professor E:
I saw you riding your bike the other day. Boy, are you slow!
You must be a lousy bike rider.

Signed,
No Offense

Dear No Offense:
Riding a bike slowly isn't easy at all. The more slowly you ride a bike, the harder it is to stay balanced. That's one reason it's hard to learn how to ride a bike. When you start out, you want to go slowly, but that just makes it more difficult. When you ride a bike, the forward movement helps keep you upright.

Here's a challenge for you. Just how *slowly* can you ride your bike? Let's have a bike race where the *last* person to cross the finish line is the winner. Anyone who touches the ground is out. No fair riding in circles! No training wheels or tricycles allowed!

Ha! You lose! I win! You will never be as good a bike rider as the amazing Prof. E. Um, what I meant to say is that it looks like you may need further practice riding your bike very slowly. Pay attention to what you do when your bicycle starts to tip over. How do you keep your balance without putting your feet on the ground?

What did you do when you started to tip over? If you were falling to the left, you probably turned the wheel to the left without even thinking about it. Then your bike made a slight turn to the left so that it was under you, and you got your balance again. If you were falling to the right, you probably turned a little to the right.

Why does turning the bicycle wheel help you get your balance back? Because even though you turn the wheel, your body tends to keep going in a straight line. When your body goes in a straight line, it pulls you back into balance. (For more on how this works, see page 160.)

Your winning friend,
Professor E

To learn more about science on the playground, visit Exploratopia *online at* www.exploratopia.com.

The Amusement Park

Ahhh . . . the roller coaster. You creep up that first hill, knowing all too well what's coming next. You zoom downhill, whiz around a curve, shoot up another hill, and then zoom down another hill. Then suddenly you are *upside down* in the loop-the-loop! It's no wonder that the roller coaster's nickname is the "scream machine."

Some people aren't too fond of the old scream machine. (Maybe you're one of them?) Some people worry about little things like falling out of the coaster when it's upside down.

But you're a scientist, and you know there's no problem! The roller coaster has been designed using scientific principles. Knowing these principles, you can predict what will happen on the ride and the effects on your helpless body. And you don't have to worry about falling out of the coaster at all. Nope, not even a little!

Getting Ready

Scientists love going to amusement parks! Where else can they observe so many scientific principles at work? (And get a really good corn dog while they're at it!) Before heading out to experiment, a scientist spends some time getting ready.

Make Your Own Roller Coaster

Design your own little roller coaster and see how fast you can make a marble go. There's only one problem — you're too big to ride this roller coaster!

Here's What You Need

✔ Scissors

✔ 12 feet of foam pipe insulation (You can buy this at a hardware store in three 4- or 6-foot lengths. Ask for the kind with the thickest walls.)

✔ Masking tape

✔ Marbles (any kind — as long as they roll easily in the foam pipe)

✔ Large, empty metal coffee cans, furniture, boxes, blocks, and other things you can stick under your roller coaster track to make hills

✔ A yardstick or measuring tape

✔ A stopwatch (if you have one) or a watch with a second hand

Here's What You Do

1. Using your scissors, cut the foam tubes in half to make two half-pipes. These will be your roller coaster tracks. Try your best not to get folds or crimps in your tracks. The smoother the track, the faster and farther your marble will go.

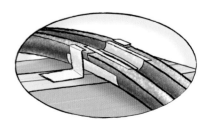

2. Using the masking tape, tape sections of the track together. Make sure the tape is smooth in the track so your marble won't get hung up.

3. Start by making a hill that your marble can roll down. Your marble is going to roll down this hill, up and down other hills, and around curves, just like a real roller coaster. You want your first hill to be tall.

4. Once you have a hill you like, make a second hill.

5. Start the marble at the top of your first hill. Let it roll down that hill and up the second hill. Does it make it to the top of the second hill and then roll down the other side? If not, try making the second hill smaller. If it does roll down the other side, you might want to make the second hill bigger. How big you can make the second hill and still have the marble roll over the hill? Make a chart like this one to keep track of your experiments.

6. After you've experimented with two hills, try adding more hills and some curves. Is it better to have a curve or a straightaway before a hill? Try both. Test your coaster every time you add a new feature, just to make sure the marble makes it all the way around the track.

7. Tape the middle parts of your track to the cans, tubes, and boxes you're using to make hills and valleys. Attach 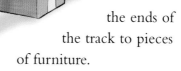 the ends of the track to pieces of furniture.

8. Once your roller coaster track is completed, send a marble for a ride. Start the marble at the top of the first hill and let it go. Does your marble complete the course? (If not, make changes to your design and fix the problem.)

How tall is the first hill?	How tall is the second hill?	Did the marble make it over the second hill?

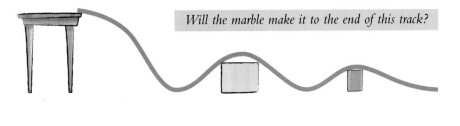

Will the marble make it to the end of this track?

How about this one?

9. Use your watch or stopwatch to time how long it takes your marble to run the course of your track. Can you think of a way to make your marble finish the course in less time? Try your idea and see if it works.

10. Experiment with other track designs. Put your hills in different places. Make a curve a straightaway or change a straightaway into a curve. Have a great time! You may have a future in roller coaster design!

What's Going On?

Did you notice where on the track your marble went fastest? If you didn't, send your marble on another ride and pay attention to its speed as it rolls uphill and down.

As your marble rolls down a hill, it speeds up. As it rolls up a hill, it slows down. You probably noticed that your marble was rolling fastest at the bottom of the first big hill and slower as it reached the top of the next big hill.

Your marble starts rolling because of *gravity,* the force that pulls you and your marble toward the center of the earth. At the top of a hill, your marble has a lot of *potential energy.* That's energy that is stored up and ready for release.

When your marble starts to roll down the hill, the potential energy turns into *kinetic energy,* the energy of motion. The faster your marble rolls, the more kinetic energy it has. As the marble rolls up the next hill, its kinetic energy turns back into potential energy, and the marble slows down. As the marble rubs against the track, some of the kinetic energy turns into *heat energy.*

You probably discovered that the first hill in your homemade coaster had to be the tallest. No hill could be higher than the first hill, since climbing a higher hill would take more energy than the marble had to begin with.

Physicists, scientists who study matter and energy, say that energy can't be created or destroyed. It can only be transformed from one form to another. When you roll your marble down a track (or take a ride on a roller coaster), you are testing this physical law. Think about that when you're on a roller coaster climbing a very tall hill. All the potential energy you are gaining is going to turn into kinetic energy as you speed down that hill — screaming all the way!

Tools for Exploration

Measuring and counting

How fast is your marble moving as it rolls down the track? Can you think of a way to measure your marble's overall speed? (If you need help, see page 358.)

Tuck your hands under your thighs and you'll feel your weight pushing down on your hands. Lean to the left, and your left hand will be squashed harder. Lean to the right, and your right hand will be squashed.

Now imagine that you are sitting on your hands while you ride a roller coaster. What will your hands feel when the train whips over the top of a hill. Will your weight push down on them harder or not as hard? What will your hands feel when the train plunges toward the bottom of a valley?

Make a chart like this one and write down what you think will happen when you are on a real roller coaster. Will your hands feel more force or less force at each point in the ride? (It's a good idea to write down what you think so that you will remember it.)

When you say what you expect will happen, you are making a prediction. *We are asking you to make predictions about what you will feel when you sit on your hands while riding a roller coaster.*

Scientists often make predictions and then experiment to see if their predictions were right. In this case, you can test your prediction by riding on the roller coaster — an experiment in excitement and terror!

When the roller coaster train is in this position	I think my hands will feel this
Racing over the top of a hill	
Reaching the bottom of a valley	
Going around a curve	

The Car Ride

Here's a scientific experiment to try in the car on the way to the amusement park!

Here's What You Do

1. Next time you're riding in a car, close your eyes and try to tell what the car is doing by feel.

2. When the car starts up and begins to move, pay attention to what you feel. Do you feel that you're being thrown forward or pushed backward?

3. Can you tell when the car speeds up? How?

4. Can you tell when the car slows down? How?

5. Can you tell when the car turns? How?

6. What does it feel like when the car is moving at a constant speed? (Try to ignore the road noises going on around you.) Do you feel like you're moving?

7. Now open your eyes.

8. When the car makes a turn, look at a tree or a building that would have been straight ahead. Notice what your body feels as the car turns. Does this feeling change when the car is going faster or when the turn is sharper?

What's Going On?

When you close your eyes, you can pay attention to body movements that you don't normally notice.

When the car started moving, did you feel like you were pressed back in your seat? We did. When the car slowed down, did you feel that you were thrown forward?

The person who could explain what you felt is Isaac Newton, the same guy who discovered that a piece of glass could break rays of sunlight up into all the colors of the rainbow. (See page 306.) Back in the seventeenth century, Newton came up with three laws of motion. These laws explain what you felt in the moving car, even though Newton discovered them long before the automobile was invented.

Newton's laws deal with motion and *inertia.* You know what motion is, but you may not know about inertia. Inertia is the tendency of an object to keep on doing whatever it is doing. (Like when you keep watching TV even though you know you should do your homework.)

Basically, Newton's laws say that you'll only start moving (or stop moving or change direction) if something gives you a push to overcome your inertia.

When you and the car are sitting still, it takes a push to make you move. The engine turns the wheels, and the wheels push on the ground. The ground pushes back on the wheels and that makes the car move. The car seat pushes on you. You feel this push as the car seat shoves on your butt (which wants to stay put).

When the car stops, you keep on moving forward until something stops you. The something that stops you could be *friction* between your butt and the car seat. (Friction is the drag that you get when two surfaces rub together.) If the car stops suddenly, friction isn't enough to stop your movement, and the pull of the seat belt stops you. (You are wearing your seat belt, aren't you?)

When the car goes around a corner, you keep moving forward until friction or the seat belt drags you along to follow the path of the car.

All those pushes and pulls you felt in the car were Isaac Newton's laws of motion in action.

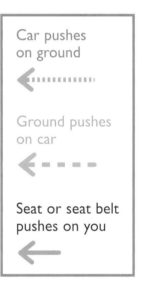

Car pushes on ground

Ground pushes on car

Seat or seat belt pushes on you

Tools for Exploration

Sharing your experience

Close your eyes while you're riding in the car, and tell the driver when you think the car is slowing down, speeding up, or going around a turn. Can you tell what's going on?

Dear Professor E:
I'M curious about this ride called the Roundabout. That's the one where people stand against the walls of this round cage and then the cage spins really fast. Then the ride moves so that it's completely on its side. Why don't the people fall out? There's nothing holding them to the wall!
Signed,
Just Checking

Dear Just Checking:

There is *something* holding the people to the wall of the Roundabout. You just can't see it. To ride the Roundabout (or any of the rides at the amusement park), you need to trust in the laws of physics. Try this:

Put a little water in the bottom of a bucket and go outside. (It'll work indoors, too. But I don't want to get you in trouble if you mess up.)

Hold the bucket by its handle. In one swooping motion, swing the bucket fast — overhead and then back down again. Around and around in a circle. Don't stop!

The secret to keeping the water in the bucket is to keep the bucket moving in a circle. If you stop your swing with the bucket overhead, the water will immediately fall out, pulled down by gravity. But as long as you keep the bucket moving fast enough, the water stays in the bottom of the bucket.

To understand why the water stays in the bucket, you need to know Isaac Newton's laws of motion. (Maybe you remember them from page 160.) According to Newton's laws, something that's moving will keep on moving in a straight line — unless a force gives it a shove in a different direction.

When you swing the bucket, you get the water and the bucket moving together. The bucket would move in a straight line, but your arm keeps pulling on it. The force of your arm pulling on the bucket keeps it moving in a circle.

The water in the bucket would move in a straight line, but the bottom of the bucket keeps getting in the way and pushing the water back toward the center of the circle.

The water stays in the bucket as long as the bucket is moving in a circle fast enough. The force that keeps the bucket moving in a circle is the pull of your arm toward the center of the circle. Scientists call this *centripetal force*. Centripetal means "center-seeking" or "toward the center." When you spin the bucket, you can feel your arm pulling in on the bucket — a centripetal force.

You may have heard about something called *centrifugal force*. Centrifugal means "center-fleeing" or "away from the center." If you were a tiny person sitting in the bucket, you would feel like a force was pushing you into the bottom of the bucket, away from the center of the circle. From the point of view of a tiny person in the bucket (or a regular-sized person in a spinning carnival ride), it *feels* like there's a centrifugal force. But when you look at the situation from outside the bucket, you see that the force is really centripetal. So scientists call centrifugal force an *imaginary force*, a product of the imagination of that little guy in the bottom of the bucket.

Your suddenly dizzy friend,
Professor E

Classic Rides

Okay, you're ready to start your experimenting at the amusement park now. Let's start out with the easy rides — the Ferris wheel and the bumper cars. If you pay attention, these rides can be science experiments (as well as a lot of fun).

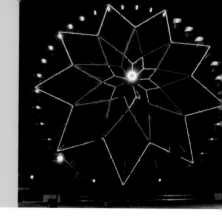

Bumper Cars

What happens when you crash your bumper car into someone else's bumper car? And what does Isaac Newton have to say about that?

Here's What You Need

✔ A bumper car ride

✔ A ticket to go for a ride

Here's What You Do

1. Before you go on the bumper car ride, predict what will happen by answering these questions.
   - When you start your car, which way will you feel you're being pushed?
   - When you crash into something head-on, which way will you be thrown?
   - When you are hit from the side, which way will you be thrown?

2. If you are having trouble answering the questions, think back to what you felt when you did the "Car Ride" experiment (see page 160). Does that help?

3. Go on the bumper car ride. Were your predictions right?

4. If your predictions didn't match what happened, don't feel bad. Scientists are always making predictions and trying experiments to see if those predictions are right. That's part of the scientific process, which is how scientists figure out how the world works.

What's Going On?

If you are wondering why you felt pushed one way or another, go back to page 160. The same forces that push you around in a regular car also push you around in a bumper car.

Of course, when you are in a regular car, you usually don't have other cars bumping into you. (At least, we hope you don't!) In a bumper car, having other cars crash into you (and crashing your car into other cars) is part of the fun.

Suppose your car is standing still when another bumper car crashes into yours. The other car transfers some of its *momentum* to your car. Momentum is the tendency of a moving object to keep on moving. When a bumper car crashes into your bumper car, it stops or slows down, but the collision makes your car move. After the crash, the other car isn't moving as fast, but now your car is moving, too.

How your car moves when another car bumps you depends on how much momentum the other car has when it hits you. A car with a couple of big kids behind the wheel packs a bigger wallop than a car that's moving at the same speed with a skinny kid driving. And a car that's moving fast will give you a bigger jolt than the same car being driven slowly by the same driver.

Here are three Ferris wheels. Can you guess the size of these Ferris wheels by comparing them to the other things in the pictures? (If you need help making an educated guess, see page 224.) Which one do you think is tallest? How far from the ground do you think you'd be if you were at the top of the tallest Ferris wheel?

Next time you're standing in line waiting to get on the Ferris wheel, see if you can you can figure out how far off the ground you're going to be when you're at the top of the Ferris wheel. You're going to be how far up? Wow! Are you sure you want to go on that Ferris wheel?

Scream Machines

Amusement parks keep coming up with new, scarier rides—like roller coasters that go upside down, or rides that drop you from hundreds of feet above the ground! Today's "scream machine" rides have been scientifically designed for maximum terror.

Waiting in Line

There are many things to do while waiting in line for the roller coaster, *besides* getting scared.

Here's What You Need

✔ One working roller coaster in plain view

✔ A watch with a second hand or a stop watch

✔ A small notepad and pencil (or a really good memory)

Here's What You Do

1. First, take a look at the hills on the roller coaster. Which hill is the highest? It may take you a while to figure this out. Some coaster tracks are as messy as a bowl of spaghetti. But you're waiting in line, so you have time to figure it out.

2. Watch the train as it travels around the track. How does the speed of the train change during the ride? Does it move faster at the top of a hill or at the bottom? As it goes up a hill, does it gain speed (*accelerate*) or lose speed (*decelerate*)?

3. Pick a spot at the top of a hill and time how long it takes the train to pass that spot. Start timing when the front of the first car passes your chosen spot on the track. Stop timing when the end of the rear car gets there. Do the same with a spot at the bottom of a valley. Where is the train traveling fastest?

Where is the train going faster? At the top of a hill, or at the bottom of a valley?

Tools for Exploration
Measuring and counting

Can you figure out how fast the train is going at different points in the ride? To figure out speed, you need to know how long it takes the train to travel a certain distance. Any ideas? If you need help, see page 358.

What's Going On?

You've probably seen roller coasters before, but this time you studied the roller coaster with a scientist's eye. Did you notice anything new?

Maybe you noticed that the hills are different sizes, and the biggest hill is always right at the start of the ride. The roller coaster train gets pulled up to the top of the first hill and then rolls or coasts through the rest of the ride. (That's why it's a roller *coaster.*)

The roller coaster train acts just like the marble in your homemade roller coaster. (See page 156.) At the top of that first hill, the train has a lot of potential energy. When it rolls down the hill, that potential energy turns into kinetic energy.

You probably noticed that the train was going fastest at the bottom of the first hill and that it slowed down as it climbed up the next hill. When the train climbed the hill, kinetic energy was converted back to potential energy. Then it rolled down the hill and sped up again.

Now here's one more thing to do while you are standing in line. Think about what you will feel at each point in the ride. What sensations will you feel at the top of the first hill? At the bottom of that same hill? Going over the second hill? Hey, no fair answering "Scared!" to all the questions.

Riding the Roller Coaster

There are many things to do and notice while riding the roller coaster, besides screaming.

Here's What You Need

✔ A roller coaster

✔ A ticket to ride!

Here's What You Do

1. Sit on your hands as you ride. (Ignore all those other crazy people waving their hands in the air. You're going to notice so much more than they are!)

2. While riding, notice where you are squashed into your seat and your butt presses harder on your hands. Notice where you feel lighter and your butt presses more lightly on your hands.

3. Is there anywhere in the ride where you lose contact with your hands? How does this make you feel?

4. Notice how you feel at the top of a hill. Do you feel heavier, lighter, or the same as always?

5. How about at the bottom of a hill? Do you feel heavier, lighter, or the same as always?

What's Going On?

Back on page 159, we asked you to predict what you would feel as you rode a real roller coaster. Were you right?

When the train rounded a turn, did you feel like you were thrown to the outside of the curve and slammed into the side of the car? That's because you kept going in a straight line until the side of the car came around and stopped you. (For more on this, see Ask Professor Exploratorium on page 162.)

When the train whipped over the top of a hill, did you feel light in your seat? When the train reached the bottom of a valley, did the weight squashing down on your hands increase?

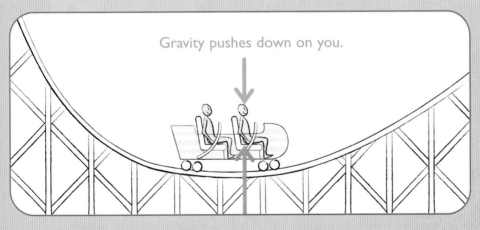

Gravity pushes down on you.

Seat pushes up on you.

You and the train were going downhill when the tracks curved upward. Remember Newton's laws of motion? (If you don't, see page 160.) Once you and the train are moving, it takes a force to make you change direction. The track pushed up on the train and the train pushed up on you, and your hands got squashed between the train seat and your body.

As the train sped over the top of a hill and dove down toward the valley, you probably felt lighter in your seat. But when the train headed downhill, you didn't push down on the seat as hard as you did before. That's why the orange arrow is shorter than before. Gravity was pulling you down, but the train was moving downward, too. The steeper the hill, the lighter you felt.

Gravity pushes down on you.

Seat pushes up on you.

**Experimenting to
test your ideas**

Did you sit in the
front, back, or middle
of the train? Do you
think the ride will feel
different if you ride in
a different part of the
train? Try it and see. (If
you want to know why
riding in different cars
makes the ride feel
different, see page 358.)

*Does your coaster go upside
down like this one?*

*If your coaster loops the
loop, pay attention to what you
feel when you're upside down.
(Yes, we know you feel terrified.
What else do you feel?)*

*When you're whirling
around a loop like this one, you
may feel like you're going to fly
out of the coaster. (Good thing
you're strapped in!)*

*To find out what causes that
feeling, read what Professor
Exploratorium has to say about
centripetal force on page 162.*

Drop Zone

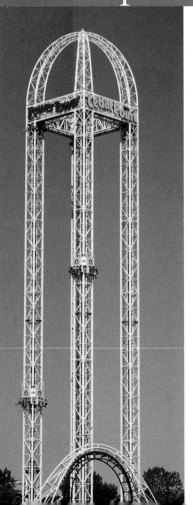

This ride takes you to an enormous height, then drops you like a
hot potato! What fun!

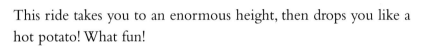

Here's What You Need

✔ A working Drop Zone ride

✔ A watch with a second
  hand or a stopwatch
  (to time the ride)

✔ A lot of nerve

Here's What You Do

1. While you are waiting in line,
   determine the time (in seconds)
   for the seat to climb the tower.

2. Determine the time (in seconds)
   for the seat to fall all the way to
   the ground.

3. Decide whether you still want to
   go on this ride. (Just kidding!)

4. While you are dropping, consider
   how your stomach feels.

5. Notice how the shoulder
   straps feel.

What's Going On?

When the Drop Zone ride dropped you, you accelerated toward the ground. The rate at which you accelerate is always the same here on earth. If you ignore air resistance, you accelerate from zero to 60 miles per hour in about three seconds.

While you are falling, you experience the same sensation of weightlessness that astronauts feel in orbit. That state of weightlessness is also known as *free fall,* which makes sense because you achieve it by falling freely.

When you were falling, did your stomach feel weird? Some of that may be due to stark terror. But your innards shift a little in free fall as well. Because your stomach and intestines are suddenly weightless, they don't snuggle together in the same way that they did when they had weight.

Did you manage to pay attention to the restraining straps and how they felt on your shoulders? While you were waiting to be dropped, the ride's restraining straps probably felt just fine. But as you went into your free fall, you probably felt the straps pushing down on your shoulders. In free fall, you no longer feel the force of gravity. Without gravity squashing you into your seat, your spine expands. For a short period of time, you actually grew taller — tall enough so that the straps pushed down on your shoulders.

After Your Trip

Since all rides are based on the scientific principles of physics, an amusement park is your very own physics lab. But, all too soon, you will have to leave this amusing laboratory and go home.

That doesn't mean your research has to stop. A top scientist can always stand to do more experimenting. What better place to experiment than your own home? Think of the advantages — no hefty admission price, lots of free food, and, best of all, you don't have to leave until you're good and ready (or until school starts again).

Now that you've experienced the real rides at the amusement park, you can copy their designs and make your own miniature amusement park rides right at home. Use your physics knowledge to build a bigger, better roller coaster. Get out those Legos and other building doodads from under your bed and experiment with designs for other rides.

Who knows? Maybe you'll be the one to come up with the next new scream machine!

To learn more about amusement parks, visit Exploratopia *online at* www.exploratopia.com.

The Beach

The first step in making a sand castle is getting the sand wet. Pack a bucket with damp sand and upend it. Then you get a nice, bucket-shaped tower for your sand castle. Do the same thing with a bucket of dry sand and you only get a pile of dry sand.

If you want to know why water makes sand stick together, you can go home and experiment with water. (See page 107.) You'll find out that water is sticky stuff. Because water sticks together, wet sand sticks together better than dry sand.

But let's save experimenting with water for another day. Instead, experiment with sand castles. How much water do you need to make the sand stick together just right? How tall a tower can you make? What happens if you add more water?

If one tower collapses, just start again. (You've got plenty of sand and water.) When you've finished making a fabulous sand castle, we have plenty of other experiments for you to try.

About Sand

Take a close look and you'll see that sand grains are tiny rocks. Some of those tiny rocks are semiprecious stones, such as jade and topaz. Most of them are made of quartz, one of the most plentiful minerals on earth and one of the hardest. Sand is tough stuff.

Magnetic Sand

You can probably find some magnetic sand on a beach near you!

Here's What You Need

✔ A magnet

✔ A small Ziploc plastic bag

✔ A container for your black sand

Here's What You Do

1. You could just stick your magnet in the sand, but you'd end up with a magnet covered with sand that won't come off. What a mess! So start by zipping your magnet up in the plastic bag.

2. Push the bag (holding the magnet) down in the sand.

3. Gently pull the bag back up. Is there any black sand sticking to the bag? The magnet attracts the sand through the plastic.

4. If you found some black sand, turn the bag inside out so that the sand is on the inside and the magnet is on the outside. Pull the magnet away and empty the sand into your container. Put the magnet back in the bag and try to get some more black sand.

5. If you don't have any black sand sticking to your bag, try another spot on the beach. If you still don't find any black sand, you may have to try another beach. You'll find black sand if your beach includes sand made when rocks made of granite broke apart. You won't find any magnetic sand on the beaches where the sand is made of bits of coral.

What's Going On?

The black sand that stuck to your magnet is made of *magnetite*, which forms when iron combines with oxygen. When grains of the magnetite touch a magnet, they become little magnets themselves, attracting other grains of magnetite. (To find out more about magnets, see page 320.)

(To find out more about magnets, see page 320.)

Tools for Exploration
Paying attention to stuff a lot of people ignore

A handful of sand may not look like much — until you look carefully. What different-colored grains can you find in a handful of sand? (If you have a magnifying glass, use it to take a really close look! Can you sort your sand grains into different colors? You can use a toothpick to sort the sand grains.) If the sand grains are too tiny to sort, can you find bigger sand grains elsewhere on the beach?

The Rock Cycle

The earth is a kind of recycling machine. Volcanoes spit out lava, which hardens to make rocks. The rocks wear away, or *erode*, to make sand — like these sand dunes.

When sand is squeezed under the right conditions, the grains stick together to make rock, or sandstone, like boulders in the photo below.

Wind and water break grains of sand off the boulders and the sandstone becomes sand again. Sand gets squeezed into sandstone and sandstone becomes sand over and over again in a never-ending cycle. Each cycle — from sandstone to sand and back again — takes about 200 million years, give or take a few million.

Geologists, scientists who study rocks, can guess how old a grain of sand is by examining its edges. A new grain of sand is sharp edged. Tumbling in the wind or rolling in the water wears down those sharp edges. Grains of sand that have been cemented together as sandstone and then chipped loose as sand a few times are the roundest (and oldest) of all.

Tiny Rocks

Andrew Jaster is a sand collector. He collects sand from all over the world and takes pictures that show the beauty of each individual grain. Sand grains are amazing when you take a really close look!

A Grain of Sand

Take a close look at any handful of sand and you'll find sand grains of many different colors and types. Some sand grains are tiny rocks, like the ones shown here.

This grain of sand from British Columbia is made of garnet, a semiprecious stone. This sand grain is 0.7 millimeters across, about 0.03 inch.

This is citrine, a kind of quartz. Quartz is one of the most common minerals on earth.

The tiny shiny flecks that you see in sand are bits of mica, like this one.

We don't know what this is. It might be another piece of mica — or it might be something else. You don't always have to know the name of something to appreciate how pretty it is.

Coral Sand

This handful of sand comes from the Cook Islands in the South Pacific Ocean. A closer look at the sand grains shows that this sand is made of bits of shell and coral.

On many tropical islands, the beach sand is made up entirely of bits of coral and broken seashells — like this one.

This sand grain was once part of a coral reef. The tiny holes were once the homes of coral polyps, the animals that built the reef.

Ocean waves pound on broken seashells, smashing them into tiny pieces — like this grain of sand that may have been part of the shell of a marine snail called a periwinkle.

You never know what you'll find in a handful of sand — until you look at it up close!

Waves and Water

People go to the beach to swim and fish and play in the water — and (in the case of scientists like you) to do a few experiments and make a few observations. To experiment with a whole lot of water, you need to visit the beach. Some experiments are too big for your bathtub!

The Basarwa Still

With a little patience and know-how, you can turn saltwater into freshwater.

Here's What You Need

✔ An early start (because this may take a few hours)

✔ A pocketknife or scissors

✔ An empty 2-liter plastic soda bottle with a cap

✔ A grown-up

✔ Saltwater

✔ A few heavy, squeaky-clean objects (marbles, pebbles, shells — anything you can use to weigh down a plastic cup and still be able to drink from it later on)

✔ A small plastic cup

✔ Sand

✔ Ice cubes

✔ A pen and notepad

Here's What You Do

1. Cut the soda bottle in two about two-thirds of the way from the top. (Ask for a grown-up's help with this.)

2. Pour about one-half cup of salt water into the cutoff bottom of the soda bottle.

3. Place your squeaky clean objects in your plastic cup, and set the cup in the saltwater. Make sure the cup is balanced so it doesn't tip over.

4. Put the cap on the cutoff top of the bottle. Then turn the top part of the bottle upside down and set it inside the bottom part. Line the bottle cap up above the middle of the cup but make sure it's not touching the sides of the cup.

5. Once the top of the bottle is arranged inside the bottom, push it down gently to make sure that it fits firmly and forms a tight seal.

6. You just made a *still,* a device that can make pure water from saltwater.

7. Put your still in a sunny place.

8. Put a few ice cubes in the upside-down top of the bottle.

9. You want the bottom of your still to be as warm as possible and the top to be as cool as possible. This is the key to a good still.

10. Every half-hour, take a look at your still. Watch for drops of water forming on the outside of the top of the bottle. When you get enough water drops, they'll drip into your plastic cup.

11. If all your ice melts, add more ice cubes.

12. After a few hours, see how much water has collected in the cup. If you only get a few drops, leave the still to work overnight (if you can).

13. When there's enough water in the collection cup to taste, carefully remove the top part of the still. (Make sure none of the clear water from the melted ice spills into the collection cup.)

14. Remove the collection cup from the bottom of the bottle. There may still be saltwater in the bottom of the bottle, but you're interested in the water in the cup.

15. Taste the water in the collection cup. Does this water look different from the saltwater? What does it taste like?

What's Going On?

Congratulations! You just turned saltwater that you can't drink into freshwater that you can drink. Now, if you're ever stuck on a deserted island with an empty soda bottle and some ice cubes, you'll know exactly what to do!

The sun and the sand heat up the saltwater. The ice cools down the bottle top. Your still works because of these different temperatures. Because the salt water is hot, some of it *evaporates* — that means the water turns from liquid into *vapor* or gas. The water vapor floats up, leaving the salt behind. When this water vapor bumps into the cold bottle top, it *condenses* — it turns back into liquid water. The liquid water drips from the top of the bottle into your collection cup.

When you have a cold drink on a hot day, you may notice drops of water on the outside of your glass. Those come from water vapor that condensed on the cold glass.

Tools for Exploration

Keeping track of your discoveries

When you put your still together, the top part of the bottle was dry. How long did it take before the first drops of water formed? What else did you notice when you checked the still? Writing down what you see may help you improve your still.

For centuries, the Basarwa people who live in Africa's Kalahari Desert have been making stills that purify water just as your still does. You use a soda bottle to hold the saltwater. The Basarwa would use a pit in the sand. You use a plastic cup to collect fresh water. The Basarwa would use an ostrich eggshell. You use an upside-down soda bottle for the top. The Basarwa might use the thin, stretchy skin from an animal's bladder. You use ice cubes to cool down the top of your still. (Lucky you! The Basarwa have to wait for the cold night air!)

Watching Waves

You can learn a lot about waves by watching them from the beach.

Here's What You Need

✔ An ocean with waves

✔ A watch with a second hand or a stopwatch

Here's What You Do

1. The high point of a wave is the *crest*. The low point is the *trough* (pronounced "troff"). The distance between two wave crests is the *wavelength*.

2. Look for something bobbing up and down in the waves — a seagull, a piece of driftwood, or a surfer.

3. When the object bobs all the way up, it's at the crest of a wave. When it goes all the way down, it's in a trough. Watch the bobbing object for a few minutes. Notice when it's on a crest and when it's in a trough.

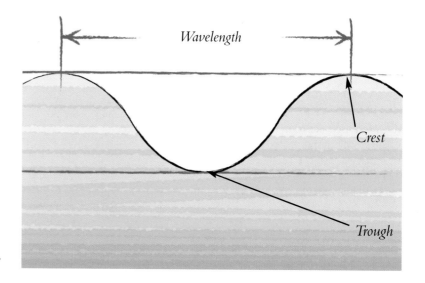

Wavelength

Crest

Trough

**Measuring and
counting**

Measuring sometimes
helps you find out
things you wouldn't
know otherwise.
With a watch, you
can figure out the
frequency of the ocean
waves and compare the
frequencies of waves
on different days.

*Have you ever watched
surfers or seagulls out in
deep water? They don't get
pushed back to shore by
every wave that comes along.
They spend most of their
time waiting, bobbing up
and down in one place. To
catch a wave, a surfer has
to paddle and paddle to
reach the edge of the wave
as it starts to break.*

*Moving waves do
not move the water itself
forward. Instead, waves
cause the water to swirl
around in a circle.*

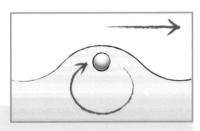

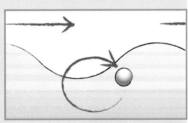

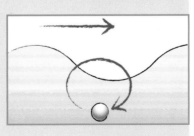

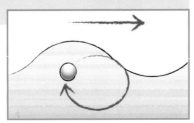

4. Use your watch to time how
long it takes for your object to
bob ten times. Start timing when
the object is at the top of a crest.
Watch while it goes down into a
trough and back up on a crest.
That counts as one bob.

5. Divide the time you measure by
ten. The answer gives you the
wave's *period,* the time it takes for
one wave to pass by, from crest
to trough and back to crest. (We
had you measure ten waves
because that's easier than just
measuring one.)

6. Once you know the wave's
period, you can figure out its
frequency. The frequency of a wave
is how often the wave goes
from crest to crest in a particular
time span. The frequency of an
ocean wave might be measured in
crests per minute. To figure
out the wave's frequency, divide
the number one by the period of
the wave, like this:

$$Frequency = \frac{1}{period}$$

So if the wave's period was
10 seconds, you get:

$$\frac{1\ wave}{10\ seconds} = \frac{1}{10}\ waves\ per\ second$$

That means $1/10$ of a wave goes
by every second.

7. It might make more sense to
measure that in minutes. To
convert into minutes you
multiply the frequency in seconds
by the number of seconds in a
minute, like this:

$$\frac{1\ wave}{10\ seconds} \times \frac{60\ seconds}{1\ minute} = \frac{6\ waves}{per\ minute}$$

That means six waves goes by in
a minute.

Dear Professor E:
I heard scientists were studying a bunch of sneakers found floating out in the ocean. What kind of funny business is that?

Signed,
A Sneaking Suspicion

Dear Sneaking Suspicion:
You're referring to the Big Sneaker Spill of 2002, where a shipload of Nike sneakers was lost at sea. This resulted in some serious science, even if it did come about in a funny way. Scientists sometimes take advantage of accidents to learn something interesting, and that's what happened here.

Curtis Ebbesmeyer is an oceanographer who studies ocean *currents*. An ocean current is sort of like a river in the ocean. It's a steady flow of water from one place to another.

Ebbesmeyer has figured out a great way to learn about currents — he maps the paths taken by cargo that falls off ships. On December 15, 2002, a storm swept thirty-three thousand Nike sneakers off a ship near Cape Mendocino, in Northern California. In early 2003, two brand-new Nike sneakers washed up on Washington's Olympic Peninsula. (One was a size 8 1/2 and the other was size 10 1/2. Darn!) Ebbesmeyer determined that the shoes had traveled in the North Pacific Current, moving more than 450 miles a month, or 18 miles a day.

Ebbesmeyer has also studied the oceangoing travels of twenty-nine thousand plastic bathtub toys and thirty-four thousand floating hockey gloves.

You can help Curtis Ebbesmeyer map ocean currents. Join his Beachcombers' and Oceanographers' International Association. Then look for interesting stuff (like sneakers or plastic duckies) that washes up on the beach and send him this information. Go to www.exploratopia.com for more details.

Currently yours,
Professor E

Curtis Ebbesmeyer, an oceanographer in Seattle, and James Ingraham, of the National Oceanic and Atmospheric Administration, studied the journeys of twenty-nine thousand bath toys that were cast adrift when the ship carrying them was wrecked in a storm off the Alaskan coast. These plastic toys made their way to Japan, the Arctic Ocean, and the Indian Ocean. The travels of the toys help these scientists figure out the movements of the ocean's waters.

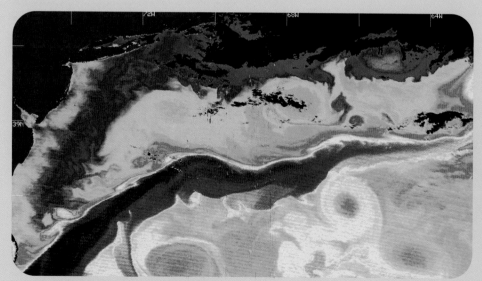

Here's a picture of ocean currents, created by a computer using information from a satellite. The black at the top is the East Coast of the United States. Different colors mark ocean waters of different temperatures. The bright red water is the Gulf Stream, an ocean current that carries warm water northward from the Gulf of Mexico. You can also see eddies of yellow (water that's a little cooler than the Gulf Stream) and green (water that's even cooler).

Wind and Weather

The beach is the perfect spot for watching the weather. You don't need fancy equipment. Look up and see what kind of clouds are in the sky. Put your hand in the air and feel which way the wind is blowing. You can learn a lot about the weather just by paying attention.

Which Way Does the Wind Blow?

Does the wind in the morning blow in the same direction as the wind at night?

Here's What You Do

1. Are there any flags around you? If not, is there anything else flapping in the breeze? If so, notice the direction that the flag or other flapper is flying. If you draw a line from the flapping end of the flag to the flagpole, your line will point in the direction that the wind is blowing from.

2. Wet your finger and hold it up in the air. The wind will feel cool against your wet finger. The side of your finger that's facing the wind will feel coolest.

3. Check the direction of the wind in the morning and in the evening. Is it the same?

What's Going On?

During the day, cool breezes often blow from the ocean to the land. In the evening, the breeze often blows from the land back to the water.

Why? During the day, the sunshine warms the land. The land then warms the air just above it. Warm air rises and cold air from above the water moves in to take the place of the warm air, making a cool sea breeze.

At night, the ocean stays warm while the land cools off. (You may have noticed this if you've ever gone for a swim at night; the water feels warmer than the air.) The water warms up the air above it. That warm air rises, and cooler air from the land rushes to take its place, making a breeze from the land to the sea.

Whenever there are two surfaces that absorb heat differently — like ocean and sand or mountain and prairie — that difference creates wind.

How Fast Is the Wind?

In 1805, an English admiral named Beaufort invented a way to measure the speed of the wind just by watching what the wind does to other things. You can use the Beaufort scale to figure out how fast the wind is blowing.

Beaufort Scale

Force 0	less than 1 mile per hour	Calm	Smoke rises straight up.
Force 1	1-3 miles per hour	Light air	Weather vanes are still, but smoke drifts.
Force 2	4-7 miles per hour	Light breeze	You can feel the wind on your face and hear leaves rustle.
Force 3	8-12 miles per hour	Gentle breeze	Leaves are in constant motion. Flags wave.
Force 4	13-18 miles per hour	Moderate breeze	The wind raises dust and loose paper, moves small branches, and makes flags flap.
Force 5	19-24 miles per hour	Fresh breeze	Small trees begin to sway. Waves form on lakes.
Force 6	25-31 miles per hour	Strong breeze	Large branches move. Umbrellas are hard to use. If you're still on the beach, it's time to pack up and head home.
Force 7	32-38 miles per hour	Near gale	Whole trees move. It's hard to walk. Flags fly straight out from the pole.
Force 8	39-46 miles per hour	Gale	The wind breaks twigs off trees. It's very hard to walk.
Force 9	47-54 miles per hour	Strong gale	The wind snaps tree branches and breaks signs and awnings.
Force 10	55-63 miles per hour	Storm	The wind uproots trees and wrecks buildings.
Force 11	64-72 miles per hour	Violent storm	Widespread damage.
Force 12	over 73 miles per hour	Hurricane	Extreme damage.

Tools for Exploration

Paying attention to stuff a lot of people ignore

Meteorologists always pay attention to which way the wind is blowing. The wind brings clouds and cold air from one place to another. To find out what type of weather is coming your way, look in the direction the wind is coming from.

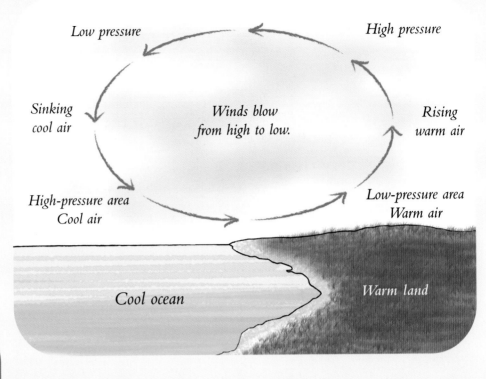

When warm air rises, it leaves behind a place where there is less air.

Meteorologists call this a low-pressure area. Cold air sinks, making what meteorologists call a high-pressure area. The wind blows from areas of high pressure to areas of low pressure.

Low pressure

High pressure

Sinking cool air

Winds blow from high to low.

Rising warm air

High-pressure area Cool air

Low-pressure area Warm air

Cool ocean

Warm land

Hot air rises. That's why hot air balloons float. That's also why the wind blows. When hot air rises, cooler air rushes in to take its place, and we feel a breeze.

Checking Out the Clouds

Looking at clouds can help you figure out what kind of weather is on the way.

Here's What You Need

✔ A pencil and a notepad (optional)

Here's What You Do

1. Watch the clouds drift by. Do you see different shapes? textures? colors?

2. If you're feeling artistic, sketch the clouds that you see.

3. If you're feeling scientific, try to identify the clouds you see, using the photos on page 183.

What's Going On?

Clouds form when warm, moist air cools off. The moisture in the air forms tiny drops of water or ice high above you. Sometimes that water and ice falls on you as rain and snow. This guide to clouds will help you predict the weather and teach you Latin names you can use to impress your friends.

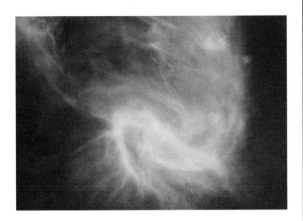

Scientists group clouds according to how high they are in the atmosphere, *the layer of air that surrounds the earth. The highest clouds are thin, curly-looking clouds, like the* cirrus *clouds in the picture. "Cirrus" comes from the Latin word for "curly." These high clouds are curly because of strong winds high above the earth.*

The high clouds to watch out for are cirrocumulus *clouds, which are arranged in a pattern like fish scales. A sky covered with cirrocumulus clouds is called a* mackerel sky. *(A mackerel is a kind of fish.) There's an old saying about this kind of sky: "Mackerel sky, storm is nigh." When you see cirrocumulus clouds, expect a storm.*

Cumulus clouds are happy-looking, puffy clouds. "Cumulus" comes from the Latin word for "pile," and a cumulus cloud can look like a big pile of cotton balls. Cumulus clouds may drop a little rain on you. But the ones to watch out for are cumulonimbus *clouds, which are tall cumulus clouds with dark bottoms.* Nimbus *comes from the Latin word for "rain cloud," which should give you a clue. Cumulonimbus clouds can bring heavy rain and snow, along with hail, lightning, and thunder.*

The lowest clouds are flat, spread-out clouds called stratus *clouds. "Stratus" comes from the Latin word for "spread out."* Nimbostratus *clouds like these are stratus clouds with dark bottoms, and they can rain on you for hours and hours!*

Taking the Long View

The beach is a great place to relax. Watch a shadow move over the course of the day. Stare out at the distant horizon. Watch the sun set. All these things will remind you that you're on a planet orbiting the sun. People are always forgetting that!

Dear Professor E:
Somebody told me that the moon makes the ocean's tides go in and out. How does it do that? And why can't the tide just stay still so I don't have to keep moving?

Signed,
Getting Wet

Dear Getting Wet:

If you spend all day at the beach, you may discover that you have to move your blanket before the day is over. Late in the afternoon, waves may be lapping at a spot that was a safe distance from the water in the morning. People who spend a lot of time at the beach know that the water level at the beach rises and falls twice daily as the tide comes in and goes out.

People noticed a connection between the moon and the tides many moons ago.

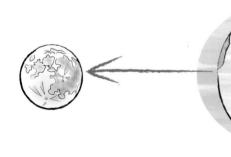

The moon orbits the earth because of gravity, a force that pulls you toward the center of the earth and pulls the earth toward the moon (and vice versa). The moon's gravity pulls on the ocean waters that are nearest the moon, making that water bulge out toward the moon. The moon's gravity also pulls on the solid earth. The ocean waters on the side of the earth farthest from the moon are left behind, making a bulge on that side of the earth, too.

As the moon orbits the earth, these bulges of water move with the moon, traveling around the globe. As one of these bulges approaches your beach, the tide will rise. As the bulge passes your beach and moves away, the tide will fall.

There are two high tides each day. The time of the high tide each day is about an hour later than it was the day before. Before you go to the beach, check the local newspaper or a Web site to find out when the tide will be at the highest and lowest points. While you're at the beach, pay attention to the water level, and be ready to move your blanket!

Glad tidings,
Professor E

Exploring Tide Pools

The ocean rises and falls as the tide comes in and goes out again. If you visit a beach with a rocky area at low tide, check for *tide pools*, places where the rocks hold puddles of ocean water at low tide. Be sure to check your tide table so you aren't caught by the rising tide. And watch out for waves!

With a grown-up, take a look in the tide pools and on the rocks around them. You'll find animals that live in the *intertidal zone.* That's the land that's covered with water by the highest high tide of the year and exposed to the air at the lowest low tide of the year.

Marine biologists, scientists who study life in the ocean, have divided the intertidal zone into four parts: the *splash zone,* the *high intertidal zone,* the *mid zone,* and the *low zone.* Each of these zones is high and dry for a different length of time each day, and you'll find different animals in each one.

Look high on the rocks for periwinkles. *These little snails live in the splash zone, where the rocks get only the spray from waves at high tide. When the rocks are dry, the snails seal themselves up so that they don't dry out too.*

Look below the splash zone for barnacles, *which look like grayish-white, volcano-shaped dots. Barnacles live in the high intertidal zone, which can be dry for more than 12 hours at a time. When the tide is out, these animals close up tight. When waves wash the rocks, the barnacles open up and feed on microscopic plants and animals in the water.*

Below the barnacles, look for mussels, *blue-black shellfish that attach themselves to the rocks so they can't be pulled loose by the waves. Mussels live in the low end of the high intertidal zone.*

Look for seaweed and sea anemones in the mid zone, right below the high intertidal zone. The mid zone dries out every day, but never for more than five or six hours at a time. When covered with water, sea anemones open up and look like undersea flowers with tentacles. When they're dry, anemones close up and look like squishy lumps.

Below the mid zone is the low zone, which is exposed to air only during the lowest tides. Here you'll find more seaweed, along with starfish and sea slugs.

The plants and animals of the intertidal zone form horizontal bands on the rocks. You can tell how high the tide rises by looking at where different plants and animals live.

Shadow Watching

Here's a great experiment to try when you're going to be at the beach all day.

Here's What You Need

✔ A sunny day

✔ A stick

✔ Two different types of objects to act as markers (we used rocks and seashells)

✔ A watch with an alarm

✔ One interesting object to mark the shadow at high noon (we used a soda can)

Here's What You Do

1. Start this activity in the morning.

2. Place your stick in the sand. Use one of your objects to mark the line of its shadow. (We used rocks to mark the shadows.)

3. Guess where the shadow will be in 15 minutes. Mark your guess with another object. (We used seashells to mark our guesses.) Set your alarm.

4. In 15 minutes, mark where the shadow is. How close was your guess? Mark where the shadow ends up.

5. Guess again where the shadow will be in 15 minutes. Set your alarm. Continue to mark the shadow every 15 minutes. Check your watch as noon approaches. Don't miss high noon!

6. Use your one interesting object to mark where your stick's shadow points at high noon. (We used a soda can to mark the noon shadow.)

7. How does the high-noon shadow look compared to earlier ones?

8. When are your shadows the longest throughout the day? Shortest? How much do the shadows move in 15 minutes?

Tools for Exploration

Making predictions

Did you guess where the shadow would be in 15 minutes? If your guess was off the first time, did you come closer on your second try?

What's Going On?

Most people don't pay attention to shadows. But the movement of shadows is evidence of something very important, something that it took people thousands of years to figure out — the earth spins like a top as it travels around the sun.

Every morning, the earth turns so that the side you are on faces the sun. As the earth spins, you see the sun come up over the eastern horizon. As the day goes on, it looks like the sun moves across the sky. But it's really the movement of the earth that makes the sun seem to move and the shadows change.

In North America, the stick's shadow will point due north at noon because at that time the sun is due south. (You can always find north at noon if you have a shadow to watch.)

Next time you are at the beach at sunset, be sure to watch for the green flash. The green flash is a flash of bright green light that you can sometimes see as the last bit of the setting sun dips below the horizon. The earth's atmosphere bends sunlight, separating the sunlight into rainbow colors. (For more on that, see page 306.) But the sun is so bright you can't really see those different colors until the sun dips so low that the horizon blocks out most of the light. Then you might catch a glimpse of the last color to dip below the horizon — green!

To learn more about exploring at the beach, visit Exploratopia *online at* www.exploratopia.com.

Part 3
Exploring Interesting Stuff

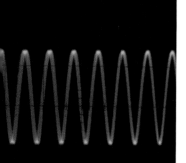

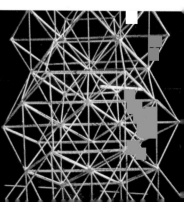

PINK GREEN BLACK PINK RED YELLOW PURPLE
BLUE GREEN BLACK ORANGE PINK RED YELLOW
PINK RED YELLOW PURPLE BLUE GREEN BLACK
ORANGE PINK RED YELLOW PURPLE BLUE
GREEN BLACK PINK RED YELLOW BLACK RED
YELLOW PURPLE BLUE GREEN BLACK ORANGE
PINK RED YELLOW RED GREEN BLACK GREEN
BLACK ORANGE PINK RED YELLOW GREEN
BLACK RED YELLOW PURPLE BLUE GREEN
BLACK RED YELLOW PURPLE BLUE YELLOW
GREEN BLACK RED YELLOW PURPLE BLUE
GREEN BLACK GREEN BLACK PINK RED YELLOW
PURPLE BLUE GREEN BLACK ORANGE PINK RED
YELLOW GREEN BLACK ORANGE PINK RED RED
GREEN YELLOW PURPLE BLUE GREEN BLACK
ORANGE PINK RED YELLOW GREEN BLACK RED
YELLOW PURPLE BLUE GREEN BLACK GREEN
BLACK PINK RED YELLOW PURPLE BLUE GREEN

Language

Take a look at this list of words, but don't read the words. Instead, name the *colors* that the words are printed in, out loud, as fast as you can. GO!

Saying the colors instead of the words was hard, wasn't it? Even though we told you not to read the words, you couldn't help it. You read each word before you named the color it's printed in. The word (which was different from the color) got in the way when you tried to name the color. Your brain was expecting the word "red" to be red, but you gave it something unexpected: the word "red" was green! When your brain gets a mixed message like that, it takes longer to make the right choice.

Back in 1935, scientist J. Ridley Stroop discovered that people take longer to name a color when the word and the color shown don't match. When the colors matched, the response was faster.

Turn this book upside down, and try this experiment again. Is it easier or harder to name the colors? Many people find it easier to name the color when they can't read the word.

Try this experiment with a small child who doesn't know how to read yet but does know her colors. Can she name the colors faster than you can? Chances are she can. For a child who can't read, the meaning of the word doesn't interfere with the name of the color.

A Little Linguistics

Some scientists study language. The fancy, hard-to-spell word for this particular science is linguistics. *Linguistics is the study of how language works — how words carry meaning, where language comes from, how it changes, how people learn language, and more. Wow! There's a lot to learn about language!*

Ping-Pong

Suppose you are an alien from another planet. Your language consists of only two words: "ping" and "pong." How much can you communicate?

Here's What You Need

✔ A piece of paper

✔ A pencil or pen

✔ A few friends

Here's What You Do

1. Take a look at the following English words and phrases. In your alien language, which of the pair would be ping and which pong? (No fair having two pings or two pongs!)

Elephant	Mouse
Italic	Bold
Ballerina	Wrestler
Comic book	Encyclopedia
Tornado	Sunny day
Hot soup	Ice cream
Hawaii	France
Scooter	Moving van

2. Write your answers on a piece of paper.

3. Ask your friend to say which word is ping and which is pong. Write down your friend's answers.

4. Collect answers from a few friends. Do people generally agree on what is ping and what is pong?

What's Going On?

For people who speak English, ping and pong are nonsense words. But even though ping and pong don't mean anything to English speakers, the sound of each word can suggest meaning.

Take a look at the answers you've collected. Did most people say that the mouse was ping and the elephant was pong? That's what happened at the Exploratorium. Most people say that the smaller member of each pair was ping and the larger one was pong. There seems to be something about the sound of ping that goes with something little. The sound of pong seems to go with something big.

Say the words ping and pong out loud and you may see what we mean. Did you automatically use a higher tone for ping and a lower one for pong? Lots of people do.

There are no correct answers to this test (our favorite kind!). When we asked people at the Exploratorium, there were food fights over the "hot soup" and "ice cream" pair. People's answers depended on what kind of soup or ice cream they were thinking of. The words "France" and "Hawaii" also received mixed responses.

"That's in! I like your sense of style."

"Don't be jokin'. As same as you!!"

"How many girls are understanding own styles?"

This is a T-shirt that a member of the Exploratorium staff bought while traveling in Thailand. The joke almost makes sense, but not quite.

If you're traveling in a country where English isn't the main language spoken, keep an eye out for interesting signs. The sign pictured below advertises a teahouse (a sort of hotel), high in the mountains of Nepal. Whoever wrote the sign knew enough English to get many of the words right. But the sign writer put those words together in ways that break the rules of English grammar. The result is wonderfully poetic.

If you want to make worthy stay, we keep on you your judgement of our reputation in lodging & cooking circle. our arangement with yak cheese and warm water bathing will be introduce 60 minutes walk from your present, at the hieght of 11600 feet sorounded with unnoticed seneries. *Himalayan lodge*

Melody of Language

The meaning of your words comes from both what you say and how you say it. Like a song, language has a melody or tune that's just as important as the words.

Here's What You Do

1. Say the word "hello" as if you're feeling very friendly. Now say it as if you're angry. With just this one word, can you show that you're surprised? Tired? Frightened? How many other different ways can you say "hello"?

2. Take the sentence "This is my dog." Draw attention to, or emphasize, different words as you say the sentence out loud four different ways: *This* is my dog. This *is* my dog. This is *my* dog. This is my *dog.* Does the meaning seem to change each time? How?

3. Say, "This is my dog?" as if you were asking a question. Does your voice change at the end of the question?

4. Here are four pictures of people with dogs — but in each one, the people are saying something different. Match each picture with the right statement. Here's what they are saying:

> *This* is my dog.
> This is *my* dog.
> This is my *dog.*
> This *is* my dog.

What's Going On?

What happened when you turned "This is my dog" into a question? Your voice probably went up at the end of the question. That's one way that people who speak English make a sentence into a question.

The same words can mean different things depending on how you say them. Your tone of voice, the places you pause, the places you speak louder, the way your voice rises and falls — all these count too. All these things are part of what a linguist would call your *intonation pattern.*

Your intonation pattern depends partly on what language you are speaking. That can lead to confusion! Speaking English with a Russian intonation pattern might sound unfriendly to someone who grew up speaking English. And speaking Russian with an English intonation pattern might sound affected and fake to someone who grew up speaking Russian!

So, it's not just what you say — it's *how* you say it!

Secret Languages

A message that is written in code (like the one to the right) is known as a cipher. Other people can't read your cipher. But that doesn't mean your secrets are safe. With a little effort, people can figure out your code. What then? You create another one, of course! Pretty sneaky.

Gsrh rh rm xlwv!

Now I Know My ZYXs

Substitution ciphers replace letters with other letters or symbols, keeping the order of the original letters the same.

Here's What You Do

1. First, you'll make a key that will help you unlock a cipher. Write down the alphabet in its regular order — A, B, C . . . (Go on and sing the little alphabet song if you want — we won't tell!) We'll call this line 1.

2. Underneath each letter of the alphabet, write the alphabet in reverse. Under Z, write A. Under Y, write B, and so on until you write Z under A. We'll call this line 2. . . .

3. The letters from line 1 will equal the letters from Line 2. That means A=Z, B=Y, and so on.

4. Look at the secret message in the green box at the top of this page. You can use your key to decode it. Find G in line 2. What letter in line 1 is equal to G? That's right: G=T. So write down a T. Now find S in line 2. S=H, so write down an H.

5. Find each letter in the message in line 2 and write down the matching letter from line 1. What does the message say? (Check your answer on page 359.)

6. Now you can use your key to write your own secret messages. Write out your message. Then find each letter in your message in line 1 of your key. Write down the code letter from line 2 that lines up with that letter. When you're done, you'll have a coded message. (When you give your friends the message, be sure to give them the key as well!)

7. Can you translate the sentence below using the reverse-alphabet method?

   Gsrh rh gsv tivzgvhg yllp
   R szev vevi ivzw!

   Why, thank you! You are too kind.

What's Going On?

Writing the alphabet backward isn't the only way to make a substitution cipher. Ever heard of the movie *2001: A Space Odyssey*? In that movie, there's a computer named HAL. Many fans of this movie think HAL was a secret cipher name. Maybe. Look at HAL's name letter by letter. In the alphabet, what's the next letter following each letter of HAL's name? It's *I-B-M*. IBM was a well-known computer company at the time the movie was made. HAL could be a substitution cipher for IBM.

Substitution ciphers actually date back to the time of the ancient Romans. Emperor Julius Caesar used them to conceal messages from his many enemies. Substitution ciphers don't always substitute one letter for another. Morse code, shorthand, and computer codes used to store characters (letters, numbers, information) are all modern examples of substitution ciphers. The trouble is that once everyone knows these codes, the codes are too easy to crack. If you want to throw off spies, you must come up with something new and improved.

Baseball signals are a kind of code. The catcher shows a certain number of fingers to call the next pitch — Fastball? Curveball? Slider? Meanwhile, the third-base coach is scratching his ear, tugging his cap, and patting his chest. What looks like a bunch of random movements are all signs telling the players to steal a base, bunt the ball, run to third, or even pay attention, because the next signal's really important! In baseball, you either crack the code or you're out!!!

Make Your Own Substitution Cipher

Choose a secret letter and create a code that's all your own.

Here's What You Do

1. Write the alphabet in its regular order — *A* to *Z*.

2. Pick a secret letter. Write that secret letter underneath the *A* of the alphabet. Follow that secret letter with the letter that comes next in the alphabet, followed by the next letter, the next letter, and so on. When you write down the letter *Z*, follow it by *A*, then *B*, *C* . . . until you catch up to the original secret letter.

3. Use this key to write a secret message just as you did in "Now I Know My ZYXs."

4. When you give your message to friends, be sure to tell them the secret letter so they can decode your message.

5. Here's a message written where the secret letter is *K*. Can you decode it?

QYYN TYL, IYE QYD SD!

Good job, you got it! We sincerely mean that. Oh, and that's also the answer to the secret message.

Alien Alphabet

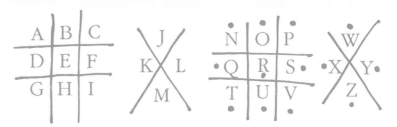

Here's the key for a different kind of substitution cipher, one that uses shapes to represent letters of the alphabet. Each letter of the alphabet is represented by the shape that surrounds it in the key.

Here's a message written in this code. Can you translate it? Check your answer on page 359.

Tools for Exploration

Keeping track of your discoveries

Cracking a code can be tough. (Nobody said being a spy was easy!) But you can make it easier by keeping track of all the possibilities you try as you try them.

Crack the Code!

You can crack a substitution cipher without knowing the key, but it takes some thought. If you want to give it a try, here's a riddle with the answer given in code.

Riddle: What's black and white and green and bumpy?
Answer: K ZSMUVO SX K DEHONY.

Can you figure out the answer? Sure you can!

The first step is to create a key. Write the alphabet in a horizontal row. Then try to figure out what some of the code letters are.

How can you do that?

The riddle's answer has two one-letter words. Take a look at the "Information for Code Crackers" box below and you'll find out that the most frequent one-letter words are *A* and *I*. Try *A* first. If *K* equals *A,* then *K* is your secret letter. Make a key, just as you did in "Make Your Own Substitution Cipher."

Try using your key to decode the riddle's answer. Do you get something that makes sense? (Check your answer on page 359.) That one was easy. Here's a tougher one — an interesting fact, hidden in a substitution cipher.

HXDA ORWPNAWJRUB PAXF OJBCNA
RW CQN BDVVNA CQJW RW CQN FRWCNA.

Uh-oh. This one doesn't have any one-letter words to help you out. But it does have a two-letter word that's used twice. Look in "Information for Code Crackers," and you'll find that could be any number of words. Hmmm . . . It's going to take a little while longer to figure out the secret letter on this one. (You might want to use a pencil with an eraser when filling in that second line.)

Do any of the three-letter words help you? How about the double letters? Keep searching the message and reading "Information for Code Crackers" until you find something that will help you. It may take a while.

Want a little help? A three-letter word (*CQN*) is used twice, and the *cq* combination is also used in the word *CQJW.* Look at the order of frequency list. What's the most frequently used two-letter combination? That's right — *th.* (*T* is also the most common first letter of a word.) A common three-letter word is *the.* (*E* is also the most common final letter of a word.) Could *CQE* be "the"? Can you figure out the message now? (Check your answer on page 359.)

Information for Code Crackers

Here's a list of the letters and small words used most frequently in English. These are listed in order of how often they are used. This information will help you crack the code on this page.

Most frequent one-letter words:	*A, I*
Most frequent two-letter words:	of, to, in, it, is, be, as, at, so, we, he, by, or, on, do, if, me, my, up, an, go, no, us, am
Most frequent three-letter words:	the, and, for, are, but, not, you, all, any, can, had, her, was, one, our, out, day, get, has, him, his, how, man, new, now, old, see, two, way, who, boy, did, its, let, put, say, she, too, use
Most frequent double letters:	ss ee tt ff ll mm oo
Most frequently used letters:	*E T O A N I R S H D L C W U M F Y G P B V K X Q J Z*
Most frequent first letters:	*T O A W B C D S F M R H I Y E G L N P U J K*
Most frequent ending letters:	*E S T D N R Y F L O G H A R M P U W*
Most frequent two-letter combinations:	th er on an re he in ed nd ha at en es of or nt ea ti to it st io le is ou ar as de rt ve
Most frequent three-letter combinations:	the and tha ent ion tio for nde has nce edt tis oft sth men

Dear Professor E:
I saw a movie the other day about these Native American soldiers that spoke in a code only they could understand. Is this a true story?

Signed,
Movie Fan

Dear Movie Fan:

All true. During World War II, members of the Navajo nation served in the United States Marine Corps as *code talkers.* These men transmitted coded messages in a language that the enemy could not crack: the Navajo language, spoken by Navajo of the American Southwest.

A coded message was made of a string of Navajo words. To decode the message, you would have to translate each Navajo word into English, and then use the first letter of each English word to spell out a message. One way to say the word "navy" in Navajo code is: *Tsah, be-la-sana, ah-keh-di-glini, tsah-ah-dzoh.* Translated, these words are as follows: "needle," "apple," "victor," "yucca" (the name of a plant that grows in the American Southwest). The first letters of each word spell NAVY.

About 450 frequently used military words were assigned Navajo words. For example, *gini* means "chicken hawk," which stood for "dive-bomber." *Besh-lo* means "iron fish," which stood for "submarine."

The Navajo code was never broken, and Marine commanders credit the code with saving the lives of countless American soldiers.

Your Frozen-Rhino-Into-Everything-Near-Denver (F-R-I-E-N-D!),
Professor E

These very intelligent-looking pigs speak a secret language called Pig Latin. Perhaps you've heard of it? (Hmm. Some secret!) Like any language, Pig Latin has its own rules. The basic rule is this: You take the first letter of a word, move it to the end, and add ay *to that letter (*piggy *becomes* iggy-pay*). When the word starts with a vowel — a, e, i, o, or u — leave the vowel where it is and add* hay *to the end of the word (*adorable *becomes* adorable-hay*). If a word starts with two letters that together make one sound (*chubby*), treat them like a single letter (*chubby *becomes* ubby-chay*). Finally, for really short words (such "as" "a," "I," "it," "on"...), just* forget about it! *I ove-lay my adorable-hay, ubby-chay iggy-pays! Don't you?*

Ets-lay ope-hay
the armer-fay is a
egetarian-vay!

Pig Latin and Beyond

Pig Latin is just one example of a *transposition cipher*, where the original letters are rearranged in some way. There's more!

Here's What You Do

1. You are going to write your message so that the letters make a rectangle. Then you are going to copy the letter from the rectangle in a way that scrambles your message. Your friend (who has the key to the cipher) will then be able to unscramble the message.

2. Start by writing your message in regular sentence form. Suppose your message is: *Meet me after school behind the gym.*

3. Count the number of letters in your secret message. It's twenty-nine, right?

4. To make a rectangle that will hold all those letters, we need to find two numbers that multiplied together will equal twenty-nine or a little more than that.

5. Nothing divides evenly into twenty-nine, but five times six equals thirty.

6. Add an *O* at the end to make your boxed message an even thirty letters.

7. Write the letter in a rectangle that is six letters wide and five letters high. Like this:

M	E	E	T	M	E
A	F	T	E	R	S
C	H	O	O	L	B
E	H	I	N	D	T
H	E	G	Y	M	O

8. Now copy the letters over again, only this time, copy them column by column. (If you copy it row by row, you'd get your original message back — anyone could read that!). By copying your message, column by column, you'd get this:

MACEH EFHHE ETOIG
TEONY MRLDM ESBTO

9. Without the key, it would be hard to know what *that* means. To decode your message, your friend needs to know the shape of your original rectangle. It was five letters high and six letters wide. Putting the height first, that could be written as 5 × 6.

10. Send your friend a note that says:

5x6 MACEH EFHHE ETOIG
TEONY MRLDM ESBTO

11. After your friend rearranges the letters to make a rectangle that's five letters high and six letters wide, the message should become clear. Did he meet you after school behind the gym? After all this effort, let's hope so!

12. Using the above system, make up a new transposition cipher message for your friend to decode.

What's Going On?

Geometric shapes (like our rectangle) are the basis for many transposition ciphers. They work because they're easy for the person reading the message to remember. Your friend simply followed your directions and copied the letters into a five (letter) by six (letter) rectangle to read the message: Meet me after school behind the gym O!

Changing Languages

The word ear *(as in an* ear of corn*) comes from the Latin word* acus, *which means "leaves that surround corn." The word* ear *(the kind you use to hear) came from the Latin word* auris, *which means "the ears on your head." These Latin words ended up sounding the same but meaning different things.*

What Do You Call It?

Even though there are plenty of available words, people still seek out new and different words for the same object.

Here's What You Do

- You're going to conduct a survey. On this page are some pictures of ordinary, everyday objects. Go around and ask people you know the following questions:

- What do you call these objects?

- Where did you grow up?

- How old are you? (Be careful of this question; some people don't like it!)

- Are you a female or a male? (On second thought, you can probably just figure this one out.)

- Write the answers down and see if you can come to any conclusions.

What's Going On?

How did your survey go? Did you get a variety of responses? Did you learn any new words? Did you notice that older people use different words than younger people? (If you want to see some of the answers people at the Exploratorium gave, see page 359.)

Many factors influence the language you use. Your age is one. Young people often use quite different words than older people. Where you live also matters. People in England call French fries *chips*, and they call potato chips *crisps*. But you don't have to live in a different country to have different speech patterns. People who come from different parts of the United States often have completely different names for the same objects.

Tools for Exploration

Explaining what you notice

Can you figure out why different people use different words for the same thing? Does where people come from make a difference? Does their age make a difference?

Zap! Yeow!

Here is a list of words describing sounds followed by a list of possible situations. Can you match the sound effect with the appropriate situation?

Sound-Effect Word	Situation
1. BTAM!	Cosmic rays hit a spaceship entering a cosmic storm.
2. BYANNG!	Captain America hits villain with shield.
3. FTIK!	Power ray hits superhero with a sizzling roar that apparently kills him.
4. FAZZH-SHRRAK!	Silver Surfer's surfboard comes shooting out to him.
5. KZZZK!	Villain's powerblast and superhero's repulsor ray collide with each other, with awesome, explosive results.
6. RAK TAC TAC TAC TAC!	The Incredible Hulk hits a super villain who slams into a rock wall.
7. SHOOM!	Arrow hits superhero's costume, snagging shoulder.

The sound-effect words in this quiz are examples of onomatopoeia (pronounced AHN-uh-MAHT-uh-PEE-uh). As we noted earlier, that means using words to imitate the sounds they represent.

All the sounds and situations in this quiz were taken from real Marvel Comic books. These onomatopoeia words can't be found in the dictionary — yet! But others have already been accepted and included in the dictionary. Look up "pow" in your dictionary. See what we mean?

You'll find the answers to the quiz on page 359.

Comic book writers make up words to write down sounds. KE-PHLATT!! Oh, my — did you just drop your book?

BING BANG BADABOUM!

Comic book writers in other languages make up sound-effect words, too. You might think that the words would be the same as they are in English — but you'd be wrong.

We looked at *Tintin,* a series of comic books that have been translated into many languages, and compared the sound-effect words. In English, a cork popping out of a bottle goes POP! In French, the same sound is CLOUC! In English, a brick falling into the water makes a SPLOSH! In German, it makes a PLUMPS! And in French, a man falling down stairs makes the sound BING BANG BADABOUM! (We don't know what that would be in English.)

Even though the words are different, they have some things in common. Leanne Hinton, a linguistics professor at the University of California at Berkeley, studied comic book words and found that comic book words followed certain language rules, no matter where the books were from. Here are some of Professor Hinton's conclusions:

- Loud sounds always have an "oo" sound in them. Boom!
- Soft sounds have a short *i.* Click!
- Short *a* is used in sort of loud but not awesomely loud sounds. Bang!
- A sound that starts quickly is represented by a consonant — most likely *p, t, k, b, m, d,* or *g.* Kzzz!
- If the sound stops quickly as well, it'll end with these same consonants — *p, t, k, b, m, d,* or *g.* Pop!
- Sounds that start rapidly but then go on for a while are usually represented by the letters *s, sh,* or *z.* Shoom!
- Sounds that slowly fade out end with *s* or *sh.* Whoosh!
- A ringing sound ends with *n* or *m* or *ng.* Clang!
- A sound that lasts a long time ends with a repeating consonant. Kkkkkk!

Richard Rhodes, another linguist at the University of California at Berkeley, studies how sound-effect words become real words. Professor Rhodes thinks language sounds fall into two categories: *wild words* and *tame words.* Wild words are sounds that aren't normally represented in words. Tame words are represented in words.

Wild words can develop into tame words over time. When you step in bubble gum (or worse), don't you usually say something like *yech!? Yech!* is a wild word. But many people all over the world say something like the sound *yech!* when they encounter something icky. Over time *yech!* has turned into the English word "yuck!" Pretty soon everyone spells it the same way. The word begins to show up in books, actors say it in movies, and then, one day, it's in the big, fat dictionary. Once a word's in the dictionary, it becomes a tame word.

Do you see any tame word possibilities among the wild words we've looked at? Personally, we're rooting for *bing bang badaboum!*

To learn more about how you can explore language, visit Exploratopia *online at* www.exploratopia.com.

What is this man doing? He's making music with a saw. That's right, a saw like the one a carpenter would use to cut wood.

A musical saw player uses a bow, like the bow used to play a violin. Stroking the saw with the bow makes the saw tremble, or *vibrate*. When the saw vibrates, it makes a sound. By bending the saw, the saw player changes the sound, making it higher or lower and making beautiful music.

Back in the 1920s and 1930s, the saw was a popular musical instrument. Even today, there are musicians all over the world who play the saw. It just goes to show — you can make music from just about anything.

Singing

Trained singers learn to control their singing voice by controlling their breath. This singer is singing loudly, but the candle flame near his mouth doesn't flicker. He's learned to make a big sound without blowing out a lot of air. What do some of the best singers do with their voices? They experiment.

You Sing Like a Bird

Some kinds of birds share songs — one sings a note and then the other sings the next note. Sounds easy enough. Give it a try. (The birds are sharing laughter right now!)

Here's What You Need

✔ A singing partner

Here's What You Do

1. Pick a song you both know and like. How about "Take Me Out to the Ball Game"?

2. You sing a word. Then, your friend sings a word. Then you, your friend, and so on, throughout the song.

3. When you get to "Cracker Jack," you can decide how to handle it. You could have one person sing the whole word. Or you could have one person sing "Crack," the other sing "er," and the first one sing "Jack." The first way is easier, but we think the second is more fun.

4. How does your song sound? Well, they say practice makes perfect. So, practice some more!

Take Me Out to the Ball Game

Take me out to the ball - game. Take me out with the crowd.

Buy me some pea-nuts and Crack - er Jack. I don't care if I ev - er get back, so it's

Root! root! root! for the home team. If they don't win it's a shame! For it's

one! two! three strikes you're out at the old ball - game!

What's Going On?

Some birds — like the African bush shrike — sing like this when they are courting each other. One bird sings every other note; the other bird fills in the gaps. We haven't heard these birds singing, but we've been told that it's almost impossible to tell that there are two birds singing. They sound like a single bird.

If someone closed their eyes and listened to you and your friend singing, would you sound like one person singing?

Don't be discouraged if you can't sing as well as the birds do. Maybe this activity is just for the birds!

Song Switcheroo

Try singing the words of one song to the tune of another.

Tools for Exploration

Sharing your experience

Sing one of your switched songs for a friend. When you're done laughing, ask your friend to help you think of other songs that can be switched. Sometimes, two heads are better than one.

Here's What You Need

✔ Your voice

Here's What You Do

1. Sing the words of "Take Me Out to the Ball Game" to the tune of "America the Beautiful." (Concentrate — you can do it!) Hey, that new version sounds pretty good!

2. How about this one? Can you sing the words of the "Marine Corps Hymn" to the tune of "My Darling Clementine?" (If you need some help, look at the words to the "Marine Corps Hymn" on page 209.)

3. Can you come up with any other songs that work to different tunes? Can you find poems that you can sing to certain songs? Some people say you can sing any poem written by the famous poet Emily Dickinson to the tune of "Yellow Rose of Texas." Try it and see!

America the Beautiful

My Darling Clementine

Marine Corps Hymn

Dear Professor E:
I like to sing in the shower. It seems to me that I sound better in the shower than I do anywhere else in the house. Is it just my imagination?

Cleanly yours,
Waterlogged

Dear Waterlogged:
Nope, it's not your imagination. When you're in the shower, you're surrounded by hard, smooth surfaces that bounce the sound of your voice back to you. That gives your voice more power, turning up the volume — especially on the low notes. Because the sounds are bouncing around, some of them take longer to reach your ears. That stretches out the sound, giving your voice a richer, fuller sound. These effects combine to make you sound great! (That is, even greater than usual.)

If you want to get out of the shower and still have the benefit of a few sound reflections, try singing into a wok! (See page 350.)

Tunefully yours,
Professor E

Marine Corps Hymn

From the Halls of Montezuma

To the Shores of Tripoli,

We fight our country's battles

In the air, on land, and sea.

First to fight for right and freedom

And to keep our honor clean,

We are proud to claim the title

of United States Marine.

You've Got Rhythm

When you sing a song, you hold some notes longer than others. Sometimes you pause before singing the next note.

Music is a way of organizing sounds. Time plays an important part — that's what rhythm is all about. You can't have music without rhythm.

The ABCs of Rhythm

Understanding rhythm is as easy as *ABC.*

Here's What You Need

✔ A watch or clock with a second hand

Here's What You Do

1. Sing the *ABC* song, the one that you learned back when you were learning the alphabet.

2. Sing the song again, but this time clap along with it, one clap for every letter. (It gets a little tricky when you get to *LMNOP,* but hang in there.)

3. Start tapping your foot to a regular beat. Then sing the song in time with your foot taps. Keep your foot taps even and steady, even if they don't match up with the words of the song. (*LMNOP!*)

4. Now speed up your foot tapping and sing the song in time with your new, quicker foot taps.

5. How long does it normally take you to sing the *ABC* song? Time yourself and see.

6. Sing the song again as fast as you can. How long did it take you? (Our best time is six seconds.)

Jumping rope can help you understand rhythm, pulse, and tempo. You have to swing the rope evenly. That's the pulse. Whatever rhymes or chants you say provide the rhythm. When someone shouts, "Pepper!" and you change the speed, you are changing the tempo.

ABC Song

A B C D E F G   H I J K   L M N O P

Q R S   T U V   W X   Y and Z

Now I know my A B C's.   Next time won't you sing with me?

What's Going On?

You just experimented with rhythm, tempo, and pulse while singing your *ABCs*. (You've come a long way since you learned that song. No kindergartner could have managed all that.)

Clapping along with the song gave you a better feel for its rhythm. You found that you had to clap faster when you got to the *LMNOP* part. The rhythm of the song isn't regular. In the "ABC Song," it takes longer to sing *G* than it does to sing *F*. Some notes are long and some are short, and that helps make the song more interesting.

When you tap your foot, you provide a background beat, or a pulse, for the song. It's called the pulse because it's like a normal human heartbeat — boom, boom, boom. The pulse is even, and it lies underneath the rhythm. Rhythm can vary, but the pulse is steady. This is also called *time*. When we sing in time with another person, we are keeping the same tempo and following the same pulse.

When you tapped your foot faster, you sang at a faster tempo. You still paused at the places where there are pauses in the song (like right after *G*), but the pause, and each note, was shorter. If you slow a song down, you sing at a slower tempo.

Tools for Exploration

Measuring and counting

Try tapping your foot to keep time to other songs. Compare your foot tapping when you sing the "ABC Song" to your foot tapping when you sing "Take Me Out to the Ball Game." Do you notice any difference between the two songs? (For more information on this, see page 360.)

Fascinating Rhythms

Want to find out how rhythmic you are? Measure your boom boom!

Here's What You Do

1. Assign a different sound to the numbers 1, 2 and 3. Use each sound the number of times indicated. Suppose 1 is one handclap, 2 is the two words "boom boom," and 3 is three finger snaps. (Feel free to come up with your own sounds if you don't like ours.)

2. Now try all the combinations of these three rhythms, moving from one group to the next as smoothly as you can:

3. 123 132 231 213 321 312

4. That would be:
   • clap, boom, boom, snap, snap, snap
   • clap, snap, snap, snap, boom boom, and so on.

What's Going On?

This activity was designed to help music students practice their rhythmic skills. It's a good way to test your rhythmic coordination. How'd you do? Lots of us at the Exploratorium are terrible at this! If you can manage this, maybe you should consider a career as a drummer!

Finding Music

Ralph Carney is a musical virtuoso, a collector of sounds, and the creator of balloony tunes, music played with the air escaping from a balloon. Today's musicians find music everywhere. So can you! Keep reading to find out how.

What Will This Sound Like?

Use a recorder to capture the variety of sounds around you.

Here's What You Need

✔ A tape recorder or another sound recorder

✔ A microphone to go with the recorder

✔ A notepad and pencil

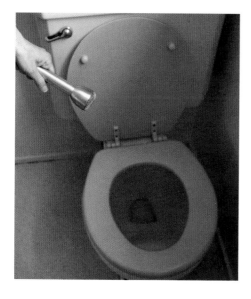

Here's What You Do

1. Use your sound recorder to record any and all kinds of sounds around you: running water, crumpling newspaper, the squeaky wheel of a grocery cart, a singing bird, a ticking clock . . . The possibilities are endless!

2. Write down each sound as you record it.

3. After you've collected a bunch of sounds, play the sounds back.

4. Can you identify all the sounds you recorded? Check your notepad to see which ones you missed. You may be surprised!

5. If you have access to the World Wide Web, search for sound samples online. You'll find many interesting sounds. Many hip-hop artists and other modern composers use samples from other music in songs of their own.

Tools for Exploration

Experimenting to test your ideas

Scientists aren't the only ones who experiment. As a musician, you can experiment with sounds, figuring out the combinations of sounds that you think work best together and putting those sounds together in a musical composition.

What's Going On?

Were you surprised when you listened to your sounds? Maybe you discovered that you couldn't figure out what created a sound just by listening to it. (Aren't you glad you wrote it down?)

Brenda Hutchinson, a composer who worked at the Exploratorium, has lots of experience with transforming everyday sounds. It all started when she was five years old and she got a tape recorder for Christmas. She immediately began to record everything.

One day she decided to investigate the sounds of the toilet. She hung a microphone in the toilet bowl and flushed the toilet. The recorded sound she got was totally unexpected. Instead of sounding like a toilet flushing, it sounded more like a goat kicking through a junkyard of cans. Much more interesting!

Isn't it amazing the way that sounds can change when you separate them from whatever it was that produced them? Brenda still can't get over it!

The Structure of Music

Composer Brenda Hutchinson listens to everything as if it were music. She records natural sounds and makes them a part of her musical compositions. Here are some questions that may help you think about the musical qualities of the sounds around you:

- Is the sound loud or soft?

- Is it high (like a flute) or low (like a tuba)?

- Does it go on for a long time or is it short?

- Does it repeat in some kind of rhythm?

- Does it sound like a flute, a piano, a violin, or some other instrument?

- Can you sing along with it? Does it have a good beat — good enough to dance to?

Asking yourself these kinds of questions will help you hear sounds as a composer does — as music. That means listening to the sound without thinking about where it came from.

Some artists make sculptures that focus our attention on sounds we tend to ignore. We are lucky to have two such musical sculptures at the Exploratorium.

The Aeolian Harp hangs in a place of honor at the entrance to the Exploratorium museum. Created by artist Doug Hollis, the harp works a little like a giant, one-way, tin-can telephone! The wind blows through the harp's long wires, making them vibrate. The vibrating wires make metal dishes attached to the wires start vibrating, and the dishes make an eerie, high-pitched hum. People standing near the Exploratorium entrance look around, trying to figure out where all the heavenly music is coming from.

The Wave Organ amplifies the sound of seawater rushing into built-in pipes as the tides ebb and flow. To hear the Wave Organ, you walk down to a sitting area by San Francisco Bay. Then you just listen. Soon you hear the symphony of sounds the Wave Organ plays for you. While the sounds of this organ are certainly impressive, you don't need the Wave Organ to listen to the sounds that water makes. Peter Richards, the artist who built this sculpture, hopes that people become more aware of what they're hearing — not just at the Wave Organ, but anywhere and everywhere.

Making Music

This woman is playing a musical instrument that's called the pipes of Pan. *According to Greek legend, the god Pan thought the wind made a beautiful sound when it blew through the reeds. So he cut some reeds and made them into a musical instrument.*

Singing Wineglass

With a little patience, you can make a glass sing!

Here's What You Need

✔ A little bit of water

✔ A drinking glass with a stem, like a wineglass (ask permission and use a sturdy ordinary one)

✔ A table or flat surface

✔ A grown-up helper

Here's What You Do

1. Wet the rim of the glass and your finger.

2. Set the glass down on a table or counter. Hold onto the base of the glass with one hand.

3. Rub your moistened finger lightly around and around the wet rim, until the glass begins to hum. (Be gentle. You wouldn't want to break the glass and cut yourself. A light touch works best anyway.)

4. Put a little water in the glass. What happens to the sound of the note?

What's Going On?

Back in 1761, Benjamin Franklin invented a musical instrument that he called the *glass harmonica*. It was built from musical glasses (like your wineglass), and he called it a harmonica because he thought the sounds it produced were *harmonious*, another word for "pleasant sounding."

Is the sound you get from your glass heavenly? No? Well, keep practicing!

Does putting a little water in the glass change the note your wineglass plays? Set up a whole row of wineglasses, with varying levels of water, and make your own glass harmonica.

Bottle Band

You can make an instant musical instrument with some empty glass bottles. To learn how, go to page 345. Then come back here to learn how you can use your new instrument to make beautiful music.

Back already? When you tried experimenting with bottles, you found out that adding water changed the pitch of the sound you heard. (The *pitch* is how high or low the note is. If you're blowing across the top of a bottle to make a sound, adding water will make the note higher. If you're tapping on the bottle, more water will make the note lower.)

By filling identical bottles with different amounts of water, you can make an instrument that can play a musical *scale*. A scale is a series of notes that go up in pitch in a regular way — like the one you get when you sing, "do, re, mi, fa, so, la, ti, do."

Try to play the notes that go with "do, re, mi, fa, so, la, ti, do." If you need a bottle to play a higher note, add a little water. If you want a lower note, pour some water out.

When you sing or play "do, re, mi," and so on, the first *do* and the last *do* are an *octave* apart. The word "octave" describes the musical distance between the notes. The first part of the word, *oct,* comes from the Latin word for "eight," which is *octo.* And if you count the notes from *do* to *do,* you'll find there are eight of them.

All around the world, people have grouped musical notes into octaves. But there are many ways to divide an octave to make a scale. If you live in the United States, the "do-re-mi" scale is probably the one you are most used to hearing. But you could divide the space between *do* and *do* with five notes, or ten notes. Use your bottles to create your own new scales.

Make Your Own Band

You can make music from just about anything! Use the suggestions from this chapter to sing, make rhythms, or build your own instruments. Experiment with all the objects and places around you. What else can you make music with? Where else can you make music?

Play the *What would happen if . . .* game. Suppose you find a flexible plastic tube on the floor. *What would happen if* you whirled it over your head? *What would happen if* you sang into the tube? *What would happen if* you blew a raspberry into the tube? *What would happen if* you banged it against something?

Making your own band should be a snap. After all, if music can be found anywhere, then a band could be made up of just about anything. All you have to do is gather some other interested folks. (Or, if you prefer, you could go the one-person band route.) Then, use all your new knowledge of musical structure to create music that's all your own.

When you're not busy making music, be sure to listen for it wherever you go. No matter the source, all sounds can be music to someone's ears. How about yours?

The Cuica

One of the most popular instruments played in the Brazilian celebration called Carnaval is the *cuica*. Build your own cuica and make your own Carnaval fun.

Here's What You Need

- ✔ A knife
- ✔ A bamboo skewer about 8–10 inches long (used for making shish kebabs and sold in grocery stores)
- ✔ Electrical or duct tape
- ✔ A large empty can with a plastic lid (we used a coffee can)
- ✔ A can opener
- ✔ A hammer and small nail
- ✔ String or rubber bands
- ✔ White glue
- ✔ A piece of damp cotton cloth (like an old towel or a T-shirt)
- ✔ A grown-up helper

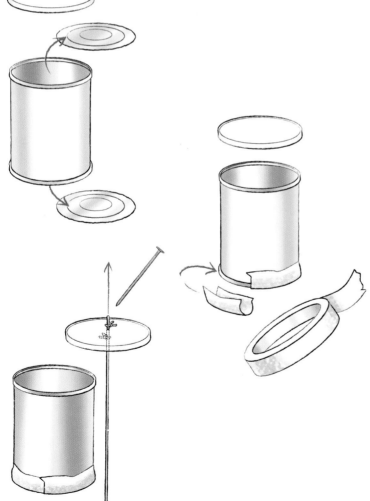

Here's What You Do

1. Cut off the sharp end of the skewer or wrap it with tape.

2. Take the plastic lid off the can and carefully put tape over any sharp edges on the empty can. Then use the can opener to cut out the bottom of the can. Put tape on any sharp edges.

3. Use a hammer and nail to make a small hole in the center of the plastic lid. Make the hole big enough to push your skewer through, but not so big that the skewer will fall through.

4. Push the skewer through the lid, leaving $1/4$ inch of the skewer sticking out the top of the lid.

5. Hold the skewer in place. Take two short pieces of string (or rubber bands) and tie two knots around the skewer — one directly above the lid and one directly below it.

6. To keep the knots from slipping, put a few drops of glue on each knot.

7. Put the lid back on the can. If the skewer sticks out the bottom of the can, break off the extra piece.

8. If the lid doesn't fit tightly on the can, put some glue along the sides of the lid to hold it on.

9. To play your cuica, hold the can with one hand and hold the damp cotton cloth in the other. The hand with the cloth will be inside the can. Rub the cloth up and down on the long end of the bamboo skewer.

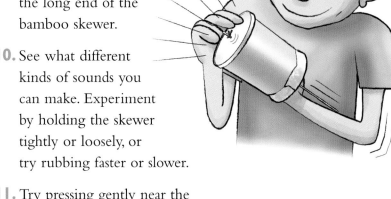

10. See what different kinds of sounds you can make. Experiment by holding the skewer tightly or loosely, or try rubbing faster or slower.

11. Try pressing gently near the center of the plastic lid while you play.

What's Going On?

Did all the cats in your area run away as you played your cuica? Well, maybe you need a little more practice before you're ready to make music. But you sure can make some interesting sounds.

While the cuica may look somewhat like a drum, it isn't played like one. During a Carnaval parade, a cuica player rubs the stick (your skewer) with one hand (your moist cloth) while the other hand holds the other end steady. The larger the cuica, the lower the pitch. Pressing near the center of the skin (your lid) changes the pitch. The hollow space of the metal cylinder (your can) works to amplify the unique sounds for all to hear!

A cuica can make an amazing variety of sounds, anything from deep croaks to high-pitched cackles. It can sound like a dog barking. It can sound like a person laughing or crying. It can sound rhythmic like a drum or tuneful like a flute. Hunters in Africa (where the cuica originally came from) use the cuica to attract lions!

The rhythmic vibration caused by the sticking and sliding of the cloth creates the sound. (For more on vibration and sound, see page 340.) The sound of chalk screeching on a blackboard is the same kind of sticking sliding effect, but you never see anyone playing *that* at Carnaval.

Palm Pipes

To figure out how to play this instrument, don't use your head. Use your hand.

Here's What You Need

✔ PVC pipe that's $1/2$ inch in diameter, cut into 9 pieces. These pieces of pipe must be cut to the following lengths: 15.8 centimeter, 14.0 centimeter, 12.5 centimeter, 11.8 centimeter, 10.5 centimeter, 9.4 centimeter, 9.2 centimeter, 7.9 centimeter, and 7.0 centimeter. (You can get PVC pipe at a hardware store. Ask the person at the store to cut the pipes to the sizes you need.)

✔ A ruler marked in centimeters (cm) and a hacksaw (if you or your helper want to cut the pipes yourself)

✔ Sandpaper

✔ A grown-up helper

✔ A permanent marker or stick-on labels and a pen

✔ 8 other people (You're going to form a band!)

Here's What You Do

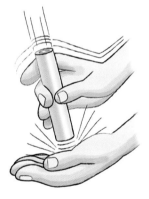

1. If any of your pieces of PVC pipe have sharp edges, use your sandpaper to sand them smooth.

2. Bang the open end of a piece of PVC pipe against the palm of your hand. Don't cover the top end of the pipe. Can you make a musical sound? If not, try again. Once you get a good sound, you're ready to perform.

3. Using your marker or labels, mark each length of pipe with the following letters and numbers:

15.8-cm pipe C_1	11.8-cm pipe F_2	9.2-cm pipe B_2
14.0-cm pipe D_1	10.5-cm pipe G_2	7.9-cm pipe C_2
12.5-cm pipe E_1	9.4-cm pipe A_2	7.0-cm pipe D_2

4. With these pipes, you can play a complete musical scale (from *do* to *do* or from C_1 to C_2). Plus you have one extra pipe (D_2), which lets you play more songs.

5. Compare the notes or pitches that you get from different pipes. The longer the pipe, the lower the note, or pitch, you get.

Tools for Exploration

Making predictions

Suppose you got a pipe that's longer than your longest one. Do you think the sound would have a higher pitch or a lower pitch than the sound of your longest pipe? Try it and see.

6. Give one pipe to each person in your pipe band, and keep one for yourself.

7. Ask each person to practice making a good note by holding the pipe vertically with one hand and banging the bottom end into the palm of the other hand.

8. First, try playing all the notes in order. Have each member of the band play a note — in this order: C_1, D_1, E_1, F_2, G_2, A_2, B_2, C_2, D_2 You've played a scale and one extra note.

9. Do it a few times, so everyone can practice making a good sound.

10. Now, try playing a song! When you're playing a song, members of the band will need to pay attention to rhythm, playing their notes at the right time. It may help to sing the song the first few times you play it, until everyone gets the rhythm down.

11. Remember that a little practice goes a long way.

12. Now, try playing for an audience. Can they figure out what song you're playing? Aww, what do they know?

13. After you play the three songs we've provided, can you figure out how to play other songs?

Songs for Your Pipe Band

Mary Had a Little Lamb

(You'll need four players and pipes C_1, D_1, E_1, and G_2)

E D C D E E E D D D E G G
E D C D E E E D D E D C

Jingle Bells

(You'll need five players and pipes C_1 through G_2)

E E E E E E E G C D E
F F F F E E E E E D D E D G
E E E E E E E G C D E
F F F F E E E E G G F D C

Twinkle, Twinkle, Little Star

(You'll need six players and pipes F_2 through D_2)

C C G G A A G F F E E D D C
G G F F E E D G G F F E E D
C C G G A A G F F E E D D C

To learn more about exploring music, visit Exploratopia *online at* www.exploratopia.com.

Math

Wow! That's a big wave! Can you figure out how big it is? Sure you can.

Look for something in the photo that you can compare to the wave. You could use the surfer or his surfboard. Let's use the surfer since you can see all of him.

This surfer looks like a grown man. The average height of an American man is about 5 feet 9 inches tall. To make our calculations simple, let's say this guy is 6 feet tall. But he's crouching a little — which makes him a little shorter. Let's say he's around 5 feet tall. Using a ruler, measure the surfer in the photo. How many of these guys, standing on top of each other, would it take to equal the height of the wave?

Since this surfer is 5 feet tall, multiply your number of guys by 5 feet to get your real-life answer. Eek! That really *is* a big wave!

What is this surfer doing in a chapter about math tricks? Well, to figure out the size of the wave, you used a little thinking plus a little guessing. A mathematician would say you made an *estimate*, a well-informed guess. Estimating is a handy mathematical skill.

Making an Estimate

Suppose you have to answer the question at left — without a calculator. How? Make an estimate. That is, find an answer that's close to the exact answer. You know 32 is close to 30, and 969 is close to 1,000. What's 30 times 1000? That's your estimate. Which choice is close to that number?

How Far?

How far did this skateboarder jump — from takeoff to landing? Can you figure it out?

Here's What You Need

✔ Your brain

✔ A ruler

✔ A piece of paper

Here's What You Do

1. Take a close look at the photograph. Can you guess the length of anything in the photo? How long do you suppose the skateboarder's arm is? You could find a person who looks like he's about the same height as this guy and measure his outstretched arm.

2. How many arms it would take to equal the gap our skateboarder jumped? Figure it out using a ruler. Or fold a piece of paper so it's just as long as the arm in the picture, then see how many pieces of paper like this you would need to fill the space between the skateboarder's takeoff and his landing.

3. Multiply the number you get by the length of the arm. The result is the distance our skateboarder jumped.

4. If you can't find a friendly guy to measure or if you would like to double check your answer, look at the photo one more time.

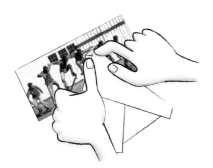

What else could you use to measure the gap? How about the skateboard itself? How long is your skateboard? How many skateboards would you need to fill the gap? Multiply that number by the length of your skateboard. If you already measured the gap using the skateboarder's arm, compare your answers. Are they pretty much the same?

What's Going On?

When you figured out how far the skateboarder jumped, you made an *estimate*, a well-informed guess.

If you want to check your estimate of the skateboarder's jump against ours, see page 360.Your answer is probably not exactly the same as ours—and that's okay. An estimate doesn't need to be exactly right, as long as it's close enough. Most of the time, an estimate is really all you need. In this case, you just want to know *about* how far he jumped. If you're off by a foot or two, that's doesn't really matter.

Do you also want to know how high the skateboarder jumped? Use your estimation skills to figure it out. X = the right answer! Can you estimate how far the skateboarder would have fallen if he had messed up his trick? All we can say is: X = ouch!

Dear Professor E:
When I was walking across Harvard Bridge in Boston, Massachusetts, I noticed some marks and numbers on the bridge. When I asked a passerby what it was all about, he said one word: "Smoots." What did he mean by that?

Signed,
Seeking the Scoop on Smoots

Dear Seeking the Scoop on Smoots:
Some people get really silly when they are measuring distances.

In 1958, some students from the Massachusetts Institute of Technology decided to measure the entire length of Harvard Bridge by using a person! His name was Oliver Smoot, and he was 5 feet 7 inches tall. While he lay down along one side of the bridge, another student marked just above his head and below his feet. That distance was equal to 1 Smoot. Then Oliver got up, lay down with his feet just touching the mark that had been at his head, and his fellow students marked his position again. They did this over and over again as they walked across the entire bridge. When they were done, they discovered the Harvard Bridge was 364.4 Smoots and one ear long.

Now, everyone in the area has come to accept the Smoot as an actual measuring unit, even the city police. They use the Smoot marks to pinpoint locations where accidents have taken place. Uh-oh, fender bender at 137 Smoots!

Oliver Smoot has gone on to bigger and better things. As a matter of fact, he is now the president of the International Organization for Standardization. They make sure that everyone agrees on the same methods of measurement. Otherwise, people all over the world would get different results when measuring the same things.

Measuring up,
Professor E

Stride Ruler

You may not have a Smoot to use as a measuring device, but you can measure distances with your own two feet. Measure the length of your average step, or stride, and you've got a built-in tool for estimating distances.

Here's What You Need

✔ A ruler

✔ Chalk

✔ A sidewalk or driveway that you can mark with chalk

✔ A calculator

✔ Your own two feet

Here's What You Do

1. Use your chalk to mark a starting line on the sidewalk.

2. Put your toes just behind this start line.

3. Take 10 normal paces forward, stopping when you've completed your tenth step.

4. Make a mark on the sidewalk next to your toe.

5. Using your ruler, measure how far you walked in 10 steps. You can measure in inches and feet or in centimeters and meters. (At the Exploratorium, we like using centimeters and meters.)

6. Divide the number you get by ten to find the average length of one step — your stride.

7. Repeat these steps two more times. You'll probably get a different stride length each time.

8. Add the three stride lengths together and divide by three to get the average stride length.

What's Going On?

Now you can use your average stride length to estimate distance. Just choose an object that's some distance away from you and walk towards it, counting your steps. Write down how many steps you took and multiply this number by your average stride length. The answer tells you how far away the object was.

Tools for Exploration

Measuring and counting

MIT students used Oliver Smoot to measure their bridge in Smoots. What can you use to measure things around your house?

Games

Playing games may not seem to have much to do with math, but even when you play a game as easy as tic-tac-toe, you think ahead, consider possible moves, and try to figure out what will happen. The skills that you use are skills that mathematicians use in solving problems.

The Oddball Game

By thinking ahead, a smart player can discover the winning moves of this game.

Here's What You Need

✔ 10 matching objects to use as playing pieces (pennies, paper clips, beans, other small objects)

✔ A partner

Here's What You Do

1. Put your playing pieces in a pile on the table.

2. One player starts by taking either one or two pieces from the pile.

3. The other player takes either one or two pieces from the pile.

4. Players take turns removing pieces from the pile. On each turn, you can take either one or two pieces, but you have to take at least one.

5. The player who is forced to take the last piece is the Oddball. Sorry, you lose!

6. Play again! And again! Keep going until you've mastered the game.

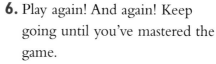

Making predictions

Suppose you started a
game of Oddball with
eleven pieces rather
than ten. Can you
figure out how many
pieces you need to
take in order to win?

What's Going On?

Thinking ahead can help you win Oddball.

Suppose it's your turn and there are only two pieces left. You don't want to take both pieces. If you did that, you'd be taking the last piece — Oddball! But if you take one piece, you leave your opponent with the last piece. So he's the Oddball!

But suppose it's your turn and there are four pieces left. If you took one piece, that would leave your opponent with three pieces. Your opponent could take two and that would leave you with one. You're the Oddball! If you took two out of the four, you'd still lose, wouldn't you? Your opponent would take one of the two left, leaving you to be the Oddball! If you're faced with four pieces, there's no way you can win against an opponent who is thinking ahead.

Now suppose it's your turn and there are five pieces. You know that four pieces means an automatic loss. Thinking ahead, you take one of the five pieces, leaving your opponent with the dreaded four. You win!

If you keep working backward, you'll find out that Oddball can be won or lost in the very first move! To figure out the pattern that lets you win, make a chart like the one at the bottom of the page.

We've filled in the numbers we already talked about. Can you fill in the blank boxes on your chart? If there are six pieces at the start of your turn, how many do you have to take to make sure your opponent gets a losing number?

Fill out your whole chart, and you'll know how to win *every time*. You'll never be the Oddball again. (To see how we filled in our chart, turn to page 361.)

(To see how we filled in our chart, turn to page 361.)

What Else Can I Try?

After you fill out the chart, Oddball will become very dull. The person who goes first can always win. After you have mastered Oddball, there are many more games like it for you to try. Some people call all these takeaway games by the same name: Nim. That name comes from *nimm,* the German word for "take."

Pieces Left at the Start of Your Turn	Do You Win or Lose?
1 piece	You lose!
2 pieces	Take 1 to win.
3 pieces	Take 2 to win.
4 pieces	You lose!
5 pieces	Take 1 to win.
6 pieces	
7 pieces	
8 pieces	
9 pieces	
10 pieces	

Simple Madagascar Solitaire

Did you lose friends by winning too many times at Oddball? Here's a game you can play by yourself. This first version is very easy, but it'll help you understand the more challenging game of Intermediate Madagascar Solitaire. (If you want, you can jump ahead and play Intermediate Madagascar Solitaire, then come back here to learn more about how it works.)

Here's What You Need

✔ A handful of stones, beans, pennies, paper clips, or other small objects to use as markers

Here's What You Do

1. Put one marker in every circle of the game board below.

2. Remove one marker from your board.

3. Jump one marker over another. You can jump over only one marker at a time. No fair jumping over an empty space! You have to jump over a marker and land in an empty circle.

4. After you jump, remove the marker you jumped over. Then, using any marker you like, jump again if you can.

5. If you end up with only one marker on the board, you win! If you have more than one marker left, and no jumps are possible, you lose!

6. Try again, starting with a different marker. Removing certain markers always leads to a winning game. How many different winning first moves can you find? Are they similar to each other in any way?

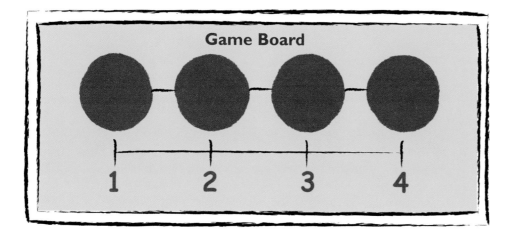

Game Board

1   2   3   4

What's Going On?

Whether you win this game depends on which marker you take away first. You always lose if you start your game by removing a marker from either end. You always win if you start by removing one of the two middle markers.

The two winning moves are mathematically the same. To see why, take a look at the picture to the left.

If you draw a line down the middle of the game board, you can see that each circle on the left side of the game board has a matching circle on the right side of the line. A mathematician would say the two halves of the game board are symmetrical. If you folded the game board in half on the dotted line, the circles on one half would match up with the circles on the other half. This type of symmetry is called *mirror symmetry*.

Mathematicians call the line dividing the game board a *line of symmetry*. Because the two sides on either side of the line of symmetry are symmetrical, the moves are symmetrical as well. Removing the marker from **2** is the same as removing the marker from **3**. Either way, you win! Removing the marker from **1** is also the same move as removing the marker from **4**. You lose!

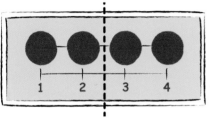

The dotted lines mark lines of symmetry. When something has mirror symmetry, the left half is a mirror reflection of the right half. The human face, for example, is more or less symmetrical. On each side of the line, there's an eye, an ear, half a mouth, and so on.

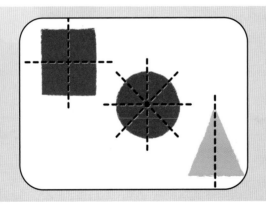

Intermediate Madagascar Solitaire

Simple Madagascar Solitaire was easy. Here's a more challenging game. You win if you end up with one marker on the board.

Here's What You Need

✔ A handful of stones, beans, paper clips, or other small objects to use as markers

✔ An Intermediate Madagascar Solitaire game board (on page 231)

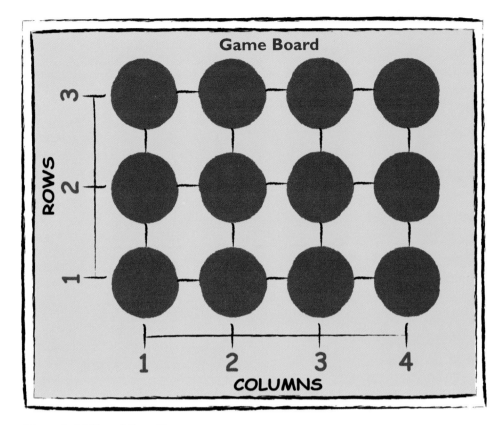

Game Board

ROWS

3

2

1

1 2 3 4

COLUMNS

Here's What You Do

1. Put a marker in every circle of the game board.

2. Start by removing any marker from your board.

3. Take a marker and jump over another marker. You can jump over only one marker at a time. You have to jump over a marker. (No jumping over an empty space.) You must land in an empty circle. You have to jump vertically or horizontally. No diagonals allowed.

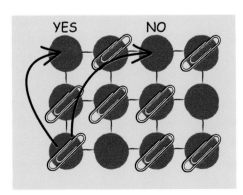

YES   NO

4. After you jump, remove the marker you jumped over. Then jump again, if you can. You can make your next jump with any marker on the board.

5. If you end up with one marker on the board, you win! If you have more than one marker left, and no jumps are possible, you lose.

What's Going On?

Did you win? Keep trying until you do. We know you can do it!

While you're playing, think about strategy. Look ahead and think about the consequences of each move. Ask yourself: If I jump here, how will that change what I can do next? Thinking ahead will help you win more often.

In Simple Madagascar Solitaire, the wrong first move can make it impossible to win a game. The same is true in Intermediate Madagascar Solitaire. But just because you lose a game, that doesn't mean that the first move was a bad one. You can start with a winning move and lose the game if you make a wrong move along the way.

What Else Can I Try?

It's hard to remember all the moves that go into a winning game. If you want to write down your moves, you can make a chart like the one below.

To keep track of your moves, write the column and the row of the marker you move and the column and the row of its new position.

When you write down a column and a row, you are using two numbers to identify an exact position. You use this same technique when you play the game of Battleship — or when you learn graphing in math class. In graphing, people talk about *(x,y) coordinates.* On the game board, the column number is your x-coordinate and the row number is the y-coordinate.

Once you've found one winning game, you can turn that into other winning games by using symmetry. (To learn about symmetry, go back and read the What's Going On? section of "Simple Madagascar Solitaire.") There are two lines of symmetry on the Intermediate Madagascar Solitaire game board. To find the lines of symmetry, trace the board on a piece of paper. See if you can find a way to fold the board in half so that the circles on one half of the board match up with the circles on the other half. The fold is a line of symmetry. (If you get stumped looking for the lines of symmetry, you can find them on page 362.)

Imagine that one of the lines of symmetry on the Intermediate Madagascar Solitaire game board is a mirror. Now imagine a mirror image of the first move of your winning game. You can win by starting with this move and playing a game in which every move is a mirror image of the move in the winning game. Give it a try!

Marker's original position		Marker's new position	
Column	Row	Column	Row

Math Magic

Magicians do card tricks all the time, but there's really nothing magic about them. Most card tricks rely on math. We'll show you our favorites and tell you how the tricks work. You can make a trick work without understanding the math. But knowing the math can help you make the trick even trickier.

Mind Reader

After your friends and family witness your amazing mind-reading ability, they'll never dare think in front of you again!

Here's What You Need

✔ A deck of cards

✔ A partner

✔ A piece of paper

✔ A pencil

Here's What You Do

1. Remove the tens and the face cards (jacks, queens, and kings) from the deck, and set them aside. While you're at it, get rid of the jokers too.

2. Shuffle the cards.

3. Ask your friend to pick a card from the deck.

4. Tell your friend not to show it to you, but to memorize the number on your card. (It doesn't matter what *suit* it is — that term refers to whether it's a heart, club, spade, or diamond. All you care about is the number.)

5. Have your friend put his card on the table, face down.

6. Now you pick a card from the deck. Don't show it to your friend.

7. Memorize the number on your card.

8. Lay your card face down on the table next to your friend's card. Your card should be on the *right side* of your friend's card as your friend sees it.

9. Give your friend the paper and pencil so that he can do some math. Tell your friend to:
- Double the value of his memorized card.
- Add 2 to that number.
- Multiply that answer by 5.

10. Now it's your turn to do a little math. No paper and pencil for you — in your head, subtract the number of your memorized card from 10.

11. Have your friend subtract your answer from his final answer.

12. Say "Are you thinking of this number?" Flip over your friend's card and flip over your card. The two cards together should make the number that your friend has calculated.

Having Trouble?

If the two cards do not match your friend's answer, the problem is probably one of two things. Either, you put your card to the left instead of to the *right* of your friend's card (and this is your *friend's* right as he is looking at the cards), or your friend needs his math checked. You now know the number of your friend's card, so say something like, "I know the magic works, so let's check your math." Then work through the math together.

What's Going On?

Can you figure out how this works? It's very tricky.

To show you, we'll run through an example of this card trick.

Suppose your friend chooses a card that has the number 3 on it. Following the above directions, your friend would do this math:

$$3 \times 2 = 6$$
$$6 + 2 = 8$$
$$8 \times 5 = 40$$

Suppose your card was an 8:

$$10 - 8 = 2$$

Your friend then does this calculation:

40 (his result) − 2 (your result) = 38

Then you flip over your friend's card. You don't know what it is until you flip it over, but when you flip it over you'll find a 3. Flip over your card and you'll find an 8 (you already knew that, of course). The two cards together spell out 38, and that's the number your friend has calculated. Amazing!

To understand why this works, you need to think about what the 3 and the 8 in 38 really mean. The position of the 3 and the 8 are important — after all, 38 and 83 are very different numbers!

In 38, the 8 tells you how many ones there are — it's in the *ones* place. The 3 tells you how many tens there are — it's in the *tens* place. In 38, there are 3 tens. Three tens is the same as 30. (30 + 8 = 38!)

When you had your friend do all that arithmetic, it was a round-about way of moving his card number to the tens place and putting your card number in the ones place. (If you want to know more about why this works, get a grown-up to take a look at page 362 with you. We explain the trick in more detail there.)

After you try this trick a few times, you'll soon realize that it doesn't matter what numbers you or your friend choose. The trick works no matter what.

Tools for Exploration
Sharing your experience and working with others
Sometimes two heads are better than one. Work with a friend to figure out how this trick works.

Buried Treasure

Try this trick a few times on your own so you can become good at it. Then, amaze your friends by finding the buried treasure. (Okay, you got us — the treasure is a card.)

Here's What You Need

✔ A full deck of cards (again, lose the jokers)

✔ A friend (when you're ready)

Here's What You Do

1. Shuffle the cards, then put them in a stack facedown on the table.

2. Deal out the cards into a stack that faces up. Count them as you deal (1, 2, 3, 4, 5, 6).

3. When you reach card number 7, memorize the number on the card. (When you do this for an audience, don't stop and stare at it, just quickly memorize.)

4. Keep counting past card number 7. When you reach card number 26, stop dealing out cards.

5. Take the stack that faces up and add it (facedown) to the bottom of the deck. You should have a full deck of cards now.

6. Now deal out 3 cards, face up, side by side.

7. Starting with the card on the left, deal out as many cards as you need to reach the number 10. For example, if the card on the left is a 3, deal out 7 more cards to make 10. If the card is an ace (that counts as a 1) — deal out 9 more cards to make 10. It helps to count aloud as you deal the cards. If your card was an ace, count: 1 for the ace, then count 2, 3, 4, 5, 6, 7, 8, 9, 10 — dealing a card each time you say a number. If your card was a 3, you say, "three" when you put down the card, then 4, 5, 6, 7, 8, 9, 10, dealing out a card for each count. It doesn't matter what's on any of those cards that you just dealt.

8. Repeat the above step for all three cards.

9. If any of the cards are 10s, jacks, queens, or kings, don't deal extra cards. These are already worth 10.

10. Have your friend add up the numbers on the top 3 cards.

11. Whatever number your friend comes up with will be the position of card number 7, the card you memorized! Say the 3 cards add up to 14, as they do in the picture here. You would say: "The fourteenth card in the deck is . . . " and then you'd say the name of the card you memorized.

12. Count down through the deck and show that you are right!

What's Going On?

Did you get your friend to shriek: "How did you do that?!" (We hope so. It's always fun to freak your friends out!) Can you figure out how the trick works? Like all good card tricks, this one seems more complicated than it really is.

Before we tell you the answer, see if you can figure it out. Think about what happens if the three cards you deal out are all 10s. Since each card is worth 10, you didn't deal out any more. And when you add up the values of those cards, you get:

$$10 + 10 + 10 = 30$$

When you count out 30 cards, you'll get to the card you memorized.

Now think about how many cards you're counting from the top of the deck. You deal out 3 cards (10, 10, and 10) and then you count out 30. So that gives you 33.

Now suppose you do the trick again, and the 3 cards you deal out are all aces. Then you deal out 9 cards on top of each of the 3 cards. So you've dealt out 30 cards (3 aces plus 9 cards on top of each ace). When you add up the aces, you get:

$$1 + 1 + 1 = 3$$

Three cards plus the thirty cards you've dealt out gives you thirty-three — the same number you got before.

If you have nothing better to do, spend a million hours doing every single combination. The number you get will always be 33.

Why does 33 take you to the card you memorized?

There are exactly 52 cards in a deck of cards. When you deal out 26 cards, exactly half the deck, your secret card is card number 7 out of those 26 cards. (You know it's the seventh card because that's the card you memorized when it was first dealt out.) Then, you put the stack with card number 7 underneath the other half of the deck. So now, instead of being 7 cards from the top (like it was at first), your secret card is 26 (the half of the deck that's on top of your secret card) + 7 cards from the top.

$$26 + 7 = 33$$

After you stack the deck, your secret card is always the thirty-third card down from the top. And dealing out 3 cards, adding as many cards as necessary to bring each up to 10, and then adding up the 3 original face-up cards will lead you to the thirty-third card.

To learn more about math games and tricks, visit Exploratopia *online at* www.exploratopia.com.

You know what a dollar bill looks like, right? Before you answer, take a look at the one-dollar bills pictured on this page. Only one of them is genuine. The others are fakes. Can you find the real dollar?

Paper Money

Don't feel bad if you're not sure which one is the real dollar bill. Most people don't pay much attention to what the money in their pocket actually looks like. That's one reason counterfeiters *often get away with their crimes. Counterfeiters are criminals who make fake money.*

Getting to Know a Dollar Bill

Here are the same dollars again. It'll be easier to find the real one this time because you are about to become a dollar bill expert.

Here's What You Need

✔ Two one-dollar bills (If you don't have any money, hit up the nearest adult for a loan. Tell him it's all in the name of science. You're not lying!)

✔ A magnifying glass (optional)

✔ A piece of writing paper

Here's What You Do

1. Compare the dollar bills to each other. Do the two bills look exactly the same? What differences do you notice?

2. Compare one of your dollar bills to the pictures on pages 238–239.

3. Look at all the symbols and pictures and numbers and letters on your dollar. Are they the same on every dollar? Compare your bills and see.

4. Look at the paper that your dollar is made of. Rub your dollar bill between your fingers.

5. Compare your dollar to a sheet of writing paper. Does the dollar paper look different? Does it feel different? What happens if you tear the sheet of paper? Crumple it? Get it wet? What happens if you do these same things to a dollar? (Don't tear too much, or there goes your dollar!)

6. Take an up close and personal look at the printing on a dollar. Use a magnifying glass if you have one. Can you find any secret symbols or words? Aha!

What's Going On?

Is your dollar bill real? Let's hope so! One way you determined that your dollar bill was real was by comparing it to another dollar bill. The second dollar looked a lot like the first one. When you compared your dollar to the pictures, you were able to match it up to just one — the picture of the real dollar!

People who are good at solving problems usually begin by examining the problem very carefully. It doesn't matter whether the person is a gardener figuring out why a plant didn't grow, an astronomer predicting the orbit of a comet, or someone like you trying to find the real dollar in a group of fakes. The first step is the same.

When the Exploratorium's team of investigators looked at a dollar bill, they found numbers in six different places on the bill. We discovered that each number revealed something about when, where, and how the dollar was made. Before you read the next section, see if you can find all six numbers on your dollar bill.

Tools for Exploration

Paying attention to stuff a lot of people ignore

If you look carefully, you can find six different numbers on a dollar bill, not counting the number one in the corners of the bill. The numbers we're talking about are different on different bills. Can you find all six numbers? Give it a try. (If you need help, see pages 242–243.)

Did You Ever Notice?

Here are some symbols and notations you may have discovered on your dollar bill.

1. Federal Reserve Number

This number is repeated four times on the front of the bill. The Federal Reserve number, like the Federal Reserve letter, matches up to a particular city. Kansas City's Federal Reserve number is ten.

2. Check Letter and Quadrant Number

Dollar bills are printed in sheets of thirty-two. The check letter and quadrant number show where in the sheet your particular dollar was positioned. This bill is B4, which means it was printed in the second row (B) and four (4) columns over.

A1	A2	A3	A4
B1	B2	B3	B4
C1	C2	C3	C4
D1	D2	D3	D4
E1	E2	E3	E4
F1	F2	F3	F4
G1	G2	G3	G4
H1	H2	H3	H4

3. Federal Reserve Seal and Letter

The letter in the center of the seal identifies the Federal Reserve Bank that issued this bill. It matches the letter at the beginning of the serial number. Kansas City's Federal Reserve letter is *J*.

4. Serial Number

Every bill has its own serial number. The bills are stamped one after another, with serial numbers that run in order. This number is repeated in the opposite corner of the bill. You may find a bill that has a star after the number. When a bill is torn or messed up in the course of printing, another bill must be substituted to make sure that a proper count is made. This so-called star note is such a substitute note. A *star note* is also used for the millionth note in a series.

5. Type of Note

Most of the bills in circulation today are Federal Reserve Notes. You may find a very old bill that is a Silver Certificate or United States Note.

6. Series Number

This number shows the year that the design for this bill was adopted, not the year the bill was printed. This 1988 series bill may have been printed in 1990. A letter is added to the year if there has been a slight change in a bill's design.

7. Red and Blue Fibers

There are tiny red and blue fibers in the blank areas on a dollar bill. These colored fibers are added during the manufacture of the paper to make counterfeiting more difficult.

8. Signatures

American paper money shows the signatures of the Secretary of the Treasury and the Treasurer of the United States who were in office when the bill was printed.

9. Treasury Seal

The Treasury Seal helps people spot counterfeit money. On counterfeit bills, the sawtooth points of the seal are often uneven or broken.

10. Face Plate Number

This number tells what plate was used to print the *face*, or front, of this particular dollar. The face plate number, along with the back plate number (see number fourteen), helps the Bureau of Engraving and Printing track down any printing mistakes.

11. Printing Plant Location

"FW" stands for the Bureau of Engraving and Printing's Fort Worth printing plant, established in 1991. If your bill doesn't show FW, it means it was printed in Washington, D.C.

12. The Great Seal

The founders of the United States designed the Great Seal. The pyramid represents the country's strength and permanence. Some symbols on the seal have been linked to secret societies. The All-Seeing Eye that tops the pyramid is a Masonic symbol. (The Masons is an organization that Benjamin Franklin and George Washington belonged to.) The triangle is a symbol of the Rosicrucian Order. (Thomas Jefferson was a member of that society.) The Latin words above the pyramid mean "He has favored our undertaking." The year 1776 is written in Roman numerals at the base of the pyramid. Beneath the pyramid are more Latin words meaning "A new order for the ages."

13. Back of the Great Seal

The eagle design on the dollar is loaded with symbols. The 13 stars above the eagle's head and the 13 stripes on the shield correspond to the original 13 colonies. The bird holds an olive branch with 13 leaves to represent peace and 13 arrows to symbolize war. The eagle's head is turned toward the olive branch, showing a desire for peace. The ribbon reads *E Pluribus Unum,* which is Latin for "Out of Many, One."

14. Back Plate Number

The back plate number is not the same as the face plate number. Different plates are used in printing the front and back of a bill.

Clever Counterfeiters

Counterfeiting is a very old practice. Back in the 1860s, America had no government-issued paper money, or *currency*. Instead, each bank printed its own currency. Because each bank designed its own bills, it's not surprising that people had a hard time identifying fakes. There were more than 7,000 different kinds of bills!

In 1862, the United States government adopted a national currency. One reason for this was to make counterfeiting more difficult. In 1865, the U.S. government established the Secret Service, specifically to catch counterfeiters. But some counterfeiters were too clever for the Secret Service. One notable counterfeiter traveled the country giving lectures as Professor Joseph Woods. In his lectures, the professor talked about the art of detecting counterfeit money. He would show drawings on which he pointed out defects of the better-known counterfeit bills. Then he would leave town. Soon after he left, his assistants would arrive and they would pass some counterfeit bills. The town folks would study the money looking for the defects that the professor had described. Of course none of these fake bills had the defects described in the professor's lecture, so the counterfeiters were able to pass them off as real!

Is It Real?

Now that you've mastered the dollar bill, you're ready for the big time. Take a twenty-dollar bill this time — is it real or is it fake?

Here's What You Need

✔ A twenty-dollar bill (If you don't have one, find someone willing to lend one to you. Just promise to give it back. Your bill may not look exactly like the one shown here. There are a few different designs in circulation.)

✔ A magnifying glass (optional)

Here's What You Do

1. Take a look at your twenty-dollar bill. What pictures, designs, and symbols do you see? How is the twenty different from the one-dollar bill?

2. Take a close look at the doodling in the strips at the top and bottom of the bill.

3. Run your finger over the surface of the bill. Compare the feel of the blank area near the picture of Andrew Jackson to the areas that are crowded with doodling. Do these areas feel different?

4. Find the series number on the bill. It's right near Andrew Jackson's picture. (See page 242 for more about this number.)

5. If you have a bill with a series number of 1990 or later, hold the bill up to a bright light. Look in all the blank areas of the bill. Do you see something there that you couldn't see before?

6. If you have a magnifying glass, zero in on the picture of Andrew Jackson. If the picture is inside an oval, look at the bottom edge of the oval. Do you see anything that you missed before?

7. Now take a look at the number twenty in the lower right-hand corner of the front of the bill. Tilt the bill so that you're looking at the number from a different angle. Does it look different?

What's Going On?

You found some of the special details that make it difficult for criminals to counterfeit a twenty-dollar bill.

The doodled areas feel different from the blank areas. That's because money is printed on presses that leave lines of ink that stay on top of the paper, raised above the paper's surface. American paper money is printed using engraved steel plates, which produce very crisp lines. The doodles won't be sharp on a counterfeit bill that was photocopied or printed on a regular printing press.

You probably noticed a few new things when you held the bill up to a bright light. If your bill has a series number of 1990 or later, you'll see a vertical line running through the paper just to the left end of the Federal Reserve Seal. The line is made from a clear polyester thread. In tiny printing, the line says USA TWENTY.

When you look at Andrew Jackson with a magnifying glass, you may see a line of teeny, tiny printing hidden in the bottom edge of the frame around the portrait. It says THE UNITED STATES OF AMERICA. Did you catch that? Don't feel bad if you didn't; not many people do.

If your bill has a series number of 1996 or later, hold the bill up to the light and look in all the blank areas of the bill. Can you find a picture that's visible only when you hold the bill up to the light? That's called a *watermark,* a picture that's put into the paper when the paper is made.

You probably also discovered that tilting your bill made the number twenty in the lower-right corner on the front of your bill change color. This number is printed with a special color-changing ink.

In 2003 the U.S. Treasury Department added new features to the twenty-dollar bill. The biggest change is the color — the newest twenty-dollar bill includes peach, blue, and light-green background colors. A big blue eagle has been added to Andrew Jackson's left and a shimmering green eagle to his right.

What Else Can I Try?

If you look at recently printed five-dollar bills and ten-dollar bills, you will find watermarks, tiny printing, and a clear polyester thread, just like on the twenty.

If you compare old bills and new ones, you'll find some other changes as well. The portraits on new bills are larger than those on old bills, as you can see if you compare the new five to an older five. Portraits can also help people identify counterfeit bills. Because people pay close attention to human faces, they are likely to notice any flaws in a portrait.

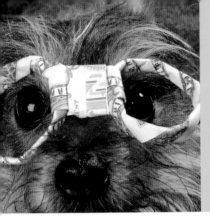

Money Experiments

Sure, paper money is useful when you want to buy something. But can you use it for anything else? How about making eyeglasses from dollar bills and putting them on a dog? Anyone can use money to buy stuff. But it takes a really creative mind to use a million dollars for something else.

Build a One-Buck Bridge

Think you can build a bridge using just a dollar bill? It'll only cost you a dollar to find out!

Here's What You Need

✔ 3 identical plastic glasses

✔ A crisp one-dollar bill

Here's What You Do

1. Line up two glasses so the space between them is just a little wider than the width of one glass.

2. Using only the dollar bill, make a bridge!

3. Use your bridge to support the third glass on top of the two empty glasses.

4. Stumped? If you don't succeed right away, put the problem aside and come back to it later. After a break, you just might come up with a fresh approach.

What's Going On?

How did you do? If you're stumped, try folding your dollar bill different ways — lengthwise, widthwise, every which way. Try fat folds and tiny ones.

Our solution for the one-buck bridge is on page 363. (But you may have come up with a different solution, and that's great!)

If you didn't make a one-buck bridge this time, keep trying. Solving problems can take time. The best, most valuable inventions often take years and years to get just right.

Tools for Exploration

Experimenting to test your ideas

Often, testing your ideas leads to even more ideas. Maybe one way of folding your dollar doesn't work, but another way will. How can you take something flimsy and make it stiff and strong?

Folding Money

Turn an ordinary dollar bill into a ring that looks like a million bucks!

Here's What You Need

✔ A crisp one-dollar bill

Here's What You Do

1. Take the bottom edge of your bill and fold it up so that just the back bottom margin shows. You'll notice that the back margins are a little bigger than those on the front. Don't panic. This is as it should be.

fold up

2. Now fold the top half down to cover the flap you've just made. Leave it short of the bottom edge by just a hair.

fold down

3. Fold the top half down again. This time it should end up exactly even with the bottom edge.

fold down

4. Turn the bill over so that the number ones in either corner are facing up and fold the right margin under.

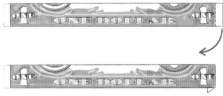

5. Now fold the shaded area so it sticks straight up, like this:

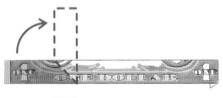

6. Fold the vertical part (that's the part sticking straight up) over to the right, as shown. Crease well.

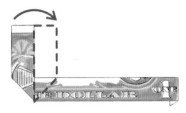

7. You don't have to do the fold shown in step 8 if you don't want to, but it will make your finished ring a little nicer. Taper the top and bottom edges of the bill a bit by folding the top and bottom edges.

8. Run a pencil over those folds to really flatten them.

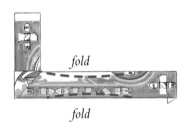

fold

fold

9. Turn the bill over and hold it in your left hand. Wrap it back around the tip of your index finger so the eagle ends up upside-down right under the vertical flap.

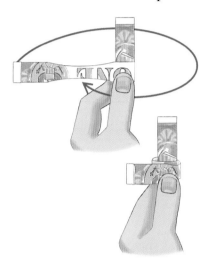

10. Pinch it all together to hold it in place.

11. Now fold the vertical flap down.

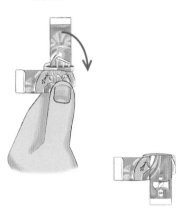

12. Next, fold the flap on the left across the front of the ring.

13. If the number one isn't centered on the flap you folded over, you can fix it. Back up a few steps and adjust.

14. To keep the number from popping up, tuck the little folded-over edge under the vertical flap.

15. Finally, turn the ring over so you can see the inside. There will be a diagonal slot behind the number one. Tuck the flap into this slot.

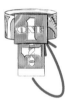

16. Congratulations! Proudly wear your Buck Ring for all to see!

Time for Change

If you've tried everything in this chapter so far, you now know more about paper money than just about anyone on the planet. But paper money isn't the only money you use. What about the coins in your pocket? Here's your chance to really get to know your change!

Loose Change

Can you tell a penny from a dime with your eyes closed?

Here's What You Need

✔ A handful of change, including one or two of each kind of coin — quarters, dimes, nickels, and pennies. If you can find them, throw in a half dollar and a dollar coin, too.

Here's What You Do

1. Take a close look at those coins. How are they similar? How are they different?

2. Don't stop at the obvious differences. Sure, they're different sizes and colors, but what else?

3. Close your eyes and give the coins a feel. Feel for ridges, grooves, raised areas, bumps, and dots. Be sure to feel the edges of each coin — there's stuff going on there, too.

4. Feeling pretty confident that you know your coins? Now, close your eyes, mix up your coins, and make change using only your sense of touch.

What's Going On?

It was probably easy finding differences between the coins when you had your eyes open. The penny is the only brown one; the rest are silver colored. Each coin has a different picture or symbol on its front and back. A dollar coin is bigger than a half dollar, which is bigger than a quarter, which is bigger than a nickel, which is bigger than a dime or a penny — those kinds of things are easy to see.

You really got more of a feel for the differences between your coins when you handled them. The sizes of the coins still help you to tell a quarter from a dime — but a dime and a penny are so similar in size, they're not so easy to tell apart by feel. But check out the edges of each coin. Quarters and dimes have tiny ridges all around the edge. You can easily feel those tiny ridges and tell the coins apart.

Blind people learn to tell coins apart by feel, but paper money all feels pretty much the same. In some countries, bills of different values come in different sizes, like coins do here. That helps blind people identify them.

Ask Professor Exploratorium

Dear Professor E:
The vending machine at my school won't take Canadian quarters. It spits them right out. How can the machine tell a Canadian quarter from an American one?

Signed,
Coinfused

Dear Coinfused:
You are right. The vending machine won't accept a Canadian quarter. The vending machine can tell the difference between the two coins.

To figure out how the machine knows the difference, try the "Smart Vending Machines" activity on this page.

Cointentedly yours,
Professor E

Smart Vending Machines

Learn how a vending machine figures out which coins are American and which aren't.

Here's What You Need

✔ Some American coins, some Canadian coins, and some coins from other countries

✔ A magnet

Here's What You Do

1. Hold the magnet near an American quarter. Does the magnet attract the quarter?

2. Now try a Canadian quarter. Aha!

3. What do you think will happen if you try this with other coins? Try it and see.

4. Are any American coins attracted to the magnet? What about the other coins?

What's Going On?

Your magnet was attracted to the Canadian quarter, but not to the American quarter. The Canadian quarter contains nickel, which magnets attract. Many foreign coins contain either iron or nickel and are attracted to magnets. (For more fun with magnets, see page 320.)

Inside a coin-operated vending machine is a coin-testing unit that rejects counterfeit, foreign, or defective coins. Many of these testers use magnets to separate Canadian coins from U.S. coins. Coin testers may also weigh the coin, check its diameter, test its electrical conductivity, and use other characteristics to find out if a coin is fake or foreign. So don't bother trying to fool a smart vending machine like this!

Tools for Exploration
Asking questions
We started out with one question — what makes a vending machine reject foreign coins? That question led us to other questions. How are foreign coins different from American coins? What happens if you bring a magnet near a Canadian quarter? How about an American quarter? Come up with questions of your own and experiment to find the answers.

Dirty Pennies

No one likes dirty money. You can make a dirty penny look as bright and shiny as, well, a new penny!

Here's What You Need

✔ A handful of dirty pennies

✔ 2 plastic cups

✔ Vinegar

✔ Salt

Here's What You Do

1. Place fifteen to twenty dull, dirty pennies into a plastic cup.

2. Cover the pennies with vinegar.

3. Sprinkle salt into the vinegar.

4. Swirl the solution so that it comes in contact with all the pennies. Your pennies become clean and shiny before your eyes.

Tools for Exploration

Experimenting to test your ideas

What could you change in your recipe? In your search for the perfect penny cleaner, change only one thing in the recipe at a time. If you make a lot of changes at once, you can't tell which change made a difference.

What's Going On?

Your pennies cleaned up beautifully in the simple salt-and-vinegar solution.

The dirty pennies were covered with tarnish. Tarnish forms when oxygen in the air reacts with the shiny copper metal in the penny. Copper and oxygen, like everything else in the world, are made of tiny particles called atoms. When an atom of copper combines with an atom of oxygen, they join to form copper oxide, which is a dull brown. Those dirty pennies weren't really covered with dirt — they were covered with copper oxide.

So how did vinegar clean the pennies? Vinegar is an *acid*. Acid reacts with copper oxide, yanking the copper atom away from the oxygen atom. When that happens, the copper oxide dissolves, leaving the pennies shiny.

What Else Can I Try?

We've given you a recipe for cleaning pennies. But any good cook could tell you that a recipe is just a starting place. What could you change to make this recipe even better?

You know that vinegar and salt will clean a handful of pennies. But suppose you wanted to clean some pennies, and you didn't have any vinegar. Do you have any other acids in your kitchen? Most acids are sour, like vinegar. How about orange juice and salt — will that clean pennies? Give it a try and see. (For safety's sake, do NOT experiment with any cleaners; stick to foods.)

Suppose you want to clean something other than pennies. Will your penny cleaner take the tarnish off other coins? What about other metals? Will it clean a rusty nail or a tarnished teaspoon? Experiment and see.

Thinking About Money

You would all agree that a dollar bill is money. What if we were to tell you that a hunk of limestone that weighs thousands of pounds is also money? It's true! On Yap, a South Pacific island, a giant limestone disk is a kind of money. At least, that's what economists say. Economists are scientists who study money. They have found that people use money for very different things.

One use is to buy things. You give someone a dollar for a candy bar. That person takes that dollar and uses it to buy a soda. Economists say that this is a *medium of exchange* — you both exchange your dollar for something else. On Easter Island, live rats were once a medium of exchange. (After being exchanged a few times, the rats ended up as dinner. Yum!)

But money means more than buying things. If you have a lot of money, you are rich, even if the money is sitting in your bottom drawer. Economists say that money used this way is a *store of value*.

That's where those giant stones on the island of Yap come in. The stone disks are chipped out of the rock on an island hundreds of miles from Yap. People load these disks into boats and carry them home. It's difficult to get such a big stone home — that's why the stones are valuable. People display these stone disks outside their houses. The bigger your stone, the more valuable it is and the richer you are.

The big stones on Yap are valuable because everyone agrees that they are. Your dollar is valuable because everyone says so. If everyone suddenly believed that old bottle caps were really valuable, then they would be. In that way, economists say money is a "*promise.*" You (and everyone else) make a promise that your money will be valuable today, tomorrow, and forever. Without that promise, that crisp dollar bill in your pocket is just a piece of fancy green paper.

To learn more about money and how you can experiment with it, visit Exploratopia *online at* www.exploratopia.com.

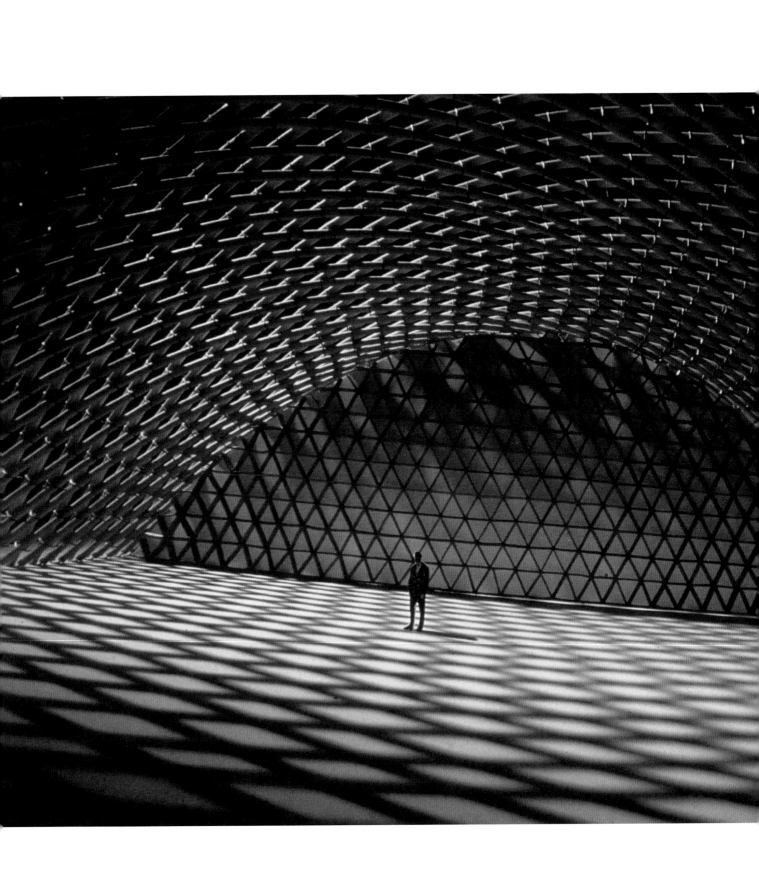

This entire building is made out of paper! The designer was Shigeru Ban of Japan. In 1995, he began experimenting with some paper tubes that were lying around in his studio. He found the tubes flexible and surprisingly strong. He used them to build temporary houses for people who had lost their homes in an earthquake.

Shigeru Ban proved that paper is a building material that is low-cost and easy to assemble. He invented a new form of architecture by experimenting with paper. What will you do?

Making Paper

In 105 A.D., a Chinese court official named Ts'ai Lun made paper using a method a lot like ours. He didn't have a book that told him how to do it. He experimented and figured it out for himself. If you don't have all the things we say you need, try to find something else that will work. Be creative and have fun!

Two artists, Pamela Paulsrud and Marilyn Sward, teamed up to create a handmade paper exhibit called "Treewhispers." They strung each piece of handmade paper together to form long columns that hang from the ceiling. Each column represents a tree. These ladies are building an entire forest from handmade paper! People from all over the world are submitting their own pieces of handmade paper to the project. Pretty amazing, huh?

Step 1: Get Ready

Making paper is easy — as long as you have everything you need!

Before You Get Started

✔ Ask your parents if it's okay if you do something wonderfully scientific and creative — that will make a bit of a mess. Ask where they would like you to work. You'll need water and electricity.

✔ Make sure you have enough time. It will take a few hours.

✔ This activity has six steps. Read all the steps and make sure you have what you need before you get started.

Step 2: Make the Mold

To make paper, you need a screen that's pulled tight and supported by a frame. Papermakers call this a *mold*.

Here's What You Need

✔ An embroidery hoop (available in fabric stores or arts and crafts stores) or an old picture frame, no bigger than 8 inches by 10 inches, and a stapler with staples. You can also make a square frame using a hammer, some nails, and 4 pieces of wood about 1/2-inch wide by 1 inch thick by 6 inches long. What else could you use? One teacher at the Exploratorium uses a splatter screen — a screen with a handle that a cook might use to keep bacon grease from splattering on the stove when bacon fries.

✔ A piece of window screen, a nylon stocking, or some other fine mesh material. Make sure your material is large enough to cover your embroidery hoop, picture frame, or square frame.

✔ A grown-up helper

Here's What You Do

1. There are many different ways to make a mold. Basically, you need something that has a screen surrounded by a stiff frame. We describe a few molds here. Choose your favorite — or invent your own!

2. If you have an embroidery hoop, here's what you do. An embroidery hoop is really two hoops in one. Take the two hoops apart and cover the smaller hoop with your piece of screen or nylon stocking. Secure the other hoop on top to hold your screen firmly in place.

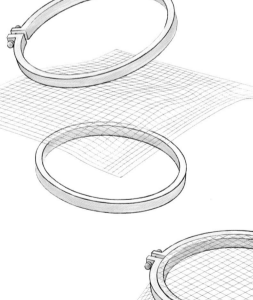

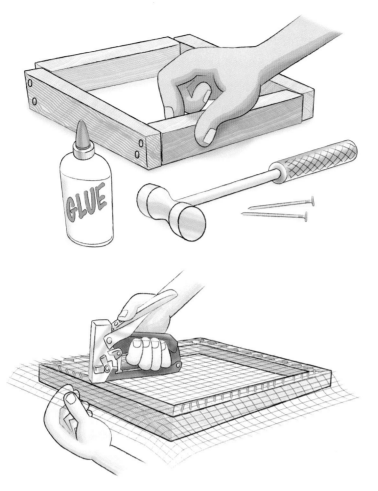

3. If you have a picture frame, have your grown-up helper take the glass out of the frame. Put your screen on top of the frame. Pull the screen tight across the frame and staple it to the sides.

4. If you don't have an embroidery hoop or a picture frame, nail four pieces of wood together to make a square. Set your screen down on top of the frame and nail or staple it in place. (You want a snug fit, without any big gaps between the wood and the screen.)

Step 3: Make Paper Pulp

Now you need some paper pulp. Fortunately, it's easy to make.

Here's What You Need

✔ Paper to recycle. You can use computer paper, typing or copy paper, tissue paper, paper towels, or construction paper. *Don't* use newspaper or the slick paper from magazines.

✔ A bucket

✔ Water

✔ A blender

✔ Cornstarch

Here's What You Do

1. Tear your paper into 1-inch squares and put them in your bucket. If someone you know uses a paper shredder, ask her for some shredded paper — it works great.

2. Add water and soak your paper squares for about a half hour, long enough to get them thoroughly wet. While your paper is soaking, set up your drying station (see Step 4).

3. Put a handful of wet paper squares in the blender and add water to cover the paper squares.

4. Put the top on the blender and blend on medium-high for a few seconds. If your blender sounds like it's working too hard, add more water and try again.

5. When your paper looks like mush or cooked oatmeal, it's pulp.

6. Add a tablespoon of cornstarch to your pulp. Blend again.

Step 4: Set Up a Drying Station

Just a little more preparation and you're ready to make paper.

Here's What You Need

✔ Lots of newspaper

✔ Paper towels

✔ An old sheet (cut into several pieces) or a few Handi Wipes

Here's What You Do

1. Find a flat surface that you don't mind getting wet — maybe a kitchen counter, a table, or the floor.

2. Put down a stack of old newspapers. Put six paper towels on top of the newspapers.

3. Put a piece of your old sheet or a Handi Wipe on top of the paper towels.

You are making paper using the fibers from old paper. The Thai Elephant Conservation Center in northern Thailand makes paper using something they have a lot of: elephant dung! Elephants eat leaves, but don't digest all the fibers in the leaves. Those fibers — treated so that they are odor and bacteria free — make great paper. Paper made from elephant dung helps the Conservation Center raise money to feed and care for their elephants.

Step 5: Make Paper

It's the moment you've been waiting for — it's time to make paper!

Here's What You Need

✔ A plastic tub that's big enough to dunk your mold in

✔ Water

✔ Rubber gloves (if you have sensitive skin)

✔ All the stuff you prepared in Steps 2, 3, and 4

✔ A sponge

✔ A rolling pin

Here's What You Do

1. Fill the plastic tub with water and set it down near your drying station. If you have sensitive skin, put on the rubber gloves.

2. Pour the pulp from the blender into the tub. Swirl it around so it mixes in with the water and doesn't clump.

3. Get the mold from Step 2. On your molds, there's one side where the screen is surrounded by a lip — made from the embroidery hoop or the wooden frame. Hold the mold with this lip *down,* and dip the mold into the tub. Slide the mold under the pulp to the bottom of the tub.

4. Stir the pulp, so the pieces are distributed evenly in the water.

5. Lift the screen while jiggling it back and forth. You want a nice even layer of pulp across the surface of the screen. If you get a lumpy mess on your first try, that's okay. Just dump it back in the tub, stir it up, and try again.

6. When you have an even layer of pulp across the screen, pull it straight up and out of the tub.

7. Hold the screen over the tub for a few minutes so the water can drain. Keep draining until the pulp is damp but not dripping.

8. Take your screen to your drying station.

9. Quickly flip the screen over and lay it on the sheet or Handi Wipe, pulp-side down.

10. Right now, your future paper is very wet. You need to remove some of the water before you try to pull the paper off the mold. Pat the back of the screen with your sponge to soak up some of that water. Be sure to pat, don't wipe. When your sponge is wet, squeeze it out over the tub.

11. Pat with the sponge and squeeze out the water until you aren't getting any more.

12. Gently peel the paper away from the mold, starting at one edge. Be careful and your paper will come away in one piece.

13. Place the paper on the sheet or Handi Wipe.

14. Put another piece of sheet material or a Handi Wipe on top of the wet paper.

15. Put some more paper towels and newspapers on top of that.

16. Roll a rolling pin over the whole thing, squeezing it as flat as you can.

17. Lift the newspaper, take out the wet, newly made paper, and lay it on a paper towel to dry. It'll take a few hours for your paper to dry completely.

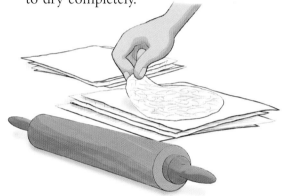

18. Now you're ready to make all kinds of paper. Try making different pulps — using different types of paper or paper of different colors. Add stuff to make your paper more interesting. (See page 262.)

Step 6: Clean Up

This is the step everyone wants to skip. But cleaning up is a very important step — if you ever want to do a messy project again.

Here's What You Do

1. Dispose of your extra paper pulp. DO NOT pour it down the drain. It will clog the drain, and people will get really, really mad at you. (You could even lose your papermaking privileges and that would be a shame. You're so good at it!)

2. If you have a sieve, you can pour the pulp mixture through the sieve. The sieve will capture the pulp so you can pour the water down the drain. Squeeze the water out of your paper pulp and put it in your recycling bin with the newspapers. (It's just paper, after all.)

3. Pick all the bits of paper out of the blender. Wash the blender, the rolling pin, and the plastic tub with soap and water. Put all your equipment away.

What's Going On?

Have you ever pulled apart a cotton ball? The stringy strands of cotton are made of *cellulose,* the tough, stringy stuff found in plants.

Paper is mostly made of cellulose, which paper makers get from cotton, wood, other plants, or old paper.

The paper you made is 100 percent recycled paper — that means it only contains material that was used in paper before.

What Else Can I Try?

You can add glitter or flowers or leaves to your paper. If you want to add flowers or leaves, press and dry them in advance. You can press a flower or leaf by putting it between some pieces of wax paper and flattening it in a book for a week. *After* the pulp comes out of the blender, add the flowers or leaves.

To make colored paper, make a pulp of colored paper and mix it with the pulp of white paper. Try leaving the colored paper in larger pieces, so you have bigger bits of color in your paper.

You can also add color by adding powdered or liquid paint, food coloring, water-based inks, tea, or herbs. Add the color to the pulp after you put the pulp in the tub. Don't put the color ingredient in the blender.

Tools for Exploration

Experimenting to test your ideas

How could you make your paper even better? Maybe you want to add some color. Or try using a different kind of paper to make your pulp. Experiment and see what happens. If one experiment doesn't make a good sheet of paper, then just try again.

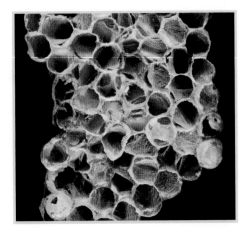

Wasps were making paper long before people ever did. Paper wasps chew wood into a pulpy paste and use it to make their nests.

Building with Paper

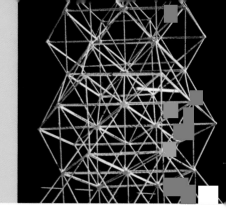

In 1994, some of the Exploratorium staff decided to see how tall a tower they could build out of newspaper and tape. There are no hidden wires or support beams in the tower. How do you think they got it to stand up straight in the air? What would make a tower of paper strong and stiff like that?

Paper Towers

How tall a tower can you build with two sheets of paper, tape, and scissors?

Here's What You Need

✔ 2 pieces of 8 ½ x 11 paper (recycled, if you have it)

✔ 2 feet of cellophane tape

✔ A ruler

✔ Scissors

✔ A friend to build with (if you want the company)

Here's What You Do

1. Build the tallest tower you can, using nothing but two sheets of paper and two feet of cellophane tape.

2. Think about towers you have seen, or take a look at the towers pictured here. Do these give you any ideas?

3. Think about what you can do with paper. You can fold it, roll it, or cut it. You can crumple it or twist it. Do any of these things help?

4. What shape might make a good tower? Can you make a tower that's triangular? Or one that's shaped like a cylinder?

5. Use your ruler to measure the height of your tower. Can you make a tower that's more than two feet tall?

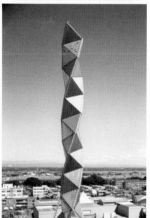

What's Going On?

Did you figure out a way to turn a floppy sheet of paper into something stiff and strong?

As you worked on your tower, did you have a plan? Did it change as you built it? Sometimes, you get new ideas as you experiment with a material — even something as familiar as a piece of paper.

Newspaper Towers

Try building a tower from newspaper. How tall a tower can you build?

Here's What You Need

✔ Lots of newspaper

✔ Tape (the stronger, the better)

✔ A room with a very tall ceiling or a place outside that's not windy

Here's What You Do

1. Experiment to see how you can make newspaper into a strong building material. At the Exploratorium, we rolled newspapers to make sturdy newspaper "sticks." We taped those sticks together to make a triangle, then we added more sticks to make a *tetrahedron,* a three-dimensional shape that has four triangular sides and four corners. (*Tetra* means "four" in Greek.)

2. We used our newspaper tetrahedrons as building blocks because they didn't collapse easily. You can try that, or experiment on your own.

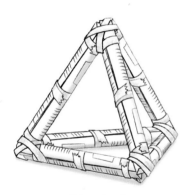

Tetrahedron

What's Going On?

Buckminster Fuller was an engineer, mathematician, and inventor. He was a pioneer in using the tetrahedron as a basic shape for building. If you want to know why tetrahedrons are so great for building, use newspaper sticks to make a tetrahedron and a cube. Which one collapses first when you push down on it?

When we built our newspaper tower, we ran into a problem. You can't climb up a newspaper tower to add more layers to the top. But paper is light, so we built the next layer on the floor and then lifted the whole tower and put it on top of the newly built layer! Our finished tower was 20 feet high!

Tricks with Paper

Paper seems so ordinary. You write on it every day. You blow your nose on it. You read books and magazines made out of it. But paper can be extraordinary, too. In fact, it can be downright tricky to deal with. Here are some experiments that show you how tricky paper can be.

Exponential Folding

It's easy to fold a sheet of paper in half. But can you fold a sheet of paper in half ten times? Want to bet on that?

Here's What You Need

✔ A sheet of newspaper (the larger, double-page size)

Here's What You Do

1. Fold your sheet of newspaper in half in any direction you want. How many layers of newspaper do you have after folding the newspaper once? Two! (So far, so good. Only nine more folds to go.)

2. Without unfolding your first fold, fold the newspaper in half again. Now you have two folds and four layers.

3. Fold the newspaper in half again. How many layers of newspaper do you have after three folds? Four folds? Five folds? You can keep track by making a chart like the one we've started for you on this page.

4. Keep folding the newspaper in half until you can't fold it any more. How many folds were you able to complete? How many layers of newspaper do you have?

Number of Folds	Number of Layers of Newspaper
0	1
1	2
2	4
3	8
4	
5	
6	
7	
8	
9	
10	

What's Going On?

Oh, man! Folding a newspaper seemed so easy! Most people think that folding a newspaper ten times will be a snap.

But at some point, usually after seven folds, most people find that they can't make the next fold. The area of the folded paper gets smaller and smaller with each fold. At the same time, the thickness of the stack of folds keeps increasing. Soon, the paper is just too thick to budge.

Did you make a chart like the one on page 265? (If you need help filling it in, see page 364.)

Do you see a pattern in the number of layers? Each time the paper is folded, you get twice as many layers as you had before. After one fold, there are two layers. After two folds, there are 2×2 layers, or four layers. After three folds, there are $2 \times 2 \times 2$ layers — that's eight layers. What do you get after four folds? Five folds?

A shorthand way to write $2 \times 2 \times 2$ is 2^3 (or 2 to the third power). The 3 is called an *exponent* and the 2 is the *base*. The exponent says how many times the base is multiplied by itself. Four folds would be 2^4 (2 to the fourth power) layers. That's $2 \times 2 \times 2 \times 2 = 16$. There are 16 layers in four folds. Five folds would be 2^5 (2 to the fifth power). That's $2 \times 2 \times 2 \times 2 \times 2 = 32$.

Most people can't manage more than seven folds. That's pretty good — that's 128 layers! One of us can fold it eight times. (We think she is a weight lifter in disguise!) That's 256 layers! How many layers would you have after folding the newspaper ten times? Well, no wonder you couldn't do it!

Ever try to make music using paper? This is a picture of a show held at the Disney Concert Hall, in Los Angeles, called "Inventions for Paper Instruments and Orchestra." In it, the musicians and the audience made music by shaking shredded paper pom-poms, waving around sheets of paper, and banging on giant paper scrolls that hung from the ceiling. What are some other ways to make interesting sounds from paper?

Dear Professor E:

So this jokester at school walked up to me the other day and said, "I'll give you a choice. I can give you $14. Or I can give you a penny today, then two cents tomorrow, then four cents the next day — and keep doubling the amount for fourteen days total. Which would you rather have?" Naturally, I say, "Just give me the $14." He walked away laughing without giving me a single cent! Did I make the wrong choice?

Signed,
Penniless

Dear Penniless:

If you do the calculation, the second choice gets you more money. Here's how much money he would give you each day:

Day 1: 1 penny	Day 6: 32 pennies	Day 11: 1,024 pennies
Day 2: 2 pennies	Day 7: 64 pennies	Day 12: 2,048 pennies
Day 3: 4 pennies	Day 8: 128 pennies	Day 13: 4,096 pennies
Day 4: 8 pennies	Day 9: 256 pennies	Day 14: 8,192 pennies
Day 5: 16 pennies	Day 10: 512 pennies	

If you add up all those pennies, he would give you 16,383 pennies, or $163.83. As you can see, $163.83 is much more than $14.00. Not that you can count on that guy to pay up anyway! But, he must have known a thing or two about *exponential growth* in order to trick you like that. As this and the folding newspaper experience (see "Exponential Folding," page 265) have shown, doubling an amount will get you to large numbers very fast!

Your Ever-Expanding Friend,
Professor E

Fifteen-Ring Lei

Make a chain of paper links, then try a problem-solving challenge!

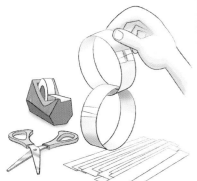

Here's What You Need

✔ Scissors ✔ Paper ✔ Tape

Here's What You Do

1. Cut fifteen strips of paper.

2. Tape one strip together at the ends to make a ring.

3. Loop the next strip through the ring and then tape the two ends together to make an interlocking ring.

4. Keep on looping and taping until you end up with a necklace of fifteen interlocking rings.

5. Here's your challenge: Turn this lei into five chains of rings. Cut your lei and retape where needed to make five chains, all of different lengths.

6. You must use all fifteen rings. Every time you cut a ring and then retape it, that counts as one.

7. Can you manage to do it with only three cut-and-tapes?

What's Going On?

This is a very tough problem. Here are a few hints to help you figure it out:

You want to make five chains with a different number of links in each chain. Figure out how many links will be in each chain when you are finished. Now, figure out where you will cut your lei to make chains of the lengths you were just thinking about.

If you still don't get it, put this aside for a while and come back to it later. That's a strategy a lot of expert problem solvers use.

If you get stumped, our answer is on page 364.

Mobius Magic

A Mobius band is a paper invention that has only one side and only one edge.

Here's What You Need

✔ Scissors

✔ A few sheets of typing or notebook paper

✔ Tape

✔ A pencil

✔ A paper clip

Here's What You Do

1. Cut a strip of paper from the long side of a sheet of paper. The strip should be about an inch wide.

2. Stick a piece of tape on one end of the strip.

3. Make a loop by bringing the end of the strip with the tape close to the end without the tape, but don't stick them together just yet.

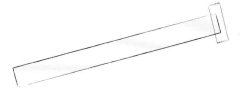

4. Flip the tape-free end over, and then attach it to the taped end. You'll have a band with a twist in it. This is a Mobius band! It may look ordinary, but it's really very weird.

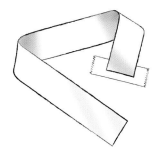

5. Use your pencil to make an X somewhere in the middle of your Mobius band.

6. Starting at the X, draw a line that goes around the band.

7. Keep going until you reach the X again.

8. Do you notice anything strange? You never picked up your pencil to move it from the inside of the band to the outside of the band. But somehow you managed to draw a line that is both on the inside and the outside. That's because the Mobius band really has only one side! Weird!

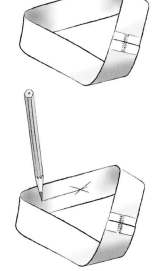

9. Now draw a number 1 at one edge of the Mobius band and a 2 across from it, at the other edge.

10. Turn the band over and put a 1 on its backside, making sure it's right under the 1 you've already made. Put another 2 under the 2 while you're at it.

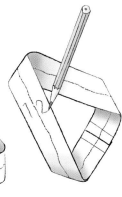

11. Now put a paper clip on the band so that it's right beside the 1.

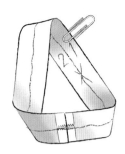

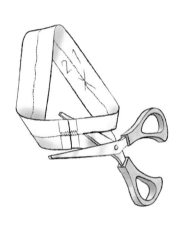

12. Slide the clip along the edge of the band. You'll pass the 2. Keep going and you'll reach the 1 again. You went from the edge of the band labeled 1 to the edge of the band labeled 2 without taking the paper clip off the band. That's because the band really has only one edge!

13. Cut the Mobius band in half, straight down the middle. Before you finish cutting, make a prediction: Will cutting one Mobius band in half produce two Mobius bands? Try it and see.

14. Start over with another Mobius band. Cut out a strip of paper from the long side of your paper. The strip should be about 1$\frac{1}{2}$ inches wide.

15. Draw two lines down the length of the strip, so that the lines divide the strip into roughly equal thirds. Do the same thing on the other side of the strip.

16. Make a Mobius band out of the strip by twisting it once and taping the ends together.

17. Now you are going to cut the Mobius band along any one of the lines. But first, make a prediction — what do you think you'll end up with? Start cutting and keep cutting until you reach the place you started.

18. What did you get? Was your prediction right? (Don't feel bad if it wasn't. This is very tricky stuff.)

What's Going On?

A regular band of paper has two sides and two edges, but a Mobius band has only one side and one edge. This is hard to believe, but you proved it yourself.

A German astronomer named August Ferdinand Mobius invented the Mobius band in 1858. Mobius's paper invention proved to be not only tricky, but useful too. Mobius bands are now used in recording equipment — they allow you to record on both sides of the tape.

The Mobius band is part of a special kind of math called *topology.* Topology deals with the ways in which things can be twisted, stretched, bent, or squished from one shape into another.

The way things connect to each other — or don't — is an important part of topology. One way to study connection is to disconnect something. That's what you did when you cut the Mobius band in half. Rather than getting two loops, you get one big loop with two twists. That's because a Mobius band has only one edge and one side. When you cut it in half, you add a second edge and a second side.

Walk Through Paper

Here's another challenge for you.

Here's What You Need

✔ A sheet of paper measuring 8 1/2 by 11 inches

✔ Scissors

✔ A lot of imagination

Here's What You Do

1. Take your sheet of paper and cut it so that you, big person that you are, can step through a hole in the piece of paper. What are you waiting for?

What's Going On?

Maybe your first attempt didn't work. That doesn't mean it's impossible. Get another piece of paper and try something else. Okay, something else, something else . . .

Put this chapter aside. Don't come back until you: (a) have figured it out, (b) have run out of paper, (c) really, really need to know the answer or else you will explode!

Did you make a hole in your paper big enough for you to walk through? Tricky, isn't it?

Before we tell you our answer, we'll tell you a legend that may help you out. A queen was shipwrecked on an island, and she begged the people who lived there for some land on which her people could live. The people of the island said that she could have all the land that she could surround with an ox hide. So the queen cut the ox hide into thin strips and used those strips to surround as much land as she could — a lot more land than the ox hide could cover.

Does that give you any ideas? (If you want to see our answer, turn to page 364.)

To learn more about paper, visit Exploratopia *online at* www.exploratopia.com.

Optical Illusions

Take a look at Greg, the kid on the left in the burgundy T-shirt, and his twin, Greg2, the kid on the right. (Just ignore Roger, the kid in the middle; he's not family.) Obviously, Greg has been taking his vitamins — he sure looks taller than Greg2.

Wait, Roger is saying that the twins are the same exact height. You're not listening to him, are you?

All right, check it out. Grab a ruler and measure Greg and Greg2. You'll see that . . . Roger is right. Greg and Greg2 are exactly the same size. But they sure don't look it. This photograph is an *optical illusion,* a tricky picture that fools your eyes.

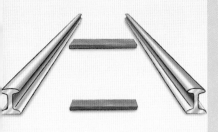

About the Size of It

Check out the drawing on the left. Which board is longer? Measure them and see. Your eyes and your brain work together to create the picture of the world that you see. Usually they do a darn good job of it. But when your eyes and brain meet an optical illusion, all bets are off. The usual rules don't apply!

Want to Buy a Rock?

Here are a couple of rocks for sale. You can have them real cheap but there's one thing you should know — there's no delivery. You want it, you carry it.

    Try to guess how big each rock is. Can you fit it in a wheelbarrow, or will you need a Mack truck? Pick your rock, and then turn to page 365 to see what you just bought.

    Did you choose a rock you can manage to move? What threw you off in guessing the size of the rocks?

    There really isn't any way to figure out the size of the rocks from the pictures on this page. One way to figure out the size of a rock is to compare the rock to objects around it. But our photographer made sure that there was nothing familiar near the rocks in the photos on this page.

    The photos on page 365 show a person near each rock. You know roughly how big a person is. By comparing the person to the rock, you can estimate how big the rock is.

How Big? How Far?

Have you ever noticed that people shrink when they walk away from you? You haven't? After you try these experiments, you'll be sure to notice that people around you are shrinking and growing all the time.

Here's What You Need

✔ Something to measure with your fingers — a car, a friend, a TV, a lamp, a house

✔ A friend

✔ A toy car, if you happen to have one

Here's What You Do

1. Close one eye. Hold your arm straight out in front of you. Find an object that will fit in the space between your thumb and finger.

2. Move closer to the object, keeping your arm stretched out straight. Does the object stay the same size as you move? Or do you have to move your fingers to fit a larger object?

3. Move away from the object. What happens?

4. Now you're going to shrink your friend. Close one eye. Hold your arm out in front of you with your hand in a fist and your thumb pointing up in the air. Ask your friend to slowly walk away from you. When your friend and your thumb look exactly the same size to you, have your friend stop walking. Cover your friend with your thumb. Now ask him to wave his arms. Look, your thumb has little arms! How many other things can you totally wipe out with your thumb? Whoa, you just knocked out a whole house!

5. Try step four again, only this time, use a toy car instead of your thumb. Can you make your friend look like he's driving the tiny car?

6. Take your toy car out and find some real parked cars. Walk around, hold up your toy car and try to make it look the same size as a real car. Can you "park" your toy car between two real cars? (Okay, because you're not really driving a car, you can't really go where the real cars go, so stay on the sidewalk!)

What's Going On?

When you see someone far away, you don't think, "Hey, there's someone really tiny!" You think, "That person is far away." When someone looks bigger and bigger as he walks toward you, your brain doesn't think, "Hey, he's swelling up!" You know that he is coming closer. You don't even think about this stuff, unless someone like us calls it to your attention.

Why bother to pay attention to this? Well, knowing about the way distance affects size helps to explain what's going on with Greg and Greg2 at the beginning of the chapter.

Take a look at that picture again. Which of the Gregs would you say is farther from you in the picture? Most people say the Greg on the left is farthest away. After all, he's standing under an arch that's behind Roger, the big guy. So your brain figures he just looks small because he's far away.

Greg2, the guy on the right, is closer to you, because he's standing right beside Roger. But if Greg2 is closer to you — and he's about the same size as the Greg who is farther away — then he must really be little! So your brain sees Greg2 as a really little guy, smaller than his distant twin. Weird!

Tools for Exploration

Making predictions

Suppose you had a tall friend and a short friend, but you wanted to have them look like they are the same size. Would the tall person have to stand farther away or closer than the short person? Make a prediction — then do the experiment to see if your prediction was right.

Tiny Buffalo

In the 1950s, anthropologist Colin Turnbull lived in the African Ituri Forest with the Mbuti people. (An *anthropologist* is a scientist who studies the history and culture of various people.) One day, Turnbull took his Mbuti friend, Kenge, out for a car ride. He drove to the edge of the forest to give Kenge his very first look at the vast grasslands beyond. A herd of buffalo grazed about a mile away. Kenge had seen buffalo before but he had never seen *anything* that far away from him. In his home, the Ituri Forest, the trees and bushes were so close together that you couldn't see more than a few yards. Kenge asked, "What kind of bugs are those?" When Turnbull explained that they were buffalo and not bugs, Kenge laughed and told him not to tell silly lies about tiny buffalo.

Trace Your Face

Think you know the size of your face? You may be surprised!

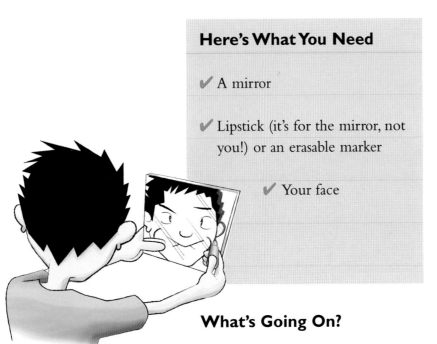

Here's What You Need

✔ A mirror

✔ Lipstick (it's for the mirror, not you!) or an erasable marker

✔ Your face

Here's What You Do

1. Hold the mirror out at arm's length. Look at your beautiful self.

2. While holding the mirror at arm's length, use the lipstick or erasable marker to trace the shape of your face on the mirror.

3. Now bring the mirror closer and closer to you. Does your face still fit in the drawing?

What's Going On?

As you bring the mirror closer to you, your reflection gets larger. But the line that you traced is getting larger, too. The two grow at exactly the same rate — so your face always fits in the shape you traced. What do you think will happen if you move away from the mirror? Will your face still fit in the shape you traced? If you have a friend handy, trace your friend's face in the mirror. Then have your friend back away from the mirror. Does your friend's face still fit the shape you traced? Can you explain what's going on? (Hint: Your friend moved, but you and the mirror didn't.)

Experiment with the Full Moon

Check your calendar to find out when the moon will be full. On the day that the moon is full, look for it low in the eastern sky just after sunset.

You're going to hold your hand out at arm's length and cover the moon. But before you do that, guess how much of your hand it will take to cover the moon. Will you need your whole fist? just two fingers? Take a guess before you do anything else.

Now, stretch your arm out and block the moon. Can you block it with one finger — maybe just the tip of your little finger?

Wait a few hours, then go out and take another look at the full moon. It'll be high in the sky, and it'll look much smaller. How much of your little finger do you think it will take to cover it? Stretch out your arm and see.

The moon looks smaller when it's high in the sky, but it's really the same size as it was on the horizon. Scientists who study optical illusions are still arguing about exactly what causes the illusion that the moon changes size. They think it has something to do with how far away you think the moon is. (For more on how this works, read about the illusion that begins this chapter on page 274.)

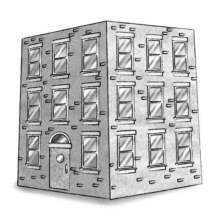

Illusion Experiments

Look at the picture on the left. (No fair using a ruler yet.) Is it farther from point A to point B or from point B to point C? Take out a ruler and measure.

Contrary to the popular saying, what you see is not always what you get.

Which line is taller — the outside corner of the building or the inside corner of the room? Use your ruler to check.

If you tried "How Big? How Far?" on page 274, you know that an object looks bigger when it's closer to you. To figure out how big something really is, your brain has to guess how far away that object is. These pictures are drawn so that one line looks like it's farther away than the other. Your brain figures that the line that's farther away must actually be bigger, since it appears to be the same size as the one that's close up.

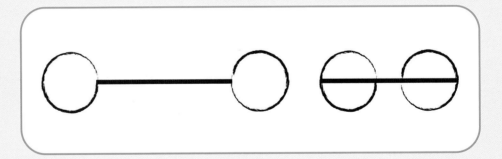

Which line is longer — the one that runs through the circles or the one in between the circles? Use your ruler to check.

Surprised? Or have you figured out by this time that you can't always believe your eyes? (At the rate we're going, you may never believe them again.)

A Swell Illusion

Here's What You Do

1. Look at the circle in the middle of each cluster of circles. Which of the center circles looks bigger?

2. Get your two dimes out. Put one dime on top of each of the middle circles. Do the dimes look like they are the same size?

3. Now take the dimes away and look at the circles again. Do the circles change in size? Keep looking at the circles for a minute. Whoa! Do you see what we see?

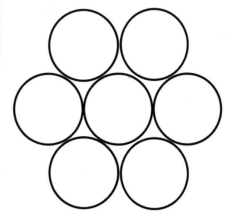

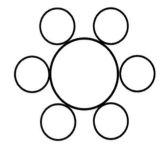

What's Going On?

The middle circles are the same size, of course. But to most people, the circle that's surrounded by little circles looks bigger than the circle that's surrounded by big circles.

Your brain automatically compares each circle with the things around it before making a guess about its size. (If you tried "Want to Buy a Rock?" on page 274, you know that this can be a good way to judge size.) The circle that's surrounded by little circles looks big by comparison. The circle that's surrounded by big circles looks little by comparison. So your brain comes to the conclusion that one circle is big and the other is small — and that's how you see them.

Many people would think that having two identical circles look different is strange enough. But here at the Exploratorium, we wanted to experiment a little more. So we tried covering the circles with dimes.

When we showed this to people, most people thought the two dimes looked the same size when they were on top of the circles. But when we took the dimes away, something strange happened. Some people reported that removing the dimes makes one of the middle circles get larger.

We've only experimented with this a little bit. What happens when you try it?

Tools for Exploration

Sharing your experience
Show this illusion to a friend. Does your friend see the same thing you do when you take away the dimes?

Dear Professor E:
I think optical illusions are cool, but I don't understand why scientists bother studying them? Don't scientists have better things to do with their time?

Signed,
Why Bother?

Dear Why Bother?
Scientists study optical illusions because they want to know what's going on inside your head! Don't take it personally — it's not just your head that interests them. It's the human brain that they want to know about.

Your eyes and brain work together to let you see the world. Usually, they do a good job of it. Your eyes send your brain information that they gather from light. (For more on that, see page 11.) Your brain takes that information and makes a picture of the world. But when you look at an optical illusion, this smoothly functioning system breaks down! The picture your brain makes doesn't match the world!

One way to figure out how something works is to look at times that it doesn't work! By studying pictures that fool your eyes and brain, scientists try to figure out some of the shortcuts that your brain takes in making sense of the world. But it isn't an easy thing to figure out. Some of these optical illusions have been around for hundreds of years, and scientists are still arguing about how they work!

Argumentatively yours,
Professor E

Take a look at this picture. All the white shapes in this pattern are perfectly square or rectangular — but they sure don't look it. The horizontal lines on the pattern are perfectly parallel. That means they run side by side, always the same distance apart, like the lines on a piece of notebook paper. But these lines don't look parallel, and they don't look straight. In fact, the lines look like they're snaking all over the place!

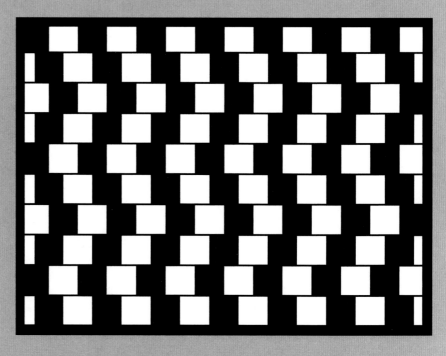

The black-and-white pattern confuses your eyes and your brain, and that means you just aren't seeing straight.

If you don't believe that the white shapes are square, try using a piece of paper to block out everything but a few squares. Do they look square now? Or block out everything except the top row of squares. Do the lines between the squares still look crooked?

Here's another way to convince yourself the lines aren't crooked. Close one eye, hold this page right under your nose, and look across the page sideways, along the lines. Told you so!

Perception of Patterns

Your eyes send information about the world to your brain. Your brain tries to make sense of that information, searching for things that look familiar. This helps your brain make sense of the world, but sometimes it leads to optical illusions — like the illusion that these kids are leaning to one side.

What do you see in this photo? A bunch of spots that don't add up to anything? Suppose we said it was a picture of a spotted dog — a dalmatian. Can you find the dalmatian? It may take a minute, but suddenly your brain will see the pattern of spots that makes the dog.

What do you see in this painting? At first glance, maybe all you see is a mountain partly covered with snow. Keep looking and you'll see something more. Bev Doolittle, a creator of camouflage art, painted this tricky picture.

Man or Mouse?

Take a look at these pictures. What do you see?

Each one of these pictures can be seen as two completely different things. You probably see one thing first. Then if you try, maybe you can see the other picture. Once you've found both pictures, you may find yourself flipping back and forth between the two. First, it's a rabbit. Then, it's a duck. Then it's a rabbit again!

Your brain works hard to make sense of the information that your eyes supply. But these pictures make your brain work overtime.

Is this a guy playing a saxophone — or the face of a young woman? If you have trouble seeing the woman, hold the picture at arm's length and squint at it. Sometimes that helps.

Do you see a fancy white vase? Or two people staring at each other, nose to nose?

Is this a rabbit, or is it a duck? It all depends on how you look at it.

Is this a man or a mouse? You decide!

Mystery Spot, U.S.A.

While writing this chapter, the Exploratorium took a field trip to the Mystery Spot, in Santa Cruz, California. According to the brochure, strange things happen at the Mystery Spot. People shrink and grow! Balls roll uphill! Tilting people are held upright by an eerie force!

What could cause such peculiar events? Some people say a meteor landed at the Mystery Spot. Others claim that it was a magnetic force field. A few people figure it has to be aliens from outer space! (Some people always blame things on the aliens!) All anyone knows for sure is that it wasn't called the Mystery Spot for nothing.

The Mystery Spot is one of many such places around the country. If you ever get a chance to visit one of these tourist attractions, go! You'd have fun, and we think you can figure out what the mystery really is. As it turns out, the happenings at the Mystery Spot are not due to aliens or antigravity forces or anything like that. They are all optical illusions.

Tools for Exploration

Explaining what you see

The tour guides at the Mystery Spot (and places like it) say that aliens or mysterious force fields cause the strange things you see there. Can you come up with any other explanation?

When Charlie is standing on the right, he looks much taller than Maya. But when they switch positions, Maya is about the same height! If you look carefully, you can see one of the reasons that Maya gets bigger. As she walks from the left to the right, she gets closer to the camera. (If you tried "How Big? How Far?" on page 274, you know all about what happens when someone gets closer.)

In the house at the center of the Mystery Spot, Trevor tries to stand straight, but as you can see, it looks like he's leaning to the left! After reading this chapter, you know that you can't always trust what you see. Trevor is a living optical illusion! The floor of the house is tilted and the walls lean to the right, making it look like Trevor is leaning to the left.

To learn more about optical illusions, visit Exploratopia *online at* www.exploratopia.com.

Light

Do you know that you have the power to bend light? Bending light changes the way you see the world and the way that the world sees you!

With a simple bottle of water, you can transform yourself into a googly-eyed monster. You can dramatically change the shape of an ordinary penny, or you can make words grow and shrink. By experimenting with bending light, you can warp the world around you. Ultimate power is yours!

Warp the World

By bending light you can make things look weird or warped, bigger or smaller, upside down or right-side up. You can make things look like they are somewhere else altogether. How can you possibly bend light when you can't even get your hands on it? It's easier than you might think.

Soda-Bottle Antics

Want to become a googly-eyed monster? Here's how.

Here's What You Need

✔ An empty, clear, plastic soda bottle (the kind that holds two liters of soda)

✔ Enough water to fill the bottle

Here's What You Do

1. Take the label off the bottle, rinse the bottle out, fill it with water, and put the cap on the bottle. You want the bottle to be as full as you can get it. If there's a little air bubble in the bottle, that's okay. Now you're ready to start bending light.

2. Put the bottle on its side on top of this page and look through the bottle at the words on the page. How does looking through the bottle change the letters? If your letters look tall and thin, can you make them look short and fat? If they are short and

fat, can you make them look tall and thin?

3. Take a look at this word through the bottle.

MOM

4. Pick the bottle up and change the distance between the word and the bottle. How does that change what you see? Can you make **MOM** into **WOW**? Experiment until you can.

5. Hold the bottle sideways (horizontally) right in front of your eyes and take a look through it. What does the world look like through the bottle? Is it right-side up or upside down? If it's right-side up, can you make it flip upside down? (Here's a hint: move the bottle away from your eyes while looking through it.)

6. If you have a small bubble in your bottle, that's great. If you don't have a bubble, take off the cap, pour out a tiny bit of water,

and put the cap back on. Turn the bottle on its side and look at these words through the bubble in the bottle. What happens to the writing? When you looked through the bottle, the words looked bigger. What do the words look like when you look through the bubble?

7. Get a penny. Open your soda bottle and drop the penny in. Turn the bottle on its side and shake it around until the penny is lying on the side of the bottle. Look down through the side of the bottle at the penny. The penny was round when you dropped it into the bottle. What shape is it now?

8. Now it's time to become a googly-eyed monster. You'll need a friend to tell you when you

are perfectly monstrous. Hold the bottle sideways a few inches in front of your eyes. Tell your friend to stare into your eyes while slowly backing away from you. When you hear the scream you will know that your friend has gone just far enough.

9. Have your friend describe what she saw. Did she sputter something like, "Eyes freaky huge, flipped over, get me out of here!"? Good — that means you did it right. Try this neat trick at the next party you go to. You might not be invited back, but it'll be worth it!

What's Going On?

Why does the world look weird through a soda bottle?

You see the world because light gets into your eyes. (You can find out more about that on page 11, but right now, just take our word for it.) When light bounces off this page and shines into your eyes, you see these words.

When nothing gets in its way, light travels in a nice straight line, from this book right into your eyes. That light makes a picture inside your eye. Your eye sends signals to your brain, and your brain makes a picture of the world in your head.

When your brain makes that picture, it figures that the light traveled in a straight line to reach you. After all, that's what usually happens.

But when you put your soda bottle between the page and your eyes, you mess things up. Light doesn't travel in a straight line into your eyes any more. Light bends as it moves from the air into the soda bottle and the water inside. Then light bends again when it moves back out into the air.

Your brain doesn't know all that. So all those bends along the way make the picture in your head a little warped. Blame it on the soda bottle — and your brain!

Tools for Exploration

Experimenting to test your ideas

Is it the bottle or the water inside the bottle that makes you into a googly-eyed monster? Can you think of a way to figure out the answer to this question? (Here's a hint: What does the world look like through an empty bottle? What does the world look like through the bottle when it's full of water?)

What Happens When Light Shines Through a Soda Bottle?

We shone lights of different colors through a soda bottle so you could see where each beam of light ends up. The blue light hits the side of the bottle closest to the top of the picture and bends down. The red light hits the side of the bottle closest to the bottom of the picture and bends up. The white light hits the middle of the bottle and goes straight through without bending.

The light that was up is now down. The light that was down is now up. No wonder the world looks upside down through a soda bottle!

If you want to find out more about what makes light bend when it shines through your soda bottle, try experimenting with lenses. (See page 290.)

Hey, Who Broke My Straw?

Take a look at the photo on the right. Is the straw in one piece or two?

Get a glass of water and a straw. Fill the glass at least halfway with water. Put the straw in the glass and let it lean against the side. Then look at the straw through the side of the glass. Does it look broken? Does moving the straw to different positions change how it looks?

The straw looks like it breaks right at the water line. Why? Because your brain takes the information from the light that gets into your eyes and makes a picture of the world. In this case, your brain makes a picture of a straw that's underwater.

The light that traveled from the water to the air got bent on its way to your eyes, but your brain doesn't know that. Usually, light travels in a straight line, so your brain says "Hey, the light traveled in a straight line, so the straw is right over there." But your brain doesn't get it quite right. The straw isn't exactly where you think it is.

Light from the part of the straw that's above water doesn't bend on its way to your eyes. In the picture that your brain makes of that part of the straw, the straw is right where it really is.

Light from the underwater part of the straw bent when it traveled through the water. So, the two pictures your brain makes don't quite match up. The section of the straw above water and the section below water appear to be in different places, so the straw looks broken.

What's Next?

Look around your kitchen and you'll find lots of other light benders.

Here's What You Do

1. Search your kitchen and recycling bin for other bottles and jars.

2. Your soda bottle is basically *cylindrical* — that means it's shaped more or less like a cylinder. (A cylinder is the shape of a soup can.) You'll probably find lots of jars shaped like cylinders in your kitchen.

3. Try to find bottles that have different shapes. Some red-wine vinegar bottles have a long neck attached to a sphere. (A sphere is round, like a ball.) Some olive-oil bottles have flat sides; they are shaped like a box.

4. Once you have a collection of empty bottles, wash them out and fill them all with water. Compare how the world looks through different jars. Be careful with glass bottles. If you break one, get a grown-up to help with cleanup.

Disappearing Puddles

You've probably heard stories of mirages in the desert. A person who is parched with thirst sees a beautiful, cool, green lake on the horizon. The thirsty person rushes toward the lake, only to see it disappear.

Next time you take a car trip in the summer, look for *mirages*. Watch the paved road far ahead of the car for a patch that looks wet. When the car gets closer, that puddle in the road will start to shimmer, and then it'll disappear.

That's a mirage! What you thought was a puddle was actually an illusion caused by bending light.

On a hot day, the sun-warmed pavement heats up the air just above the road. When light from the blue sky hits this layer of hot air, the light bends upward. From a distance it looks like this blue light from the sky is reflecting from a pool of water on the road. So you say, "Hey, that must be a pool of water!" As you get closer, that tricky light doesn't get into your eyes anymore, and the pool of water disappears.

Lens Experiments

Ever looked through a magnifying glass? The glass in a magnifying glass is called a lens, and lenses are the best light benders around. To be an expert light bender, you need to experiment with a lens or two (or three or four). . . .

Search your house and see if you can find a magnifying glass or two. (If you can't, you can buy one at the drugstore or the hardware store.)

Ask a grown-up to help you search for other lenses. There are lenses in eyeglasses, cameras, binoculars, slide projectors, and telescopes. (Be sure to ask permission before removing any lenses from someone else's equipment!)

The more lenses you have for your experiments, the better! How many can you find?

Looking Through Lenses

Looking through a magnifying glass can give you a new view of the world.

Here's What You Need

✔ A magnifying glass or other magnifying lens

✔ Any other lenses you can find

Here's What You Do

1. Look at your finger through the magnifying glass. Hold the magnifying glass about a foot from your face and about an inch from your finger. Then move the lens away from your finger and notice how that changes what you see.

2. You can also try moving your face closer to and farther away from the magnifying glass.

3. A magnifying glass makes your finger look bigger, but if the lens is too close, it won't magnify much. If the lens is too far away, your finger will look blurry. Experiment to find the distance that gives you the best view of your finger. Can you see the tiny ridges on your fingertips? (For more about those ridges, see page 55.)

4. Try looking through your magnifying glass at other things, like color pictures in the newspaper, your TV screen, that dust bunny under your bed . . . You'll probably find a whole lot of things you never knew existed. (Maybe you were better off not knowing! Oh well, too late now. Might as well keep going.)

5. Now hold your magnifying glass at arm's length and look at a picture on the wall. Start with your lens an inch from the picture. Keeping your lens at arm's length, look through it as you move away from the picture. As

you move away, the view through the lens will blur, then flip over!

6. Look through any other lenses you've found, one at a time. Do these lenses make things look the same as your magnifying glass? Do any of your lenses make these words look smaller? If you find a lens that does that, set it aside in its own special category. Most of the lenses you find will probably make these words look bigger, just as the magnifying glass did.

7. Stack two lenses and look through both of them at the same time. How does that change what you see? Microscopes and telescopes use more than one lens in combination.

What's Going On?

When you look through a lens, the world looks different. Things might look bigger or they might look smaller. Or maybe they look blurry. Or, if the lens is in your eyeglasses, things that originally looked blurry may look sharp.

Tools for Exploration
Measuring and counting
Take a look at the photo of the magnifying glass on this page. Can you figure out how much bigger the magnifying glass makes the lines look? (Here's a hint. You'll need a ruler. If you need more help, see page 365.)

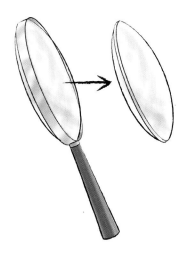

Your lenses change the way things look by bending light before it gets into your eye. You found out about that already when you experimented with a soda bottle. (See page 286.)

How does a lens make the light bend? Take a look at your magnifying glass. What does the glass part look like from the side? If there's a metal rim around the glass and you can't see it from the side, use your fingers and feel the magnifying glass. If it's like most magnifying glasses, it will be thicker in the middle and thinner at the edges. A lens that is thick in the middle and thin at the edges is called a *convex lens*.

Because the lens is thick in the middle and thin at the edges, the surface of the lens curves. This curve makes light bend.

Here's why. When light hits a piece of glass straight on, the light doesn't bend. But if light bumps into that same piece of glass at an angle, the light bends. The bigger the angle, the more the light bends.

This also happens when light moves from inside a piece of glass into the air. If the light meets the air at an angle, the light bends. The bigger the angle, the bigger the bend.

A lens is a piece of clear stuff that's carefully shaped so it bends light in a particular, predictable way. Take a look at the photo below to see what we mean.

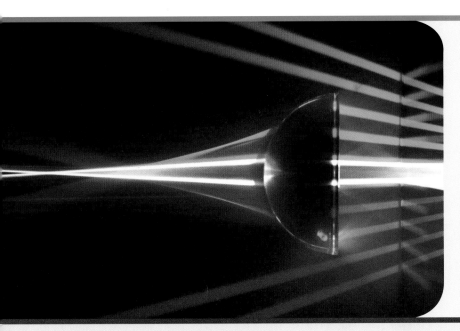

We took this picture to show you want happens when a bunch of beams of light bump into a convex lens. This convex lens is curved on one side and flat on the other. The beams of light, coming from the right, shine through the clear plastic of the lens and bump into the curved surface where the plastic of the lens meets the air. Beams of light that meet this surface straight on keep on going straight. That's what happens to the two beams of white light shining through the center of the lens. The green beams and the blue beams of light meet the curved surface at an angle. Those beams bend.

Did you find a lens that makes things look smaller? If you did, take a look at it from the side. What you've got is a concave lens. Concave lenses are thicker at the edges and thinner in the middle. Concave lenses are hard to find around the house, but if anyone in your family wears eyeglasses, check to see if those lenses are concave. Concave lenses curve in — like the opening to a cave. (Remember: con-CAVE.) Convex lenses curve out — like the rear end of a bear investigating the cave.

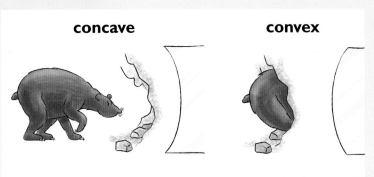

concave   convex

This is a broken lens from an old lighthouse, viewed from the side.

Dear Professor E:

What's all this fuss about curved lenses? I happen to have a magnifying lens that's completely flat. Try and explain that, buddy!

Signed,
The Magnifying Magician

Dear Magnifying Magician:

Back in 1820, a Frenchman named Augustin Fresnel (that's pronounced fray-NELL) was making really big lenses for lighthouses. These lenses had to be strong enough to focus lantern light into a narrow, bright beam that could be seen by a ship at sea. But ordinary lenses made of glass were too thick and heavy.

Fresnel knew that the surface of the lens was the important part. He knew that light bends when it moves

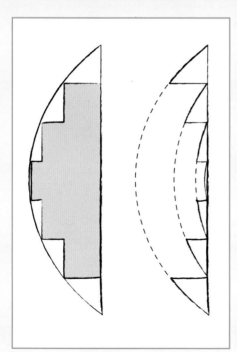

into a lens or out of a lens. The curve of the lens's surface is what makes the light bend. All the glass in the middle didn't matter, except to hold the surface in place. So Fresnel eliminated the glass in the middle, making a lens that was all surface.

The picture on the left shows the curve of a convex lens. The blue part is all the glass that really doesn't matter when it comes to bending light. Fresnel designed a lens that looked like the picture on the right. The Fresnel lens is all surface and no middle.

Today you can buy plastic Fresnel lenses to use as magnifying lenses. I bet this is what you have. Have you noticed that, if you run your finger over its surface, you can feel lots of little ridges? Each of those ridges is part of the light-bending surface of the lens. That's why it can still magnify even though it's flat. Don't mean to burst your bubble, but there's no magic here, just some really cool science.

Your Fresnel lens friend,
Professor E

Making Pictures from Light

By bending light with a convex lens, you can make a picture that looks just like the real thing. Lenses in cameras and movie projectors do just that.

Here's What You Need

✔ A dark room

✔ A TV set

✔ A partner

✔ A sheet of white paper or cardboard

✔ A magnifying lens

Here's What You Do

1. Draw the curtains or close the shades to make the room as dark as possible. (Or wait until it's dark outside and turn off the lights.) Turn on the TV set.

2. Have your partner hold the white paper or cardboard about 5 feet from the TV. If you don't have a partner, prop the paper or cardboard on a chair facing the TV. This cardboard is like the screen in a movie theater — it will reflect a picture made of light. The TV is like the movie projector.

3. Hold your lens in between the TV and the cardboard. Start with your lens up close to the cardboard and gradually move it away.

4. When your lens is the right distance away, you'll see the moving pictures from the TV on your cardboard screen, with one big difference — the picture on the screen is upside down!

What's Going On?

Your TV set produces light. That's why you can watch TV in a dark room. The picture on your cardboard screen is an image, a picture made from light.

When your TV is on, take a look at the screen through your magnifying glass. You'll see many bright bars or dots of color. Light spreads out in all directions from each of these spots of color. If you hold your cardboard screen near the TV, you can see some of this light, but you don't see an image. To make an image of the TV picture, you need to bend some of the light that's spreading out so that it comes back together and looks just like it did on the TV set.

That's where your lens comes in. A lens's job is to gather the light shining out in all directions from each spot and bend that light so it all comes back together in a single spot again. So light from the spot on top of a TV actor's head ends up on one spot on your screen, while light from the actor's eyes becomes yet another spot. All these spots of light blend together in your eye to make an image. Why is the image upside down? Take a look at the photo on page 292. Light that shines into the top of a lens bends downward. Light that shines into the bottom of the lens bends up. So the image you get is flipped upside down!

The picture on your TV set makes a good image because the TV picture is brightly lit and the room is dark. You can make images of other things that are brightly lit.

Make an image of a bright light in a dark room. Put the lens between a cardboard screen and the light and move the lens around until you get the distance just right.

Make an image of a brightly lit window in a dark room. Experiment and see what other images you can make.

Tools for Exploration

Asking questions

Can you make the picture bigger? Can you make it smaller? What do you do to change the size of the picture? What will happen if you cover half of the lens? Think of other questions you'd like to ask, and experiment to find out the answers.

How Do Eyeglasses Work?

In the thirteenth century, Italian glassmakers began making lenses and selling them to scholars with bad eyesight. The glassmakers knew that a chunk of glass that curved out on both sides made things look bigger. Those glassmakers also knew that the secret of a lens is in the curve of its surface.

Do you need to wear eyeglasses or contact lenses? If you do, it's probably because your eyes are not focusing light in the right place. Remember when you used a magnifying glass to make an image on a cardboard screen? (See page 294.) If you didn't hold the screen in just the right place, the image was blurry.

In each of your eyes, there's a lens that makes an image on your retina, the layer at the back of your eye that senses light. (For more on that, see page 11.) If the lens in your eye doesn't make a sharp image, you'll see a blurry view of the world.

When you put on eyeglasses, you are using two lenses together: the lens in your eye and the lens in the glasses. The lenses in glasses bend light before it gets into your eyes. Just the right amount of light-bending can make the image on your retina sharp, letting you see the world in focus.

The same eyeglasses don't work for everyone. The lenses need to be specially made for your eyes only. Some people are *nearsighted*. That means they can see things that are nearby, but things that are far away look blurry. A nearsighted person needs eyeglasses with concave lenses to bring far-off things into focus.

People who are *farsighted* can see objects that are far away, but things that are nearby look blurry. A far-sighted person needs eyeglasses with convex lenses to magnify things that are nearby and bring them into focus.

Finding the Focal Length

You brainy, analytical types will want to find out how much that lens of yours bends light. You can use this valuable information when you are making images (like those on page 294) or taking a closer look at stuff (like on page 290).

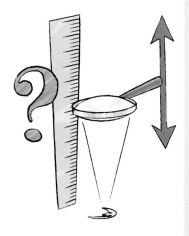

Here's What You Need

✔ A magnifying glass or some other convex lens

✔ A piece of white cardboard

✔ A ruler

✔ A clear night with a moon in the sky (If you're not sure when the moon will be out, check out page 131.)

Here's What You Do

1. Go outside, put your cardboard on the ground, and take a look up at the moon.

2. Hold your lens between the cardboard and the moon. Move the lens closer to and farther from the cardboard until you see an image of the moon on the cardboard.

3. Use your ruler to measure the distance from the lens to the screen. That's the *focal length* of the lens.

What's Going On?

When you were experimenting with lenses, you probably noticed that sometimes things looked upside down through the lens and sometimes they looked right-side up.

To know whether something will look upside down or right-side up through a lens, you have to answer two questions. First, is the object I'm looking at within the lens's focal length? Second, is my eye within the lens's focal length?

When your eye is within the lens' focal length, things you see through the lens look right side up no matter where they are. When your eye is outside the lens's focal length, the things you look at will be right-side up when they are inside the lens's focal length — and upside down when they are outside the lens's focal length.

A soda bottle has a very short focal length. That's why you only have to move it a few inches from your eyes to become a googly-eyed monster with upside-down eyes. Convex lenses that don't magnify much (like the lenses of reading glasses) have a really, really, really long focal length.

Knowing the focal length can help you figure out how to use a lens to do experiments in this chapter. To use a lens as a magnifier, hold the lens *less* than its focal length away from what you want to magnify. To make an upside-down image, hold a lens *more* than its focal length away from the object (like the TV) you are using to make an image.

Tools for Exploration

Measuring and counting

Do all your lenses have the same focal length? Measuring the focal length gives you a new way to compare your lenses.

Making Light Benders

The lenses you've been using are probably made of glass or plastic, but just about any clear substance can be transformed into a working lens. You can make lenses out of water, ice, and even Jell-O. Keep reading to find out how.

Droplet Lenses

A drop of water makes a fine magnifying lens.

Here's What You Need

✔ Clear plastic wrap

✔ A newspaper

✔ An eyedropper

✔ Water

Here's What You Do

1. Tear off a piece of plastic wrap and put it on top of a sheet of newspaper.

2. Using the dropper (or your finger if necessary), put drops of water in random spots on the plastic wrap.

3. Look at the words on the newspaper through the drops. Do the words appear bigger through the drops?

4. Look at the drops from the side. Notice that they're curved out. You just made yourself a bunch of convex, or magnifying, lenses!

What Else Can I Try?

Compare drops of different sizes and see which ones make the best magnifiers. Next time it rains, look around and you'll find tiny magnifying lenses everywhere!

Tools for Exploration

Comparing two things

Which drop makes a better magnifying glass — a big drop or a little one? Experiment and find out.

Jell-O Lenses

Make a batch of colorful lenses you can eat!

Here's What You Need

- ✔ A small (3 ounce) package of light-colored Jell-O or other brand of sweetened gelatin (use lemon, pineapple, anything you'll be able to see through)

- ✔ A measuring cup, a stirring spoon, and a small mixing bowl

- ✔ Cold, hot, and boiling water

- ✔ A grown-up assistant to help you make Jell-O

- ✔ Several different containers that can be Jell-O molds. We used a ladle, an ice-cream scoop, and a set of measuring spoons. You need something with a rounded bottom. Containers with flat bottoms will *not* work. Use a variety of containers so you'll be sure to get some good lenses.

- ✔ A refrigerator

- ✔ A piece of clear plastic or glass (suggestions: deli container lid, flat-bottomed glass baking dish, pie plate — ask your grown-up assistant for more suggestions)

- ✔ A butter knife

- ✔ A newspaper

Here's What You Do

1. Ignore the recipe on the Jell-O box. You're going to make super-charged Jell-O.

2. Pour the Jell-O into a bowl. Have your assistant add 3/4 cup of boiling water. Mix until all the Jell-O powder dissolves.

3. Have your assistant pour the mixture into the containers. (Use a spoon to pour into the smaller molds.)

4. Put the containers into the refrigerator for at least four hours to set. (You may need to prop up some molds so the Jell-O doesn't spill all over the place.)

5. When the Jell-O has completely set, wet the piece of clear plastic or glass. A little bit of water will keep your future lenses from sticking to the surface.

6. Have your assistant run hot water over the outside of the Jell-O–filled containers. Turn each container upside down over the clear plastic or glass and tap gently to remove the Jell-O.

7. For stubborn ones, run more hot water over the molds or loosen the edges with a butter knife. That should do it.

8. Wet your fingers and turn each blob of Jell-O so that its flat side is facing down on the clear plastic or glass.

9. Set the plastic or glass on top of a sheet of newspaper and look through your Jell-O blobs at the words.

10. Pick up the plastic or glass and move it slowly away from the newspaper while looking through the Jell-O. What happens as you move the Jell-O away and then back toward the words? If some of your Jell-O blobs magnify the words, call those lenses. (Call the other blobs snacks and eat them.)

11. Compare your different Jell-O lenses. Which ones make the best magnifiers? How do they differ from the ones that don't make such good magnifiers?

12. If you wear glasses, take them off for a minute and see which Jell-O lenses you can see through the best. This will be good to know because if you ever lose or break your glasses, you could just whip up a temporary Jell-O pair. Looking good!

To learn more about light, visit Exploratopia *online at* www.exploratopia.com.

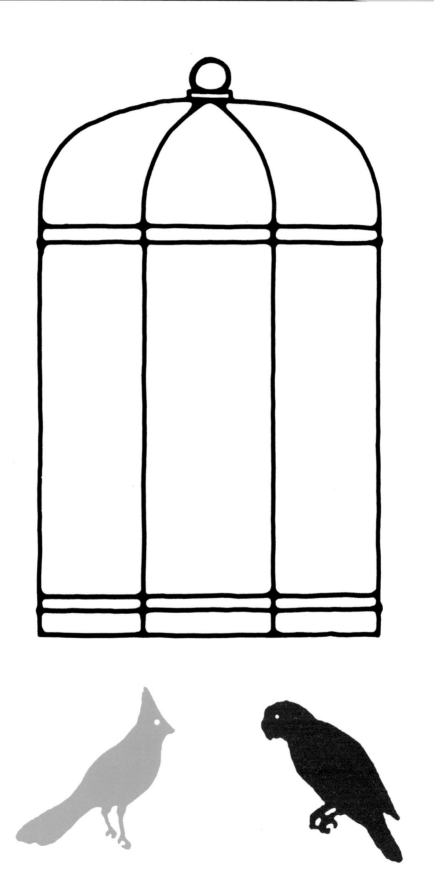

Color

You're going to use the power of your steely gaze to scare these birds back into the cage. Here's how you do it.

Stare into the eye of the red bird for about twenty seconds. It's hard to stare and watch the clock at the same time, so you might want to count the seconds out loud.

Now stare at the birdcage. Did you get the red bird into the cage? What do you mean *kind of?* You got a fuzzy looking, bluish-green bird? How odd! If you didn't see a bird when you looked in the cage, turn the lights up so that the book is in bright light, and start again.

This time, stare into the eye of the green bird for twenty seconds. Then look into the cage. Did you get the bird into the cage? What color is it?

These sneaky birds that you see in the cage are really not in the cage at all. They're inside your eyes. To find out more about these birds, turn the page.

Color Vision

*The bird that you saw in the cage is an **afterimage**, an image that you could still see even after you stopped looking at the original. Scientists have been experimenting for years to figure out why people see afterimages and how people see color.*

Afterimage

You can create art that's only in the eye and the brain of the person who sees it.

Here's What You Need

✔ A red marker, pencil, or crayon

✔ Blank sheets of white paper

✔ As many other colored markers, pencils, or crayons as you can get your hands on

Here's What You Do

1. Use your red marker to make a red spot about the size of a quarter.

2. Stare at the red spot for twenty to thirty seconds.

3. Look away from the spot and stare at a blank part of the white paper or wall.

4. Do you see a spot? What color is it? If the spot vanishes, blink to bring it back.

5. Step closer to or farther from the wall or move the white paper closer to or farther from your eye. Does the spot change size?

6. The spot you see on the white surface is an afterimage. A red spot makes a blue-green after-image. Use your other colored markers to make spots and see what color afterimage each colored spot makes.

7. Make a chart like the one on page 303 to keep track of how the colors change.

8. Now make your own custom afterimages. Can you put a blue fish in the fishbowl in the corner of page 303? A red heart on the forehead of the one you love? (No one will ever know but you!)

What's Going On?

When you shift your stare from the red spot to the wall, it looks like the spot is on the wall. But the afterimage is actually in your eyes and brain.

Why do you see an afterimage and why is the color different from the original? You see color when light-sensitive cells (called *cones*) in your eyes are stimulated by light. There are three types of cones, and each type is most sensitive to a particular color. One type is most sensitive to red light, another one to green light, and yet another to blue light.

When you stare at the red spot, the cones that respond to red light let your brain know that they are seeing red: "Hey, brain, it's red. Still red. Yep — it's as red as it ever was."

After a while, those red-sensitive cones stop responding to the red light. They quit letting the brain know that they are seeing red. (Scientists would say that those cells have *adapted* to the stimulus.) At about that time, you looked away from the circle and at the white wall. White light reflecting from the wall shone into your eyes.

Usually, when white light reaches your eyes, all three types of cones respond. That's because white light is made up of red light and blue light and green light — and all the other colors of the rainbow. (For more on that, see page 306.) But after staring at the red circle, your red-sensitive cones don't react to the white light. So you see white

Original Color	Afterimage Color
red	blue-green

light without red light — a mixture of green and blue light that makes a greenish-blue color in the same shape as the original red circle. (For more about how the colors of light mix, see page 317.) After a while, your red-sensitive cones recover and the afterimage fades.

The color of your original image (whether it's a bird, a spot, or an American flag) determines which type of cones stop responding and what color afterimage you see.

The afterimage in your eye is the same size whether you see it on a piece of paper that's a foot from your eye or a wall that's 15 feet away. But when you change the distance between your eye and the surface where you see the after-image, its size seems to change. That's because your eye and brain calculate the size of something by considering the size of the image in your eye and the distance to the object. When the afterimage is far away, it looks big. (For more on this, see page 274.)

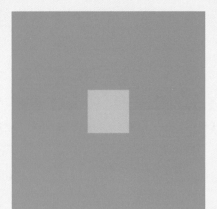

Do these blues look like the same color? If not, what's the difference?

The two blue squares are exactly the same color. If you don't believe us, take some white paper and cover up the background, so that all you see are the blue squares. Now do they look the same?

A color will look darker or lighter depending on the color that's around it. The fancy term for this is simultaneous color contrast. When the cones in one part of your eye see blue light, the nearby cones become less sensitive to blue. Because of this, a blue square that's on a background with some blue in it will look less blue than it really is. That means a blue square on a bright yellow background will look bluer than the exact same square on a blue-green background (because blue-green contains some blue).

So now you know. If your conceited teenaged sister (they're not all conceited, just yours) wears blue eye shadow to bring out her baby blue eyes, she's going about it all wrong. She needs color contrast to make the blue look bluer.

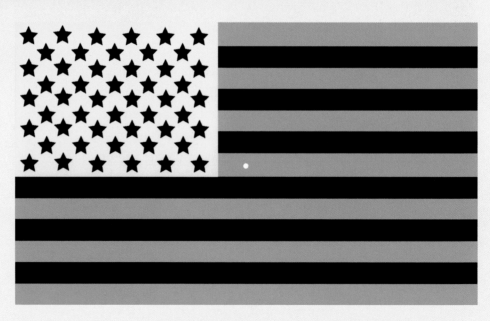

Here's an up close and personal picture of the human retina, created using a method called confocal microscopy. The bright green shapes are the cones, and the red shapes packed between them are the rods, the light-sensitive cells that let you see in dim light. To make this picture, scientists stained a piece of a retina with dyes that glow when laser light shines on them. A computer detected the glowing light from the dyes and drew this picture, one point at a time.

Hey, this flag is done in the wrong colors! Or is it? Stare at one spot in the middle of the flag for twenty seconds. Then shift your gaze from the picture to a blank white wall. Do you see the afterimage? Our afterimage flag is based on one created by the artist Jasper Johns. Does this give you ideas for making afterimage art of your own?

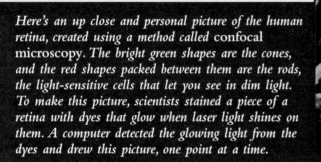

Bees don't see the same colors you and I see. Most people see red, orange, yellow, green, blue, indigo, and violet. Bees don't see red, but they see ultraviolet, a color that's just outside the range of the colors you can see. The picture above is how you see a dandelion. The picture below shows how a bee sees the same dandelion. Ultraviolet markings on the flower show the bee where to go for pollen. You wouldn't know where to go for pollen because you can't see the ultraviolet color. Oh well, you probably wouldn't want that pollen anyway!

Dear Professor E:
When my teacher asks us to use a red marker, I can't tell which one that is. Am I color-blind? (I can see all the other colors just fine.)

Signed,
Seeing Red (Not!)

Dear Seeing Red (Not!):
You create a world of color with the light that enters your eyes. But the colors you see may not be the same ones your best friend sees. About one out of 20 men and one out of 200 women are color-blind in some way, including yours truly, Professor E. It just means they don't see all the colors as well as most other people do. Some people have eyes that aren't very sensitive to red, and they can't tell the difference between purple and blue. Others, like you and I, are even less sensitive to red, and for them, red may look black or gray. Other people have eyes that aren't sensitive to green. A very, very small number of people are completely blind to color, seeing the world in black, white, and shades of gray.

Let your teacher know what colors you have trouble seeing so she can help you and any other color-blind students in your class.

Your friend (whose favorite color is blue anyway),
Professor E

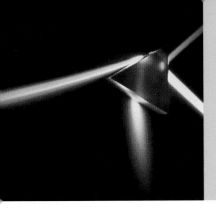

Making Rainbows

Isaac Newton discovered that sunlight contains all the colors of the rainbow. He used a wedge of glass called a prism *to separate light into rainbow colors. Newton called this the* color spectrum. *Then he used a prism to bring the colors back together to make a single beam of white light.*

Garden-Hose Rainbows

Feeling a little blue? Sprinkle yourself up an instant rainbow!

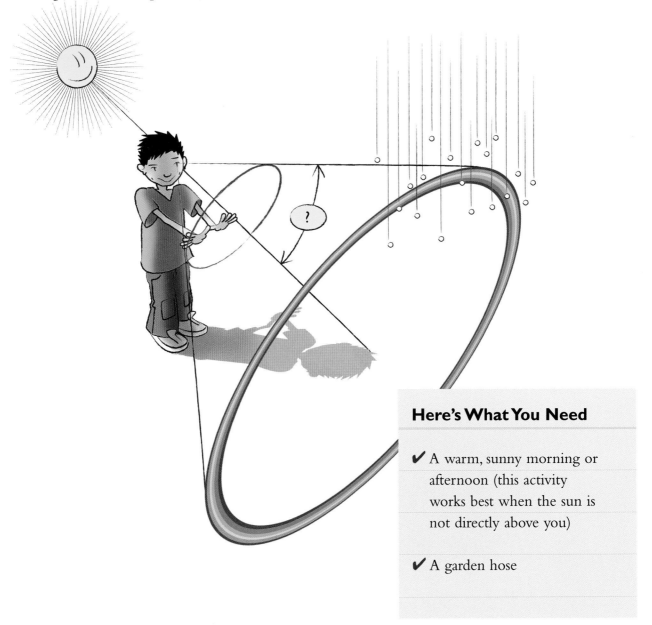

Here's What You Need

✔ A warm, sunny morning or afternoon (this activity works best when the sun is not directly above you)

✔ A garden hose

Here's What You Do

1. Stand with your back to the sun and find your shadow.

2. Run water through your garden hose.

3. Put your finger over the nozzle so that the water sprays out in a fine mist, and spray the water in front of your shadow.

4. Fiddle with the position of the spray to find just the right angle. You'll know you've got it when a beautiful rainbow appears just for you!

5. If you have trouble finding the rainbow, get a friend to hold the hose and try this trick. Stand with your back to the sun facing the spray of water drops. Hold both hands in front of you. Touch your thumbs together and spread your fingers out. Place the tip of one little finger so that it is in the center of the shadow of your head. You'll see a rainbow where the tip of your other little finger lines up with the spray. Using this trick, you can find a rainbow in a sprinkler, water fountain, or waterfall — anywhere that drops of water are falling in sunlight.

6. Look carefully. Can you see a second rainbow outside the first one? If you can, you're seeing a double rainbow.

What's Going On?

Like Isaac Newton, you have just demonstrated that white light contains all the colors of the rainbow. Whenever light moves from air into something clear (like a drop of water from the hose), the light slows down. When light hits the clear stuff at an angle, the light bends when it slows down. Different colors bend by different amounts and separate into the colors you see in the rainbow.

The rainbows that you see in the water drops are made by light that both bends and reflects from the drops. When light enters a raindrop, it bends and separates into colors. When the light hits the far side of the raindrop, some of it reflects back out. When the reflected light leaves the drop, the remaining light bends some more, spreading the colors out even more.

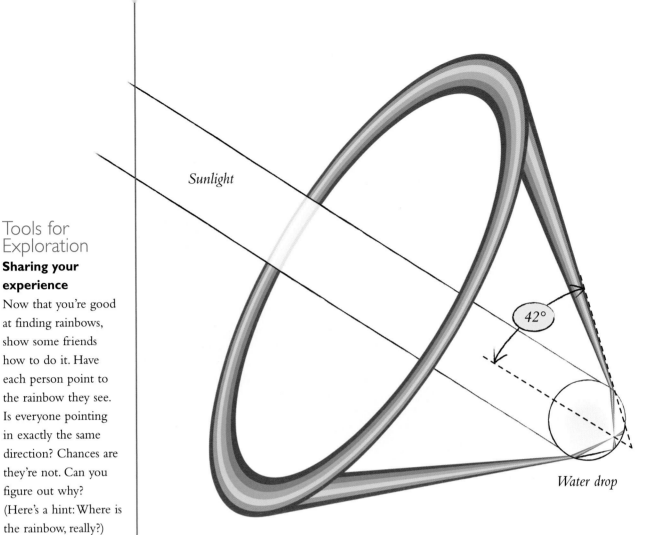

Sunlight

42°

Water drop

Tools for Exploration

Sharing your experience

Now that you're good at finding rainbows, show some friends how to do it. Have each person point to the rainbow they see. Is everyone pointing in exactly the same direction? Chances are they're not. Can you figure out why? (Here's a hint: Where is the rainbow, really?)

When light reflecting from many water drops gets in your eyes, you see a rainbow. The rainbow is in your eyes, not out in the world.

Did you try our trick for finding the rainbow? It works because the light always reflects from the water drops at the same angle — about 42 degrees. When you hold out your hands as we described, your little finger is in exactly the right position to line up with this rainbow angle.

The bending of light as it moves in and out of a water drop is called refraction. *This word comes from the Latin word* fractus, *meaning "break up."*

Many Ways to Make Color

Bending light to create a rainbow is just one of many ways to make color.
There are lots of different ways to make a colorful world!

Many of the colors you see come from pigments, chemicals that absorb the light of some colors and reflect other colors. The skin of these red cherries contains red pigment, which absorbs all the colors in sunlight except for red. The red light is what's left over. So where does this red light go? The cherries reflect the red light, that red light gets into your eyes, and you see red!

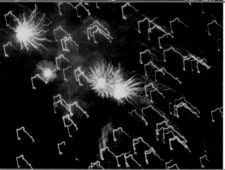

Some colors, like the cheery, red glow of a campfire or the bright colors of these fireworks, come from burning chemicals that produce colored light. Each exploding skyrocket scatters bits of burning material called stars. Gunpowder keeps these stars burning. Chemicals give these stars their bright colors — different chemicals make different colors. If you want to see colored fireworks closer to home, watch for yellow flames the next time a pot of salted water overflows on the stove. Burning salt makes yellow flames. (No fair asking to make spaghetti just so you can see them!)

When electricity flows through certain gases, the gases give off colored light. That's what makes the aurora borealis. (See page 324.) A neon sign is a little bit like a down-to-earth version of the aurora borealis. The glass tubes of this neon sign contain different gases. When an electric current flows through these gases, they give off colorful light. The color depends on the kind of gas in the tube.

If the earth didn't have air surrounding it, the sky wouldn't look blue. It would look black, like the sky that astronauts see when they look up from the surface of the moon. The earth's atmosphere is made up of molecules of several gases. (Molecules are clumps of atoms, and atoms are those tiny particles that make up your body and everything around you.) When white light from the sun bumps into gas molecules in the earth's atmosphere, blue and violet light are scattered, spreading out in all directions. Some of that light gets into your eyes. Because your eyes are more sensitive to blue light than to violet light, the sky looks blue. On the moon, there's no gas to scatter the light, so the sky has no color.

At sunset, sunlight enters the earth's atmosphere at an angle, and it has to pass through a lot of air to reach your eyes. As the sunlight travels through the air, light at the blue end of the rainbow spectrum is scattered away, leaving the red and orange light to reach the earth. That's why sunsets look so colorful.

Mixing Waves

Have you seen colors on city streets after it rains? A thin film of gasoline or oil on a wet street reflects light from both its top and bottom surfaces, creating shifting, shimmering colors. You can see the same kinds of colors in other places if you keep your eyes open.

Light reflecting from the front and back surfaces of a soap bubble makes beautiful colors.

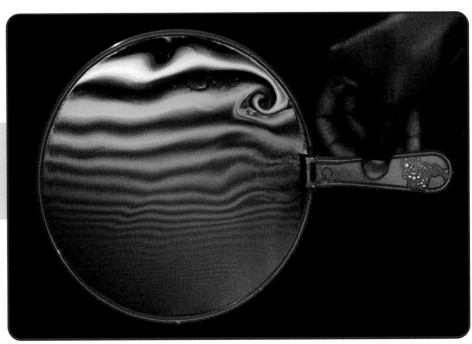

Soap-Film Stars

Forget about taking a bath (for now). You can capture the shimmering effect of soap bubbles anytime you want.

Here's What You Need

✔ Dishwashing liquid

✔ White paper

✔ Water

✔ A table

✔ A shallow dish or saucer

✔ A brightly lit place

✔ A black, plastic film can

✔ A pencil

Here's What You Do

1. Make a bubble solution by mixing 1 part dishwashing liquid to 16 parts water. (Example: 1 tablespoon dishwashing liquid added to 16 tablespoons of water)

2. Fill your shallow dish 0.5 centimeter to 1 centimeter deep (1/4-inch to 1/2-inch deep) with the bubble solution.

3. Remove the lid from the film can.

4. Place the white paper on a table.

5. Dip the open side of the film can into the soap solution.

6. Slowly pull the film can out of the solution.

7. Hold the film can horizontally over the white paper in a brightly lit place.

8. Watch the colors form and move around on the soap film. Look at the soap film even more carefully. Do you see bands of color?

9. After a while, what happens to the top of the soap film? Does it disappear or does it just become invisible? Test it by poking a pencil point into the black region. Does it break? If so, there must have been something there.

What's Going On?

If you experimented with making rainbows, you already know that white light is made of light of many different colors. Like the colors of a rainbow, the colors in the soap film (and the colors in the oil slick) come from white light. When white light reflects from a soap film or an oil slick, some of the colors in the white light get brighter and others disappear.

Light is tricky stuff. For hundreds of years, scientists have been trying to understand some of the things it does. One way to understand light is to think of it as being made up of waves, like the waves in the ocean.

Scientists sometimes measure waves — whether they are water waves or light waves — by measuring the distance between the crests of two waves. That distance is called a *wavelength*. (See page 177 for more about wavelength and ocean waves.)

White light is made of light waves of many different wavelengths. Each wavelength is light of a different color. Red light has the longest wavelength of all the colors you can see, and violet light has the shortest wavelength.

A soap film has two sides. When sunlight shines on a soap film, some of it reflects from the front of the film and some of it reflects from the back of the film. These reflected waves meet up. The illustrations on page 312 show how these waves make color when they meet.

Tools for Exploration

Making predictions
Can you tell when your soap film is just about to pop? Watch how the colors change over time. Do you notice anything that happens right before the soap film pops?

Colors Appear When Light Waves Interfere

Soap films reveal the colors that make up white light. Light waves reflect from the front and the back of a soap film. These reflected light waves meet up to make the colors you see. These colors are called *interference colors*, because they are made when light waves interfere with each other.

Different colors of light are made of waves with different wavelengths. The wavelength is the distance between the crests of the waves. Red light has the longest wavelength of all the colors you can see, and violet light has the shortest wavelength.

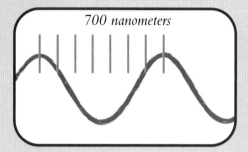

700 nanometers

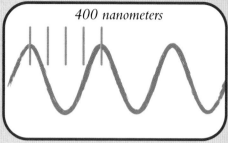

400 nanometers

When white light reflects from a soap film, light waves meet and overlap. This makes some colors of light get brighter and some colors disappear.

Which colors get brighter and which disappear depends on two things — the wavelength of the light and the thickness of the soap film. Each color you see on the soap film marks a different thickness of film.

The thinnest film — one that's only a few millionths of an inch thick — looks black because all the reflecting light waves cancel each other.

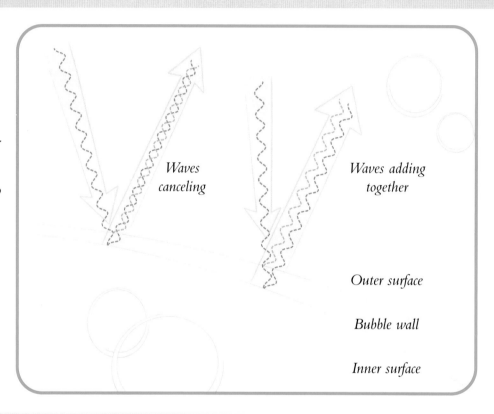

Waves canceling

Waves adding together

Outer surface

Bubble wall

Inner surface

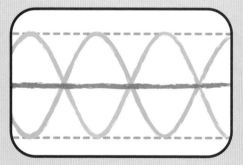

If the peak of one wave matches up with the valley of another wave, the waves will cancel each other and that color of light will disappear.

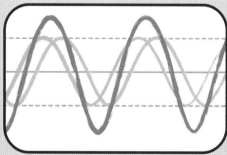

If the peak of one wave matches up with the peak of another wave, the waves add together and that color of light gets brighter.

Reflections of a CD

Create color just by interfering with a few light waves.

Here's What You Need

✔ A compact disc (better known as a CD — use an old one; you don't have to play it)

✔ A bright, sunny day or, if that's not possible, a dark room and a flashlight

✔ A piece of white paper

Here's What You Do

1. Find the blank side of your CD (the side that doesn't have any printing on it). Before you take your CD outside, look closely at this side of the CD. You'll see bands of shimmering color.

2. If it's a sunny day, hold the CD in the sunshine. Reflect light from the CD onto a sheet of white paper. Be careful not to let light shining on the CD reflect into your eyes or anyone else's eyes. Sunlight reflected into your eyes can hurt you!

3. If there is no sunshine, go to a dark room and shine your flashlight at the CD. Position your piece of white paper so that the light reflecting off the CD shines onto the paper.

4. Did you capture a color design or two or three . . . ?

5. Tilt the CD back and forth and see how that changes the reflections. How many different designs and shapes can you make with your reflected light?

What's Going On?

Like the colors in a soap film or an oil slick, the colors that reflect from a CD are interference colors. When light waves reflect off the ridges on your CD, they overlap and interfere with each other. To learn about how this makes colors, see page 312.

Mixed-Up Colors

*What happens when you mix all the colors? Some say it looks black —
the more colors you add, the darker the mixture will get. Some say white —
white light is made up of all the colors of the rainbow. What is the correct
answer? Well, it depends on whether you mix paint or light.*

That Old Black Magic

Separate the black ink in a marker into the secret colors that make it up.

Here's What You Need

✔ Scissors

✔ A white coffee filter

✔ A black marker (washable,
not permanent)

✔ Water

✔ A cup or mug

Here's What You Do

1. Cut a circle out of the coffee
filter, about the size of your
spread-out hand. (It doesn't have
to be perfectly round.)

2. With the washable black marker,
draw a line across the circle,
about 1 inch from the bottom.
(Do circles even have a bottom?
Use your best judgment!)

3. Put enough water in the cup to
cover the bottom.

4. Curl the paper circle so it fits
inside the cup.

5. Make sure the bottom of the
circle is in the water.

6. Watch as the water flows up the
paper.

7. As the water flows past the black
line, do you see some different
colors?

8. Leave the paper in the water
until the colors go all the way to
the top edge. How many separate
colors can you see?

9. Try this experiment again with
a different black marker (and a
cup of fresh water). Does this
marker make the same colors as
the first one?

What's Going On?

The ink in most impermanent markers is made of water and a mixture of colored pigments. When the water in the ink dries, it leaves the pigments on the paper.

When you dip one edge of your coffee filter in water, the filter soaks up the water. As the water flows up the paper, it dissolves the dried pigments and carries them along. The water carries different colored pigments at different rates — some travel farther and faster than others. That's why the black ink separates to reveal the colors that were mixed to make it. The last color near the top of your filter is the pigment that was carried the farthest.

This experiment gives you one answer to the age-old question: What happens when you mix all the colors together? Mixing all the color *pigments* gives you black.

Colored Shadows

Not all shadows are black. They can be colored, too.

Here's What You Need

✔ A grown-up to help you

✔ Three lightbulbs or floodlights in red, green, and blue — available at drug and variety stores. (100-watt General Electric Party Lights work well. You could also try Christmas-tree lights.) Keep in mind: The bigger the bulb, the more dramatic the effect.

✔ 3 light sockets

✔ A plain white surface (a white wall, poster board, or paper taped to cardboard) to act as a screen

✔ A darkened room

✔ Scissors

✔ An index card

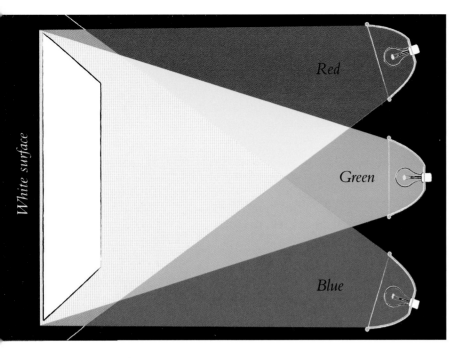

White surface

Red

Green

Blue

Here's What You Do

1. Arrange the lightbulbs as shown in the picture.

2. Set the three bulbs at the same approximate distance from the screen so that the light from all three bulbs falls on the same general area.

3. Make the room as dark as possible.

4. Turn on the bulbs.

5. Adjust the positions of the bulbs until the screen looks more or less white where the three lights mix.

6. Hold your hand between the bulbs and the screen. Do you see shadows? How many shadows?

7. Move your hand until you see three distinct shadows. What colors are the shadows?

8. Move your hand close to the screen so that the shadows overlap. What colors do you see where the shadows overlap?

9. How many different colors can you find in your shadows? With our three lights, we can make shadows of six different colors, plus black. Can you make six colors?

10. Block one of your colored bulbs so that no light from it reaches the screen. What happens to the light on the screen?

11. Try blocking the other lights, one by one, and notice how the light on the screen changes.

12. Cut a hole in an index card that's big enough for you to see a patch of color. Hold the card so that the light from the three bulbs shines through it. Do you see three separate color patches on the screen? Move the card closer to the screen. Can you get the colors to overlap? Can you see mixtures of each pair of colors?

What's Going On?

When you experimented with making rainbows (see page 306), you took white light and separated it into many colors. In this experiment, you took three colors of light and put them together to make white light. When your three lights (red, blue, green) are all shining on the screen, they mix to make light that looks more or less white.

With these lights, you can make shadows that are: blue-green (called *cyan*), blue-red (called *magenta*), yellow, blue, red, green, and black.

Where do all these colors come from? When your hand blocks light from one of the three bulbs, a shadow of your hand is cast on the wall. If that bulb were the only one turned on, your shadow would look black, as it normally does. But light from the other two bulbs shines into that shadow, filling it with a mixture of the two colors. When the blue and green lights mix, you get a cyan shadow. Red and blue lights mix to make magenta. Red and green lights mix to make yellow — which may seem kind of strange. The light-sensitive cells in your eye that respond to yellow light also respond to a mixture of red and green. So red light and green light mixed together make you see yellow. (For more on your color vision, see page 305.)

Where the shadows overlap, your hand is blocking two lights. For instance, in the spot where your red-blue shadow overlaps your blue-green shadow, you are blocking all the light except the blue light. So that spot looks blue. In the overlapping shadows, you can see blue and red and green.

Where your body blocks all three lights, your shadow will be the ordinary black shadow you are used to seeing. Ho-hum! Black shadows seem so boring in comparison to all those colored shadows.

So What Happens When You Mix All the Colors Together?

At the beginning of this section, we asked what would happen if you mixed all the colors together. If you experimented with "Colored Shadows," you saw that mixing colors of light together gives you white. If you experimented with "Black Magic" (or with the paints in your paint box), you saw that mixing colors of pigment together gives you black. So everyone who answered "black" or "white" is quite right. The only wrong answer was from that wise guy in the back who said "tangerine stripes and lavender polka dots!"

To learn more about color, visit Exploratopia *online at* www.exploratopia.com.

Electricity & Magnetism

A lightning bolt — whether it's a big flash of light on a stormy night or a little spark between your hand and a doorknob — is made of electric charges, jumping from one place to another.

Where do those electric charges come from? They're all around you! Everything is made up of tiny particles called *atoms*. Atoms are made up of even tinier particles — *electrons, protons,* and *neutrons.* Electrons have a negative electric charge and protons have a positive electric charge. *Neutrons* are neutral — they have no electric charge at all.

When you put a positive electric charge and a negative electric charge together, the charges cancel each other. Most of the time, electrons and protons hang out together. That's why most things don't seem to be electrified. But when the charges don't cancel each other — watch out!

Magnets

A bolt of lightning and a refrigerator magnet have a lot in common. Magnets are much easier to experiment with than lightning bolts, though.

This giant magnet looks like it's growing hair, but that's really black sand. To find out how to collect your own black sand, check out page 172.

Plan Ahead

In most chapters, you can do the experiments with stuff you can find around the house. But for some of the experiments in this chapter, you need special equipment. It's not expensive, but you'll need to make a trip to RadioShack or some other store that stocks wires and magnets and electric gizmos.

Here's a list of the experiments that need special equipment. If you want to do these experiments, plan ahead and make sure you get the things you need. It may seem like a hassle, but these experiments are worth the trouble!

Name of experiment	Special stuff you need
Magnetic Poles	2 donut-shaped or disk-shaped magnets about 1 inch in diameter (available at an electronic hardware store like RadioShack)
Where's North?	2 donut-shaped magnets about 1 inch in diameter (available at an electronic hardware store like RadioShack)
Complete Circuit	Some insulated wire, a 1.5-volt flash lightbulb, and a 1.5-volt D battery (available at hardware stores)
Electromagnet	At least 3 feet of insulated wire, and a 1.5-volt D battery (available at hardware stores)
Stripped-Down Motor	Insulated copper wire (at least 3 feet), 2 or 3 donut-shaped or disk-shaped magnets about 1 inch in diameter, a 1.5-volt D battery, and 2 alligator clip leads (available at RadioShack)

Magnetic Poles

Magnets stick to your refrigerator without glue. They sometimes stick to other magnets, and sometimes they push other magnets away. Weird!

Here's What You Need

✔ A few magnets (Donut magnets will work fine. Or you can use other magnets. You can use any magnets *except* those thin refrigerator magnets — the ones that bend easily. Those don't work well.)

✔ A compass

Here's What You Do

1. Bring your two magnets near each other. Do you feel anything happening between them?

2. Can you get the magnets to stick together?

3. Can you get one magnet to push the other magnet away? (Hint: If your two magnets keep sticking together, turn one around and see if they still stick together.)

What's Going On?

Sometimes your magnets stuck together (they *attracted* each other) and sometimes they pushed each other away (they *repelled* each other).

Every magnet has two poles — a north pole and a south pole. The north pole of a magnet will stick to the south pole of another magnet. Opposites attract!

The north pole of a magnet pushes the north pole of another magnet away. And the south pole of a magnet pushes the south pole of another magnet away. Similar poles repel!

Magnets come in all shapes and sizes. It may take some experimenting to figure out where the poles of each magnet are. Once you've figured out where the poles of each magnet are, you can use a compass to figure out which pole is which. The south pole of the magnet will attract the north pole of the compass needle.

By the way, maybe you are wondering why we said you shouldn't use a flexible refrigerator magnet in this experiment. We wanted you to use a magnet that had a north pole and a south pole that were easy to find. Those flexible refrigerator magnets have many, many north and south poles arranged in a striped pattern on the side of the magnet that sticks to the refrigerator. Each stripe is only about as wide as a dime's thickness — not very wide. When you play with flexible refrigerator magnets, it's hard to tell they have poles at all!

Tools for Exploration

Making predictions
After you've played with your magnets for a while, can you predict which end of one magnet will push away the end of another magnet? You might want to mark your magnets with markers or tape to help you figure out which end is which!

Where's North?

If you have a magnet, you can find north.

Here's What You Need

✔ A piece of string or thread that's about 2 feet long

✔ A donut-shaped magnet that's about 1 inch across (available at RadioShack)

✔ A table

✔ A compass

✔ Colored sticky dots or masking tape

Here's What You Do

1. Tie a piece of string to your magnet and hang the magnet from the edge of a table. If your table is metal, make sure that the magnet is far from the legs or any other pieces of metal.

2. Bring your compass near the magnet. When you bring the compass near the magnet, the compass needle will point to the magnet. The compass needle is a magnet, too. The north pole of the compass needle points to the south pole of the magnet hanging from the table. (For more about magnets and their poles, see page 321.)

3. Now move the compass far enough from the magnet so the needle doesn't always point to the magnet. You'll have to experiment to find the right distance. When you get far enough away, the compass needle will point north, no matter where the magnet is.

4. When you are far enough from the magnet, set your compass on the floor and go back to the magnet that's hanging from the table.

5. Hold your arms straight out. Point the fingers of your left hand through the hole in the magnet. Do your arms line up with the compass needle?

6. Put a sticky dot or a piece of masking tape on the side of the magnet that's facing north. That's the magnet's north pole.

What's Going On?

Did your magnet line up with the compass needle? Give your magnet a spin and wait until it stops moving. Does it line up with the needle again? Is this an accident? Nope!

If you tried the "Magnetic Poles" experiment, you know that magnets pull and push on each other. The north pole of a magnet pushes the north pole of another magnet away. The north pole of a magnet pulls the south pole of another magnet toward it.

But here's something you may not know: The earth itself is a giant magnet. Like your magnet, the earth has a north pole and a south pole. The compass needle (which is a magnet) and your magnet both feel the pull of the earth's magnetic poles and line with those poles.

Things can get a little tricky when you start talking about the earth's magnetic poles and the poles of a magnet. The end of the compass needle that points to the earth's North Pole is called the north pole of the compass needle. But you know (since you've been reading this book) that the north pole of one magnet pushes away the north pole of another magnet. What gives?

Blame the geographers, the folks who figured out maps and compasses and directions hundreds of years ago. Originally the pole of the compass needle that points to the earth's North Pole was called the north-seeking pole. But over the years, that got shortened to the north pole of the needle. The other pole (the south pole, of course) points to the earth's South Pole.

So the north pole of a magnet attracts the south pole of another magnet. But the north pole of a magnet attracts the North Pole of the earth and points north.

Dear Professor E:

My family and I went on a trip to Alaska. Every night the sky would light up in these glowing rainbow colors. Why would the sky look any different in Alaska?

Signed,
Wish I Had a Camera

Dear Wish I Had a Camera:

Does this look something like what you saw? It's the *aurora borealis,* or northern lights, nature's own light show. These lights shine when the *solar wind* (a stream of particles from the sun) blows through the earth's magnetic field. The meeting of the solar wind and the magnetic field makes an electric current. The current makes gases in the earth's atmosphere glow like the gas in a neon light. (To learn about neon lights, see page 309.)

The best place to view these lights is near the Arctic Circle. To the north of Barrow, Alaska, the aurora borealis can be seen almost every cloudless night in the fall, winter, and spring. There's a similar light show, the *aurora australis,* near the South Pole.

Tripping the light fantastic,
Professor E

Is this antigravity? Nope, just the power of magnetism.

Get five donut magnets like these and try to make your own tower of floating magnets. What do you have to do to make a magnet float? If you have trouble, check out page 366.

Some engineers put the principle of these floating magnets to work when they created the maglev train. *Maglev is short for* magnetic levitation. *Powerful magnets keep a maglev train floating a few inches above the tracks. Since maglev trains don't have wheels that rub against the tracks, they can move really fast — up to 300 miles per hour!*

Separating Charges

Experimenting with electricity can be a hair-raising experience! A Van Der Graaf generator, like this one, pulls atoms apart and builds up an electric charge. All the hairs on the girl's head have the same charge—and they are trying to get as far away from each other as possible!

Charge It!

With a plastic comb and a couple of pieces of ordinary tape, you can rip atoms apart.

Here's What You Need

✔ Scissors

✔ Scotch Magic Transparent Tape (Don't try any other kind — only the Scotch brand will work. Tape that's 3/4 inch wide works the best.)

✔ A table

✔ A plastic or rubber comb

✔ A piece of wool or human hair

✔ A marker or pen

Here's What You Do

1. Cut off two pieces of tape about 4 inches long.

2. Stick one piece of tape on top of the other piece to make a tape sandwich — with one smooth side and one sticky side.

3. Pull the tapes apart quickly. (Watch out! They'll try to grab you!)

4. Hang the separated tape pieces straight down from the edge of a table.

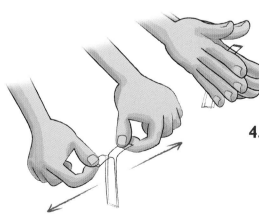

5. Rub the comb with wool or comb your hair.

6. Hold the comb next to one of the pieces of tape. What happens?

7. Hold the comb near the other piece of tape. What happens?

8. Did you find one tape moved toward the comb and one moved away? Good! Mark the tape that moved toward the comb with a plus sign and the tape that moved away from the comb with a minus sign.

9. Now bring your finger near the tape with the minus sign. What happens?

10. Bring your finger near the tape with the plus sign. What happens?

What's Going On?

When you pulled your tape sandwich apart, you also ripped apart some atoms!

Like everything else in your house, the tape is made of tiny particles called *atoms*. Atoms are made of even tinier particles called *electrons*, *protons*, and *neutrons*. These particles are *subatomic* particles. That means they are smaller than atoms. Both electrons and protons are electrically charged particles. Electrons are negatively charged and protons are positively charged.

When you pull the tape apart, you are pulling some electrons away from their protons. So one piece of tape ends up with more electrons, which gives it a negative charge. The other one ends up with more protons, which gives it a positive charge.

Positive charges and negative charges like to stick together. That's why the two pieces of tape are attracted to each other. (As you discovered when you experimented with magnets: Opposites attract!)

Similar charges push away other similar charges. Negative charges push away other negative charges, and positive charges push away other positive charges.

When you run a comb through your hair, you pull electrons from your hair and give the comb a negative charge. The comb will push the negatively charged tape away and will attract the positively charged one.

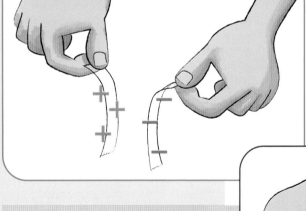

Is your finger electrically charged? If it attracts the negatively charged tape and repels the positively charged one, it's positively charged. If it repels the negatively charged tape and attracts the positively charged one, it's negatively charged.

But what if it attracts both pieces of tape? It means that your finger has no charge at all. Charged objects attract uncharged objects.

Super Sparker – The Electrophorus

With an electrophorus, you can touch electricity (ouch!), hear electricity (snap!), and see the electricity (wow!).

Here's What You Need

✔ Tape or glue (Elmer's glue or hot-melt glue)

✔ A foam cup (Paper or plastic cups won't work.)

✔ Disposable metal pie pan

✔ A piece of Styrofoam that's larger than the aluminum pie pan. You could use a slab of packing material, a stack of Styrofoam dinner plates, or some blue home insulation. The thicker the Styrofoam, the better it will work.

✔ A wool sock, wool ski sweater, sheep (or anything else covered with wool), or a lot of nice clean hair

✔ A table

Here's What You Do

1. Tape or glue the foam cup into the middle of an aluminum pie pan. This cup will be your handle. When you pick up the pie pan, use the cup.

2. Now you're going to charge the Styrofoam by rubbing it with the wool or with your hair for a full minute. (Time yourself or count off the seconds.)

3. After you rub the Styrofoam with the wool, hold the Styrofoam up to your face or over your arm. Do you feel the electric charge pulling you to the Styrofoam? Can you see the hairs on your arm sticking straight up?

4. Put the Styrofoam down on the table. Holding the foam cup handle, place the aluminum pie pan on top of the newly charged Styrofoam. Now you are ready to make sparks!

5. Lightly touch the metal pie pan with your finger. Did you feel anything? Did you hear anything?

Turn out the lights in the room. Remove the pie pan by picking up the foam cup handle. Touch the pie pan with your finger. Do you hear, feel, or see anything? Using the handle, set the pie pan down on the Styrofoam. Touch it again. Did you see the spark this time?

6. Using the handle, pick up the pie pan. Touch the metal pie pan with your finger, and you'll get another spark. Repeat these steps as many times as you like. If you run out of sparks, recharge the Styrofoam by rubbing it on your head or rubbing it with wool.

What's Going On?

This is an *electrophorus*. As you discovered, an electrophorus makes sparks. The word electrophorus comes from Greek words meaning "charge carrier." In this experiment, there are three things that carry charge: the Styrofoam, the pie pan, and you!

When you rub the Styrofoam with wool or hair, the Styrofoam attracts electrons from the wool or hair. The Styrofoam becomes negatively charged. When you put the aluminum pie pan on the Styrofoam, the electrons on the Styrofoam push away the electrons in the pie pan. Some of the electrons in the pie pan are *free electrons* — they are free to move around inside the metal. These free electrons try to move as far away from the Styrofoam as they can. When you touch the pie pan, some of those free electrons leap to your hand. You feel a shock, you hear a snap, and if the room is dark, maybe you see a spark.

Once those free electrons jumped from the pie pan to your hand, the pie pan was short on electrons. When you lift the pie pan away from the Styrofoam, your pie pan will attract any and all nearby electrons. So when you hold your finger close to the metal pie pan again, some electrons jump from your finger back to the pie pan, making another great spark.

When you put the pie pan back on the Styrofoam, you start the whole process over.

What Else Can I Try?

You can use the charged Styrofoam to move other objects. Place an empty, dry soda can on a smooth surface. The charged Styrofoam will attract the uncharged can since charged objects attract uncharged objects. This attraction will pull the can toward the Styrofoam.

Tools for Exploration
Asking questions
Can you figure out whether the Styrofoam is positively or negatively charged? If you experimented with detecting charge (see "Charge It!," page 325), think about how that might help you answer this question. If you didn't, you might want to try it now!

Electricity at Work

You can make electricity do all kinds of work for you. It's a fair exchange:
You put work in when you pull the electrical charges apart. When the electric
charges come back together, those charges work to make lightbulbs light up,
motors turn, computers compute, and all kinds of other useful stuff.

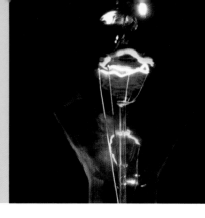

This is an ordinary light bulb. It's also known as an incandescent *light bulb.* Incandescent means it produces both heat and light.

Inside the glass bulb is a thin wire called a filament. When electric charges flow through the filament, the wire heats up and glows, making light. The flow of electric charges is called an electric current.

Incandescent lightbulbs depend on heat to make the filament glow. Making that heat is a waste of energy.

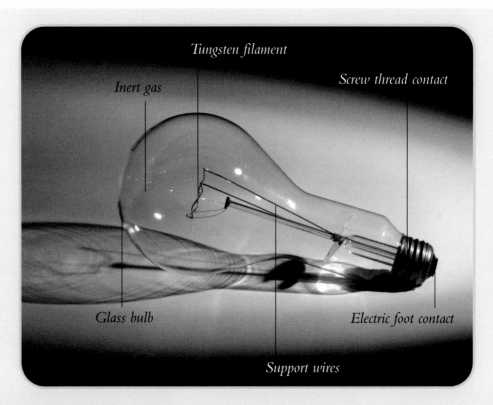

Inert gas

Tungsten filament

Screw thread contact

Glass bulb

Electric foot contact

Support wires

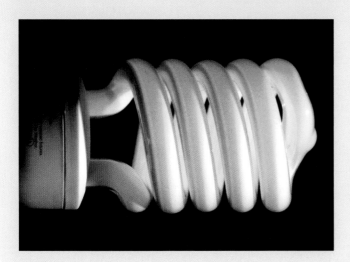

Compact fluorescent bulbs, like this one, don't depend on heat to make light. They produce more light for less energy, and can last more than ten times longer than incandescent bulbs!

In a compact fluorescent bulb, an electric current passes through mercury gas that is trapped inside the bulb. When this happens, the gas gives off some visible light and some ultraviolet light, a kind of light that your eyes can't see. (For more on ultraviolet light, see page 305.)

The stuff that lines the inside of the compact fluorescent bulb changes the ultraviolet light into light you can see. This stuff contains a substance called a phosphor. If you've ever played with glow-in-the-dark stickers, then you already know about phosphors. Glow-in-the-dark objects contain a type of phosphor.

Take a close look at the bottom of an incandescent light bulb. On the sides, you'll see metal screw threads. On the bottom, you'll see a metal bump in the middle of some black plastic. Metal is a conductor — that means electricity flows through it easily. Plastic is an insulator — it stops the flow of electric current. Electricity enters the light bulb through the metal bump, flows through the wires and the filament inside the bulb, then leaves through the metal screw threads.

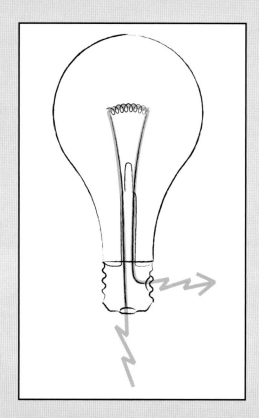

Next time you plug in a lamp, take a look at the plug. It has two prongs. An electric current flows through one prong of the plug, through a wire in the electric cord, into the lightbulb, and through the filament, making it glow. After the charges flow through the filament, they flow out of the lightbulb, through another wire in the lamp's electric cord, and back into the other prong in the plug. An electric current won't flow unless it can make a complete circle—a path known as an electrical circuit.

Complete Circuit

Can you make a lightbulb light up with a battery and some wire? With a little experimenting, you sure can!

Here's What You Need

✔ A 1.5-volt flashlight bulb
(available at the hardware store)

✔ A 1.5-volt D battery

✔ Tape

✔ Paper and pencil

✔ Some wire

Here's What You Do

1. Take a close look at your flash-light bulb and compare it to the picture of a full-sized lightbulb on page 329. Like a full-sized lightbulb, a flashlight bulb lights up when an electric current flows through its filament.

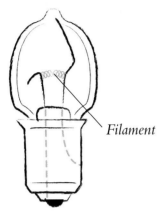

Filament

2. Can you see the filament in your flashlight bulb? Where do you think the electric current flows into and out of your flashlight bulb? Take a look at the close-up of the incandescent lightbulb on page 330. Does that give you any clues?

3. Take a close look at your battery. It has a bump on one end and a little dent on the other. These are the terminals of the battery.

4. To make the bulb light up, you need to create a path that lets an electric current flow from one terminal of the battery, through the flashlight bulb, and back to the other terminal of the battery.

5. Use your wire to connect the bulb to the battery in different ways. Remember, you want to make a path for the electric current.

6. If you're having trouble getting your bulb to light, don't give up. Look at the lightbulb photos again. Keep fooling around and trying different things.

7. No luck? Take a look at the pictures below. Some of these arrangements will make your bulb light up, and some won't. Try them all and see which ones make the bulb light up. Once you get your bulb to light one way, try to find another way that works. There's no one right answer. (If you want to see one arrangement that works, turn to page 366.)

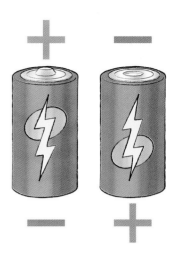

What's Going On?

As we mentioned before, for an electrical current to flow, you need to provide a complete path for the charges to follow. This path is called a *circuit*. You create a circuit for electric charges every time you turn on a lamp.

When your flashlight bulb lit up, you had a complete electrical circuit. Only complete circuits will light the bulb.

Tools for Exploration

Keeping track of your discoveries

Draw a picture of every way you connect the bulb and the battery with the wire. Your pictures will help you remember everything you've tried and which ways worked. Why do you think different arrangements work or don't work? Do your pictures help you figure that out?

Electromagnet

An *electromagnet* is a magnet created by an electric current.

Here's What You Need

✔ A grown-up helper

✔ A pair of scissors or nail clippers

✔ A 3-foot-long insulated wire (the kind with the plastic coating on it)

✔ A steel or iron nail (find a nail that is attracted to a magnet, and that nail will work for this experiment.)

✔ Tape

✔ A 1.5–volt D battery

✔ Paper clips or other small metal objects (for example, straight pins or small nails)

Here's What You Do

1. Have your grown-up helper use the scissors or nail clippers to remove the plastic coating from both ends of the wire.

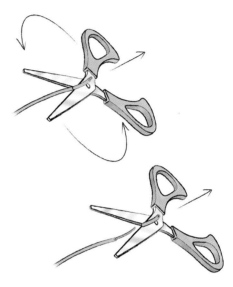

2. Wrap the wire around your iron nail twenty times.

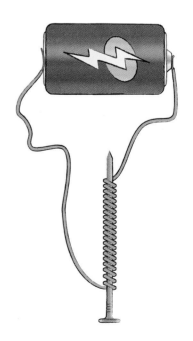

3. Hold or tape one bare end of the wire to the positive (+) terminal of the battery. Hold or tape the other end of the wire to the negative (–) terminal.

4. Bring the end of the nail near one of your paper clips. Does the paper clip stick to the nail? You've made an *electromagnet* — a magnet created by the flow of an electric current. (If the paper clip doesn't stick to the nail, check to make sure that the bare copper ends of the wire are making contact with the terminals of the battery, then try again. If it still doesn't work, make sure your battery isn't dead.)

5. Can you pick up the paper clip with your electromagnet?

6. Once you've picked up a paper clip, try hooking other paper clips to that paper clip, as shown in the picture at right:

7. How many paper clips will your electromagnet hold up?

8. Wrap the wire around your nail ten more times. With more wraps, is your electromagnet stronger or weaker? Measure its strength by seeing how many paper clips it can lift.

What's Going On?

In 1820, a Danish schoolteacher named Hans Christian Oersted discovered that electric charges moving through a wire create a *magnetic field*. Maybe you've heard or read about *force fields* in science fiction books and movies. A magnetic field is a kind of force field — it lets a magnet exert a force on steel objects around it.

Electric current flowing through your wire-wrapped nail creates an electromagnet. As you just demonstrated, your homemade electromagnet is strong enough to pick up paper clips and other small metal objects. Electricity can make magnetism. (It works the other way around too — magnetism can make electricity.)

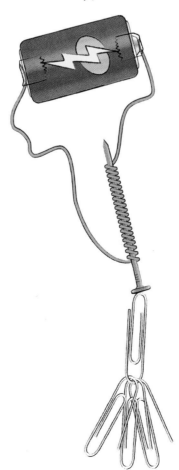

Tools for Exploration
Measuring and counting
The more times you wrap the wire around the nail, the stronger your electromagnet will be. How many wraps of wire does it take to make an electromagnet that's strong enough to pick up five paper clips? Can you make it strong enough to pick up ten paper clips?

Stripped-Down Motor

Make a simple electric motor and then watch it spin!

Here's What You Need

- ✔ Some copper wire from the hardware store
- ✔ A 1.5-volt D battery
- ✔ Wire cutters (optional)
- ✔ A grown-up helper
- ✔ Sandpaper

- ✔ Two jumbo metal paper clips
- ✔ A paper or foam cup and some tape
- ✔ 3 or 4 disk or donut magnets
- ✔ Masking tape

- ✔ 2 more metal paper clips (these can be regular-sized or jumbo)
- ✔ A rubber band
- ✔ 2 alligator clip leads
- ✔ A ruler

an inch across and to have six to eight loops. An easy way to make a neat coil is to wrap the wire around your battery and then slide it off. Make sure all the loops are neatly lined up side by side.

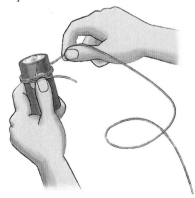

Here's What You Do

1. You're going to make a motor with very simple materials. It's a little tricky. Making your motor run may take some time and patience. But it's worth the trouble.

2. First, make a coil of copper wire. You want your coil to be about

3. Squeeze the loops together to make a coil of wire, then wrap the ends of the wire around the coil a couple times. Do this with both ends on opposite sides of

the coil. You want about 1$\frac{1}{2}$ inches of wire sticking straight out on either side of the coil. Make sure these "handles" are exactly opposite each other. Use your wire cutters to cut off the extra wire. Or, cut the wire by bending it back and forth until it breaks in two. You should now have a coil with two handles sticking straight out.

4. If you are using copper wire that has plastic insulation, have a grown-up helper strip the insulation off the ends of the wire sticking out of the coil. Take off all the insulation on each handle, from the end of the handle to the coil of wire.

5. Sometimes copper wire is covered with a thin coating of enamel, a kind of insulation that's nearly invisible. Rub your wire handles with sandpaper. This will remove the invisible enamel coating.

6. Your coil should look like this:

7. Now you need to make a holder for your coil of wire. Unfold and twist one end of each of your jumbo paper clips like this:

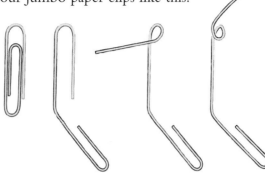

8. Turn your cup upside down and stack two magnets on the bottom of the cup. Attach your other magnet inside the cup, right under the first two magnets. This will hold the first two magnets in place.

9. Tape the paper clips to either side of the cup, like this:

10. Balance your coil of wire in the coil holder by putting the "handles" through the loops in the paper clips. Make sure the coil can spin without bumping into the magnets. You may have to adjust the paper clips. When you're done, the coil should clear the magnets by less than $\frac{1}{4}$ inch. (That's not much. Use your ruler to check.)

11. Give the coil a push with your finger to make it spin. Adjust the coil and the clips until the coil stays balanced and centered while it's spinning on the clips. Balance is very important!

12. You're almost done. Now you need to make a battery holder. Use your rubber bands to attach two paper clips, one on each end of the battery. We wrapped the rubber bands around the middle of the battery. Make sure that the rubber band is really tight, so that it pushes the paper clips onto the terminals of the battery.

13. Now you are ready to put your motor together. Clip one end of one alligator clip lead to a paper clip at one end of the battery. Clip the other end of that lead to one of the paper clips that hold the coil. Use the other clip lead to connect the other paper clip connected to

the battery to the other paper clip holding the coil.

14. Does your coil start to move? When you spin the coil with your fingers, can you feel it push back when you push it toward the magnets? If it doesn't, you may not have an electric current flowing. Squeeze the paper clips against the battery with your hand. Now does it spin? When you get your motor working, it should spin away merrily like a little machine.

15. Don't leave your motor running unattended. It can get very hot.

What's Going On?

You just made a real, working motor! As simple as this design is, it contains the three things that are found in almost every electric motor — a coil, a magnet, and an electric current.

When you hooked your coil of wire to the battery, you sent an electric current flowing through the wire. This turned the coil of wire into an electromagnet. (For more on electromagnets, see page 332.)

Like any magnet, the electromagnet has a north pole and a south pole. As you discovered if you played with magnets, the north pole of a magnet will push the north pole of another magnet away and will attract the south pole of another magnet. The north pole of the magnets on the cup attracted the south pole of the electromagnet and got the coil spinning.

TROUBLESHOOTING
Your Stripped-Down Motor

Troubleshooting means figuring out what's causing problems and coming up with solutions. Chances are, you'll need to do some troubleshooting on your stripped-down motor. Even the Exploratorium's expert motor makers have to do some tinkering to get a motor running well. (At the Exploratorium, we think part of the fun is figuring out why something isn't working and fixing it so it works.)

Here are some tips that will help you (and your grown-up helper) figure out how to make your motor run:

✔ Check your connections. Make sure that the paper clips are touching the terminals of the battery and the bare ends of the wire are touching the paper clips.

✔ Get a permanent marker and color the top half of one of your handles. For more on why this works, visit www.exploratopia.com.

✔ Make sure your coil of wire is balanced. The handles should be right in the center of the coil so that the half-circle of wire on one side of the handles is the same size as the half-circle of wire on the other side of the handles.

✔ Make sure the handles are perfectly straight and in-line with each other.

✔ Make sure the paper clip supports are exactly level.

✔ Make sure the paper clip supports are securely attached to the cup.

✔ Make sure the coil is centered above the magnet.

Keep experimenting until you get your motor spinning!

Tools for Exploration
Experimenting to test your ideas
If your motor doesn't spin right away, you get a chance to practice troubleshooting. That's what you're doing when you try to figure out why your motor doesn't spin and what you need to do to make it spin. Read the instructions again and check each part of the motor. What do you think could be wrong? How could you make it right?

To learn more about electricity and magnetism, visit Exploratopia *online at* www.exploratopia.com.

Sound

What's making all that noise? WHAT?! You'll have to speak up; we can't hear you over all this drumming.

Can you figure out what's making all this noise? No, it's not the drummer. Search more to find the sound source. WHAT? Church door?! No, no, we said SEARCH MORE! Here's a clue. Poo?! What do you mean, poo? We said CLUE!

Now listen — every sound begins with a *vibration*. VIBRATION! That's a fancy word that means something is shaking. So, what's shaking here?

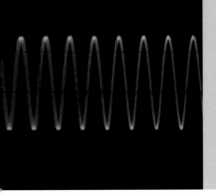

What's Shaking?

Sound starts with a vibration. The boom of a drum starts when the drummer pounds on the drumhead and makes it vibrate. That vibration travels through the air into your ears. Your ears send a signal to your brain. And your brain tells you that someone is pounding on a drum. Without vibrations, there is no sound.

Feeling the Vibes

Want to find a vibrating object that makes sound? Look no farther than your own body.

Here's What You Do

1. Find your *Adam's apple* (yes, girls have them, too) by putting your hand on your throat and then swallowing. That lump that bobs up and down as you swallow is your Adam's apple or, if you prefer, your Eve's apple.

2. Place your fingertips over your Adam's apple and softly say "ahh." Feel the vibration?

3. Now softly say "eee." Notice any difference in the feel of the vibration?

4. Say "ahh" and "eee" much louder this time. How does that make your Adam's apple react?

5. Say "zip" followed by "sip," "vine" followed by "fine." Notice any difference between the two similar words?

6. Now give some other parts of your body a chance to shake it up. Put your finger lightly on your lips and say "mmm."

7. Put your hand on the back of your neck and say "ing."

8. Put your hand on your chest and say "ahh."

9. Put a finger on each side of your nose and say "nnn."

10. Put your hand on top of your head, spin around, and say "whee!" (Okay, the spinning around part is optional — you don't have to do it.)

What's Going On?

Inside your Adam's apple is your *larynx,* or voice box. Inside that are two folds of tissue called *vocal cords.* When you hum, your vocal cords move — they vibrate. That's the vibration you feel when you put your hand on your Adam's apple.

When you speak, you exhale air from your lungs. The moving air pushes on your vocal cords and makes them vibrate. The vibrating vocal cords make the air vibrate. Your mouth, tongue, and lips shape the vibrations of the air.

Tools for Exploration

Comparing two things

You felt your throat vibrate when you made different sounds. Can you make a sound that doesn't make your throat vibrate? Try humming, whistling, and singing. What other sounds can you try?

Sound Detector

Got a balloon? Then you've got yourself a sound detector.

Here's What You Need

✔ An inflated balloon

Here's What You Do

1. People sometimes describe sounds as low pitched or high pitched. The booming of a bass drum is low pitched. The screech of a whistling teakettle is high pitched.

2. Take your balloon out somewhere where there are low-pitched sounds. We took ours to a busy street with lots of buses and diesel trucks rumbling by. (Being smart — like you — we stayed off the road and out of harm's way.)

3. Once you are in the noisy spot of your choice, hold your balloon tightly between your hands as a truck (or bus, or T. rex, or whatever low-pitched object you can find) goes rumbling by. Did you feel your balloon rumble as well?

4. Bring your sound detector out to an area with high-pitched sounds. We chose the screaming little kids section at a school recess. (Again, we were smart enough to stay out of the way. Screaming little kids are scary!) Does your balloon detect the high-pitched sounds?

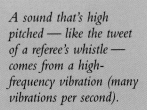

Some animals, including elephants and whales, make infrasonic sounds. These very low-pitched sounds travel for long distances, letting whales and elephants communicate with each other at great distances.

What's Going On?

Did you feel your balloon vibrating when a truck (or the low-pitched noise source of your choice) rumbled by? Your ears and the balloon both picked up the rumble of the truck — but the balloon also picked up vibrations that were too low for your ears to detect. These vibrations are called *infrasonic* sounds. (If you check your dictionary, you'll find out that *infra* means "below" and *sonic* means "sound.")

Some sounds, such as thunder and the rumble of a truck, are made up of infrasonic and non-infrasonic levels, meaning you can hear some but not all of the sound. However, even when you can't hear infrasonic sounds, you can *feel* them.

By the way, there's a word that comes in handy when you are talking scientifically about sound. That word is *frequency*, which means the number of times something happens in a certain period of time. When you're talking about sound, frequency means the number of vibrations that happen in a second. The higher the number of vibrations, the higher the frequency and the higher the pitch.

The sounds made by those shrieking little kids had frequencies up to 3,000 vibrations per second. The rumble of a bus contains sounds with frequencies as low as 40 vibrations per second. (To find out more about what frequencies you can hear, turn to page 28.)

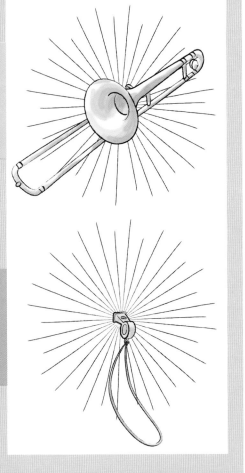

A sound that's low pitched — like a low note from a trombone — comes from a low-frequency vibration (fewer vibrations per second).

A sound that's high pitched — like the tweet of a referee's whistle — comes from a high-frequency vibration (many vibrations per second).

Frozen Vibrations

Turn on your TV! The sound vibrations are on!

Here's What You Need

✔ An assortment of rubber bands

✔ A television set

Here's What You Do

1. Choose a wide rubber band. Stretch it and pluck it. Does the rubber band vibrate as you pluck it? Can you tell anything about the direction of the vibration or is it just one big wiggle?

2. Turn on your TV and tune it to a channel where there's nothing but snow or a blue screen. Turn off the lights in the TV room.

3. Stretch your rubber band *vertically* in front of the TV screen, as in the picture above right.

4. Hold the rubber band just a few inches from the TV screen and pluck it. Do you see a series of wiggles appear on the band as you pluck? Are they moving up or down the rubber band?

5. Pluck the band again and see if you can count how many wiggles appear.

6. Sometimes counting is difficult. Look at the picture to the right. We would say that the wiggling rubber band on the left has one wiggle in it. It wiggles to the right and then to the left and ends up back where it started for one complete wiggle. We would say the rubber band on the right has two wiggles — because it includes two complete versions of one wiggle.

7. If you're having trouble, don't pull the rubber band as tight. (A looser rubber band will have fewer wiggles — making it easier to count. Make sure the rubber band is held vertically (up and down) and not horizontally (sideways). To see the waves, look at the rubber band, not the TV screen. The screen just helps you see the movement of the rubber band.

8. Experiment with different tensions (adjust the tightness or looseness), lengths, and thicknesses of rubber bands to find the best effects.

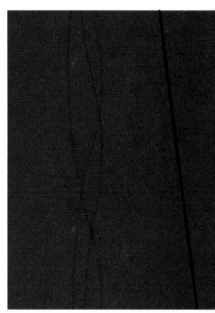

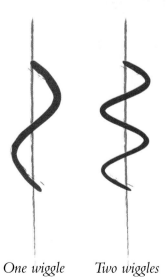

One wiggle   *Two wiggles*

You can use your TV to figure out about how fast your rubber band is vibrating. First, stretch the rubber band so that it reaches from the top of your TV screen to the bottom. Then pluck the rubber band and count the number of wiggles you see. If you multiply this number by 60 flashes per second, you get the approximate frequency of the sound produced by the vibrating rubber band. What happens to the wiggles if you pull the rubber band tighter?

What's Going On?

When you pluck the rubber band with the room lights on, you'll see a blur. The rubber band's vibrations are too fast for your eyes to see. But when you hold the rubber band vertically in front of the TV screen and pluck it, you see waves as the rubber band moves back and forth.

The light of the TV screen seems to slow down the movement of the rubber band. That's because the light from the TV screen isn't a steady light. A moving spot of light paints the picture on the TV screen, so the light on each part of the screen comes and goes. The dot is moving so fast that you don't even see it moving! Your eyes and brain blend together all the places that the dot has been, and you see a picture on the screen.

The light from this moving spot lights up different parts of the vibrating rubber band at different times. When the light is shining on the band, you see it; when the light is off, you don't.

As the light from the TV moves from the top of the screen to the bottom, it captures the rubber band at different points in its movement.

It takes the spot of light that paints the TV picture about $1/60$ second to travel from the top of the screen to the bottom. If the rubber band moves back and forth once in this time, you'll see one complete wiggle in the rubber band. If the rubber band moves back and forth twice, you'll see two complete wiggles.

*Wiggle a pencil back and forth
in front of your TV screen.
How many pencils do you see?*

Sorting Sounds

Some people say that you can hear the roar of the ocean by putting a seashell to your ear. You can hear a similar sound in a paper cup or an empty tin can!

The air around you is filled with sounds. The seashell (or paper cup or tin can) sorts some of these sounds out of the hum of background sound.

Sounds of a Bottle

Here's your chance to make some beautiful music.

Here's What You Need

✔ 4 or more identical glass bottles. (If you want to make a musical scale, you'll need 8 bottles — one for each note.)

✔ Water

✔ Something to tap the bottles with — maybe a pencil, a ruler, or a chopstick

Here's What You Do

1. Leave one bottle empty. Fill each of the other bottles with a different amount of water.

2. Tap on the empty bottle. What does it sound like?

3. Tap on the bottle with the smallest amount of water in it. Is the sound higher or lower than the sound you heard when you tapped the empty bottle?

4. Before you tap on the next bottle, think about what you expect to hear. Will the sound be higher or lower? (You're making what scientists call a *prediction* — you're guessing what will happen.)

5. Tap the bottle and see if your prediction was right.

6. Tap on the other bottles and compare the sounds they make. Does more water in a bottle make the sound higher or lower?

7. Arrange your bottles from the one that makes the lowest-pitched sound to the one that makes the highest-pitched.

8. Now you're going to change the way you play your bottle instruments. Instead of tapping, blow across the mouth of each bottle to make a hooting sound.

9. Start by blowing across the top of the empty bottle. If you don't get a sound, experiment until you do. Try blowing harder. Try changing the angle at

which you're blowing. Ask a grown-up for help. If all else fails, put some water in the bottle. (It's easier to get a sound from a bottle containing water.)

10. What do you think will happen when you compare different bottles? Which bottle do you think will make the lowest note? Which one will make the highest note?

11. Blow across the mouth of each bottle and listen to the sound.

12. Arrange the bottles from lowest pitch to highest pitch.

Tools for Exploration

Experimenting to test your ideas

Suppose you wanted to arrange your bottles to make a musical scale, like the scale you get when you sing *do re me fa so la ti do.* How would you change the water levels to make the right notes? Try it and see.

What's Going On?

When you tap on a bottle with a pencil, the bottle vibrates and makes a sound. The pitch of that sound (how high or low it is) depends on the frequency of the vibration — the number of times the bottle vibrates in a second.

When you put water in a bottle and tap on it, the bottle and the water vibrate together. With water in the bottle, you have to get more stuff vibrating — the bottle *and* the water. Because there's more stuff to vibrate, it vibrates more slowly and makes a sound with a lower frequency. Bottles with more water make a sound with a lower pitch.

When you blow across the mouth of a bottle, the bottle and water don't vibrate. Instead, the air inside the bottle vibrates, just like the air in your mouth vibrates when you whistle. The more water there is in the bottle, the less air there is. When there's less air, the bottle makes a sound with a higher pitch.

This set of porcelain bowls is an Indian musical instrument known as jaltarang. *When filled with water and tapped with bamboo sticks, the bowls play a scale.*

Whistle a high note. Now whistle a low note. What do you do differently when you whistle (or try to whistle) the low note? Chances are you make the space inside your mouth bigger by changing the position of your tongue or dropping your jaw.

When you whistle, the air rushing past your lips vibrates, making a sound that contains many different frequencies. (See page 342 if you don't know what we mean by frequency.) When this complex whistling

sound echoes off the inside of your mouth, some frequencies add together and get louder. The addition of many sound vibrations of a particular frequency to make a louder sound is called resonance. *The size of the empty space inside your mouth helps determine which frequencies get louder. By changing the size of that space, you make one sound in the mixture of sounds louder. That's resonance at work.*

How Sound Travels

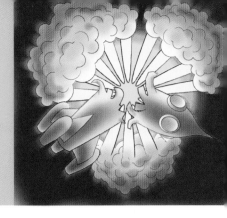

Every sound begins with a vibration that makes a sound wave. Sound waves travel through air. If there's no air, there are no sound waves. That's why scientists snicker in science fiction movies when spaceships explode with a noisy Boom! In outer space, there is no air — and that means no sound!

You can't see a sound wave. But you can use a Slinky to make a wave that's a lot like a sound wave. Hold one end of the Slinky and have a friend hold the other end. Pull the Slinky toward you and then push it away. When you do this, you squash some of the Slinky coils together and then pull them apart. Those squashed-together coils bump into other coils, causing the place where the coils are squashed together seem to move down the Slinky to your friend and then bounce back to you. That place where the coils are squashed together is a compression wave. It's called a compression wave because the coils are compressed, or squashed together.

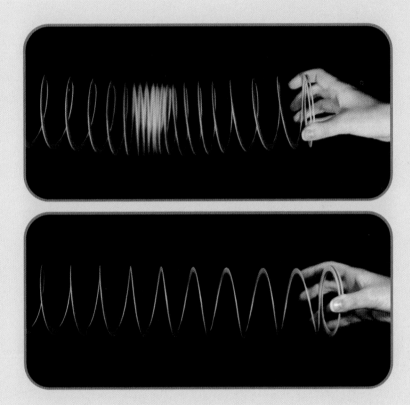

When you push and pull on your Slinky, you are like a vibrating object pushing and pulling on the nearby air. The compression wave that travels down the Slinky is like a sound wave traveling through the air. In a sound wave, the air itself is squeezed together.

Let's Play Telephone!

If you've always wanted a phone of your own, here's your chance. Only with this phone, you'll have the added opportunity to experiment and predict.

Here's What You Need

✔ Two paper cups

✔ Two paper clips

✔ String

✔ A friend to talk to

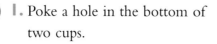

Here's What You Do

1. Poke a hole in the bottom of two cups.

2. Pull the string through the bottom of each cup.

3. Tie a paper clip onto the end of the string in each cup to prevent the string from falling out.

4. Hold one cup up to your ear and give the other cup to your friend.

5. Have your friend walk away from you until the string is tight.

6. Have your friend hold his cup up to his ear. Now you've got a telephone!

7. Take turns plucking the string while listening through the cup.

Is the sound you hear when you pluck the string different from when your friend plucks it? How does the sound change when you pull the string tighter? How does it change if you pinch the string?

8. Have your friend listen with the cup to his ear while you talk to him. Can you hear what he's saying?

9. Experiment with other types of cups: insulated foam, plastic, and waxed paper. Try tin cans and juice cans (big cans or little cans).

10. Now experiment with different kinds of string, using whatever cup or can you liked best. You can try kite string, metal wire, fishing line, skinny string, and fat string. (When experimenting, always make only one change at a time. In this case, because you are testing string, you would keep the cup the same and change the string.) Compare how different kinds of string affect the sound you hear.

Cup	String	Result
Paper cup	Kite string	Okay
Tin can	Kite string	Better or worse?
Foam cup	Kite string	Better or worse?

What's Going On?

Suppose you say "Hello!" into your cup. The vibration of the word "hello" starts the air vibrating in your cup. That vibrating air starts the cup vibrating and the cup starts the string vibrating. The vibrations travel through the string and into your friend's cup.

The string starts your friend's cup vibrating which stirs up the air inside his cup. The cup helps direct the vibrating air into his ear. He'll hear "Hello" as soon as his ear transmits the vibration to his brain. It seems instantaneous, but it's not — it's just that your ear and your brain are a very speedy team.

This process works best if the string can vibrate freely. If you pinch the string or if it's too loose, the sound vibrations will die out before reaching the other end.

Ask Professor Exploratorium

Dear Professor E:
Why do ambulance sirens sound so weird? I think they're really annoying!

Signed,
Fingers in My Ears.

Dear Fingers in My Ears:
Next time an ambulance or a fire engine whizzes past you with its sirens screaming, don't put your fingers in your ears. Listen carefully to the siren. Did you ever notice that the sound changes when the vehicle passes you? The pitch drops from higher to lower.

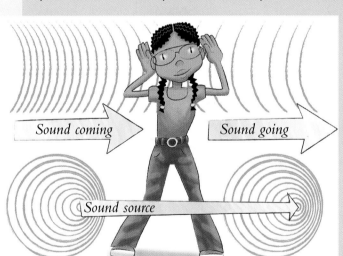

Sound coming

Sound going

Sound source

As that siren approached you, the sound waves hit your eardrums more frequently than they would have if the ambulance were standing still. The more frequent the sound waves, the higher the frequency and the higher the sound's pitch. After the ambulance rushed past you, the siren was moving away from you and the sound waves hit your eardrum less frequently. The lower the frequency, the lower the pitch.

This change in pitch is called the *Doppler effect*. The Doppler effect was named for Austrian scientist Christian Doppler. Doppler discovered it as he was studying sound waves. (That's a really neat thing about being a scientist — if you make a discovery, they sometimes name it after you!) In 1842, Doppler hired the trumpet section of the Vienna orchestra and rented a freight train. He had half the trumpet players stand on a flat car and half stay in the station. Both groups played the same note as the train traveled through the station. A musician in the station noted that the pitch of the trumpets on the train was different from that of the trumpets in the station.

The Doppler effect of the piercing sound of a siren is not meant to annoy you, but get your attention.

Your attention-grabbing friend,
Professor E

Talk to a Wok

Capture the sound of your beautiful voice by talking and singing to a wok.

Here's What You Need

✔ A large wok (if you don't have one, try using a big, shiny, metal bowl, or a deep, curved frying pan, or even a soup pan — just raid the kitchen and see what you can come up with)

Here's What You Do

1. Hold the wok in front of you at arm's length.

2. Slowly bring it toward you as you speak or sing into it.

3. Experiment with the distance between you and the wok to get the best sound.

4. At one point, do you suddenly hear your voice get louder? Great! That's your *reflecting point*.

5. Hold the wok at your reflecting point and sing away. (Who needs a microphone when you have a wok?)

What's Going On?

A moving sound wave spreads out in all directions. It will get weaker and weaker as it moves farther and farther away from the original sound source. At least, that's what happens if nothing gets in the way.

In this experiment, the wok acts like a mirror for the sound waves. The curved bowl of the wok reflects sound waves back at your head. Your voice got louder at the exact point where it was reflected back to you by the inside of the wok.

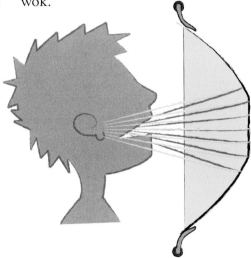

Tools for Exploration

Comparing two things

You've been talking to the bowl of the wok. Turn the wok around and try talking to the back of the wok. How does this change what you hear? (If you want to know more, see page 367.)

Speed of Sound

It takes time for a sound to get from one place to another. In a thunderstorm, you see lightning, then hear the thunder a few seconds later. To find out how far away the lightning struck, count the seconds between the flash and the thunder and multiply by 350 meters (about 1,000 feet).

As Sound Travels

It takes time for sound to travel from place to place. You're about to prove it!

Here's What You Need

✔ A noisemaking device (a big bell, hammer and pipe, a trumpet or other musical instrument, a well-trained dog that will bark on command — we know you have something noisy you can use)

✔ A quiet friend (someone who won't interfere with your other noisemaking device)

✔ A pair of walkie-talkies

✔ A large, quiet, open space (a park, hiking or bike path, empty parking lot, school yard)

Here's What You Do

1. Take your walkie-talkie and noisemaking device in hand.

2. Turn on both walkie-talkies. Take one and give one to your friend.

3. You and your friend walk away from each other. Go as far as you can without getting out of sight and out of hearing range. As you move away from your friend, you might want to shout every now and then to make sure he can still hear you.

4. Talk on your walkie-talkies when you're ready to start your noise.

5. You be the transmitter. Click and hold the transmit button on the walkie-talkie. Then make one loud noise with your noisemaking device. (We had Nick the Dog bark once into our walkie-talkie.)

6. Did your friend hear the one noise twice? Once over the walkie-talkie followed by once through the air? Isn't that the coolest?

At the Exploratorium we used a fine noisemaking device to measure the speed of sound: Nick the Dog! Nick, a sleek black labrador retriever, "speaks" on command. His bark provided a loud, crisp noise just perfect for this experiment. Good boy, Nick! Here's your treat!

7. Switch roles. Let your friend be the transmitter. Did you hear the sound both over the walkie-talkie and through the air?

What's Going On?

The receiver (your friend) should hear the noise twice, once immediately over the walkie-talkie and then again in the air as it travels toward him. If you're having trouble hearing the separate sounds, move farther away from your friend. Or try another noise, a louder one this time. Or you might need a different noise — one that starts and ends abruptly. Make one change at a time so you know what makes the difference. Don't give up too soon! Keep trying different possibilities until you succeed. Hearing the same sound twice is just too cool to pass up.

Why do you hear the sound twice? The walkie-talkie transmits the sound at the speed of light, and light is the fastest thing around. So you hear the sound through the walkie-talkie right away. It takes the sound longer to travel through the air to reach you.

Oh, and just in case you were wondering if you could use a cell phone rather than a walkie-talkie — forget about it! A cell phone takes too long to transmit the sound. Use a walkie-talkie for this experiment. You can always call your friends later.

Timing Your Sound

Using a stopwatch, walkie-talkies, and a starter pistol, Eric Muller, a teacher at the Exploratorium, has his physics classes measure the speed of sound.

Eric stands about 150 meters (that's about 490 feet) away from his class with a walkie-talkie and a starter pistol. The class has a walkie-talkie and a stopwatch. Eric clicks the transmit button on his walkie-talkie, and then fires the pistol.

The class has a stopwatch ready and the walkie-talkie on. When they hear the *BANG!* over the walkie-talkie, they immediately start the stopwatch. When they hear the *BANG!* through the air, they stop the stopwatch, recording the time between the two sounds. It all happens fast, but the class can usually measure a difference between the arrival time of the sound through the walkie-talkie and the arrival of the sound through the air.

The walkie-talkie transmits the sound at the speed of light. In empty space, light travels at about 300,000 kilometers per second. So it takes the sound about 500 millionths of a second to travel from the pistol to the class via walkie-talkie. That's so fast that it seems like no time at all!

Traveling through the air, it takes the sound about half a second to reach the class.

To figure out the speed something is traveling, you divide the distance traveled by the time it took to travel that distance. If it takes a car an hour to drive 60 miles, you would divide the distance (60 miles) by the time (1 hour), like this:

$$\text{speed} = \frac{60 \text{ miles}}{1 \text{ hour}} = 60 \text{ miles per hour}$$

So to calculate the speed of sound, the class divides the distance (150 meters) by the time (0.5 seconds), like this:

$$\frac{150 \text{ meters}}{0.5 \text{ seconds}} = 300 \text{ meters per second}$$

According to the measurements of other scientists, the speed of sound is 340 meters per second when the air temperature is 20 degrees Celsius. So a measurement of 300 meters per second isn't too bad!

You can measure the speed of sound at home using Eric's method, but you'll need something that makes a sound loud enough to be heard from a distance and sharp enough to make one quick sound.

To learn more about sound, visit Exploratopia *online at* www.exploratopia.com.

Hints, Tips, & Answers

Chapter 5 Your Brain

That Messy Brain (page 73)

The names of the states, in alphabetical order, are:

Alabama	Indiana	Nebraska	South Carolina
Alaska	Iowa	Nevada	South Dakota
Arizona	Kansas	New Hampshire	Tennessee
Arkansas	Kentucky	New Jersey	Texas
California	Louisiana	New Mexico	Utah
Colorado	Maine	New York	Vermont
Connecticut	Maryland	North Carolina	Virginia
Delaware	Massachusetts	North Dakota	Washington
Florida	Michigan	Ohio	West Virginia
Georgia	Minnesota	Oklahoma	Wisconsin
Hawaii	Mississippi	Oregon	Wyoming
Idaho	Missouri	Pennsylvania	
Illinois	Montana	Rhode Island	

Improve Your Memory — Part One — My Memory With No Help (page 74)

Improve Your Memory — Part One — My Memory With a Story (page 74)

Improve Your Memory — Part Two (page 75)

Crossing the River (page 78)

First, you take the chicken to the other side. Then you go back for the dog. You leave the dog on the far side of the river and take the chicken back with you. You leave the chicken on the first side of the river and take the grain over. Then, you go back and get the chicken. Most people assume that once they start taking things across the river, they can't bring anything back.

Stick Squares (page 79)

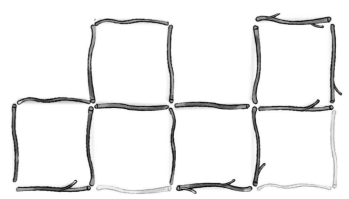

The Ping-Pong Contest (page 79)

For a tournament with three players, you need two scorecards. For a tournament with five players, you need four scorecards. For a tournament with 205 players, you'll need 204 scoreboards. To find the number of scorecards you need, just subtract one from the number of players in the tournament. Everyone in the tournament will lose one game — except the winner!

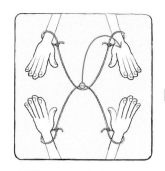

Sacks of Gold (page 80)

Divide the sacks into three groups of four each. Put four sacks on each side of the balance. If the two groups are equal, you know that the odd sack must be in the group that's not on the balance. But you still don't know if the odd sack is heavier or lighter than the others. To find out, remove one of your groups of four "standard" sacks and replace it with the group that contains the odd sack. If the group with the odd sack is heavier than the standard group, you know the odd sack is heavier than the standard sack. If the group with the odd sack is lighter, so is the odd sack.

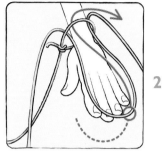

But wait — what if you compare two groups of sacks and find out that they are not equal. What then?

First, note which group is heavier. Remove that group and replace it with the third group. If these two groups are equal, you know that the group you removed was the group with the odd sack — and you know that the odd sack is heavier than the standard sack. If the new group is heavier, you know that the group on the other side of the balance contains the odd sack, and you know the odd sack is lighter than the standard sack.

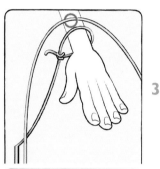

Now, set all your standard sacks aside, and weigh two sacks from the odd group against the other two sacks from the odd group. One pair will be heavier than the other.

You know from your earlier experiments whether the odd sack is heavier or lighter than the others. Therefore, you know which pair of sacks contains the odd sack.

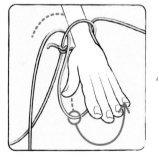

Now you can put one sack from this pair on each side of the balance. Since you know whether the odd sack is lighter or heavier than a standard sack, you can identify the odd sack.

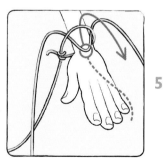

Tangled Up with a Friend (page 81)

To get loose, you need to put your friend's hand through the loop without the rest of his body coming along. Slide the string that joins your wrists up through the loop of string that's tied around your friend's wrist (shown in Picture 2). Put your friend's hand through the loop. Be sure you're going in the right direction (shown in Pictures 3 and 4). Pull the loop out (shown in Picture 5).

We warned you — this is tricky even after you know the answer.

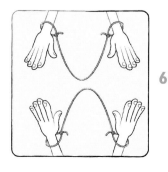

Chapter 7 The Bathroom

Alphabet Flip (page 105)

The nine letters that are horizontally symmetrical are B, C, D, E, H, I, K, O, and X.

The eleven letters that are vertically symmetrical are A, H, I, M, O, T, U, V, W, X, and Y.

Chapter 10 The Amusement Park

Make Your Own Roller Coaster (page 156)

Tools for Exploration

Here's how we figured out the speed of our marble.

Our foam track came in pre-measured lengths. So we figured out the length of our roller coaster track by adding up the lengths that we used.

Then we used a stopwatch to time how long it took for a marble to roll from the beginning of our track all the way to the end.

Finally, we divided the length of the track in feet by the marble's time in seconds. That gave us the average speed of the marble in feet per second. Sometimes the marble went faster and sometimes it went slower, but this measurement gave us the average speed.

Waiting in Line (page 165)

Tools for Exploration

Here's how you can figure out how fast the train is going at different points. First, guess how big each car is and count the number of cars in the train. (You can use the size of the people in the car to help you estimate the length of the car. For more on estimating, see page 224.) Multiply the number of cars by the length of each car and you have a good idea of the length of the train.

Now choose a spot on the track to focus on, like the top of a hill or the bottom of a hill. Use your watch to time how long it takes the train to pass that point.

Divide the length of the train by the time and you'll get the train's speed, or *velocity*. Velocity equals distance divided by time. (Miles per hour is one way of measuring velocity. Feet per second is another way.) This way of estimating the train's velocity lets you compare the speed of the train at different points. Even if your estimate of the train's length is off, your time measurement will still tell you where the train is going the fastest.

Riding the Roller Coaster (page 166)

Tools for Exploration

Try riding in front of the roller coaster train, in the middle, and at the back of the train.

Each position will feel a little different. That's because the speed you are moving at the top of a hill or the bottom of a valley depends partly on where you are in the train.

Think about the speeds of the different cars at the top of a hill. The first car goes over the top and the rest of the train follows. After the middle of the train passes over the top of the hill, the train starts picking up speed. By the time the last car whips over the top, the train is going much faster, and the riders in that last car feel like they are about to be launched into orbit.

Now think about the speeds of different cars at the bottom of a hill. When the middle of the train reaches the bottom, the train is going as fast as it's going to go. The train has started to climb the next hill and slow down. So the riders in the first half of the train feel squashed harder into their seats than the riders in the back car.

Chapter 12 Language

Now I Know My ZYXs (page 195)
When you decode the message, it says: THIS IS IN CODE! But you already knew that!

Alien Alphabet (page 197)
Decoded, this message says: MEET ME AFTER SCHOOL BEHIND THE GYM.

∧□□⊓ ∧□ ⌐⊏⁊□□ ⊑⌐∪∪∪<
∪□⊓⌐⌐⊐ ⊓⁊□□ ⁊<∧

Crack the Code! (page 198)
The answer to the riddle is: A pickle in a tuxedo. The secret letter for this substitution cipher is *K*.

The interesting fact is: Your fingernails grow faster in the summer than in the winter. The secret letter for this substitution cipher is *J*.

What Do You Call It? (page 201)
Here's what people at the Exploratorium call these objects (clockwise from top left).

Soda or pop
Thongs or flip-flops
Submarine (sandwich) or poor boy
Seesaw or teeter-totter
Sofa or couch or davenport or chesterfield
Pancakes or hotcakes or flapjacks
Sneakers or tennis shoes

Zap! Yeow! (page 202)

1. BTAM! The Incredible Hulk hits a supervillain who slams into a rock wall.

2. BYANNG! Captain America hits villain with shield.

3. FTIK! Arrow hits superhero's costume, snagging shoulder.

4. FAZZH-SHRRAK! Villain's power blast and superhero's repulsor ray collide with each other, with awesome, explosive results.

5. KZZZK! Power ray hits superhero with a sizzling roar that apparently kills him.

6. RAK TAC TAC TAC TAC! Cosmic rays hit a space ship entering a cosmic storm.

7. SHOOM! Silver Surfer's surfboard comes shooting out to him.

Chapter 13 Music

The ABCs of Rhythm (page 210)

Tools for Exploration

Measuring and counting

Did you compare the pulse of the "ABC Song" with the pulse of "Take Me Out to the Ball Game"? Maybe you noticed that the foot taps to the "ABC Song" seem to come in groups of 4 and the foot taps to "Take Me Out to the Ball Game" seem to come in groups of three. The "ABC Song" is written in what musicians call 4/4 time. That means that the song has four beats per measure. (When you look at written music, a measure is the space between the vertical lines on the five horizontal lines of the musical staff. When you are listening to music, a measure is a way of breaking up a stream of steady beats into smaller groups.) "Take Me Out to the Ball Game" is written in 3/4 time, which means that there are 3 beats per measure.

If you look at the music for the two songs, you'll see 4/4 at the beginning of the "ABC Song" and 3/4 at the beginning of "Take Me Out to the Ball Game." But you didn't need to look at the music to hear the difference. All you had to do is tap your foot in time!

Can you figure out whether "Bicycle Built for Two" is in 3/4 time or 4/4 time? How about "Frère Jacques"?

Chapter 14 Math

How Far? (page 224)

To estimate how far the skateboarder jumped, we could have used the length of his arm or his skateboard. But we decided to use the height of the skateboarder. Then we figured out that it would take two skateboarders, laid head to foot, to fill the distance that the skateboarder jumped. If the skateboarder is 6 feet tall, then he jumped 12 feet. That's an impressive ollie!

The Oddball Game (page 227)

Here's the completed chart showing how to win at Oddball.

Pieces Left at the Start of Your Turn	Do You Win or Lose?
1 piece	You lose!
2 pieces	Take 1 to win.
3 pieces	Take 2 to win.
4 pieces	You lose!
5 pieces	Take 1 to win.
6 pieces	Take 2 to win.
7 pieces	You lose!
8 pieces	Take 1 to win.
9 pieces	Take 2 to win.
10 pieces	You lose!

Do you see a pattern? If you played the game with twelve pieces, would you want to go first or second?

Intermediate Madagascar Solitaire (page 230)

Here are the moves for one winning game of Intermediate Madagascar Solitaire. Can you find others?

Marker moved		New position	
Column	Row	Column	Row
4	1	REMOVED	
2	1	4	1
2	3	2	1
4	3	2	3
4	2	2	2
1	1	3	1
4	1	2	1
1	3	1	1
1	1	3	1
2	3	2	1
3	1	1	1

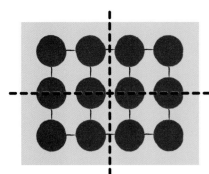

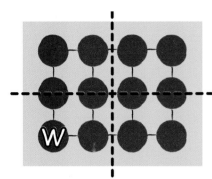

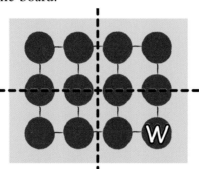

The dashed lines show the lines of symmetry on the Intermediate Madagascar Solitaire game board. If you were to fold the game board on a line of symmetry, the circles on one side would match up with the circles on the other side.

There's a vertical line of symmetry. The left half of the board matches the right half.

There's also a horizontal line of symmetry. (That line may have been harder for you to spot because it cuts across the middle of the circles in the second row.) The top half of the board perfectly matches the bottom half of the board.

The lines of symmetry can help you play a winning game on the Intermediate Madagascar Solitaire game board. The *W* on one board marks a winning first move, and the *W* on the other board marks the mirror image of that move. You can win a game if you start by removing the marker on either of the circles marked with a W. Can you find another mirror image of this move?

Mind Reader (page 233)

We gave you a simple explanation of the Mind Reader trick on page 234. Here's a more mathematical explanation for those of you who are more mathematically inclined.

To see what's going on, let's go through the steps of the trick one at a time. Because it doesn't matter what number your friend chooses, we're going to represent that number with a square like this ■. This ■ could be any number from one to nine.

First you told your friend to double his number. That means he multiplies his number by 2, like this:

2 × ■

Next you told your friend to add 2, which gives you this:

(2 × ■) + 2

Then you told your friend to multiply by 5, so you get this:

([2 × ■] + 2) × 5

That may look pretty complicated, but you can make it look simpler. What you are really doing is adding two numbers — (2 × ■) and 2 — and then multiplying the result by 5. That's the same as multiplying each number by 5 and then adding them together. That means that this:

([2 × ■] + 2) × 5

is the same as this: ([2 × ■] × 5) + (2 × 5)

is the same as this: (10 × ■) + 10

By doing all that math, your friend multiplied his number by 10 and then added 10 to the answer. So if his number was 3, he now has:

(10 × 3) + 10 = 40

You don't need to know what number he gets — as long as you know that it's 10 times his original number plus 10. Then you need to have him subtract enough to make the 10 that you had him add on equal the number on the card you chose.

Let's say your number was 8. You want him to get to 38. How do you do that? Well, you subtract your number from 10. So if your number was 8, you subtracted your number from 10 and got 2. Then you asked your friend to subtract 2 from his number.

His number was 40.

40 - 2 = 38

Voila! Your friend ends up thinking of 38. You turn over the cards and there's the answer: a 3 and an 8. Magic! (Or maybe a little bit of math.)

Chapter 15 Money

Getting to Know a Dollar Bill (page 240)

Did you find all six numbers? If you missed a few, check out the picture on page 242. The numbers you were looking for are:

1. Federal Reserve Number

2. Check Letter and Quadrant Number

3. Serial Number

4. Series Number

5. Face Plate Number

6. Back Plate Number

Together, these numbers tell you a lot about your particular dollar bill.

Build a One-Buck Bridge (page 246)

This is how we built a one-buck bridge. We folded the dollar bill back and forth to make pleats. All these folds make the dollar bill stiff — and strong enough to hold up a glass! Did you come up with the same answer, or did you build a different one-buck bridge?

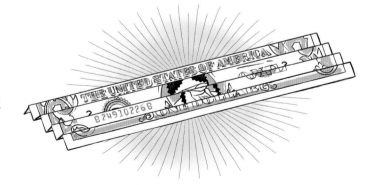

Number of folds	Number of layers of newspaper
0	1
1	2
2	4
3	8
4	16
5	32
6	64
7	128
8	256
9	512
10	1,024

Chapter 16 Paper

Exponential Folding (page 265)

The chart at left shows how many layers of newspaper you have after folding.

Fifteen-Ring Lei (page 268)

Are you ready to check your answer against ours? We figured out that the only way to make chains of five different lengths was to make the following five chains:

A chain of five links

A chain of four links

A chain of three links

A chain of two links

A chain of one link

Then we started by cutting a link. We left that link as a strip of paper, and then counted out a chain of five links. We cut the sixth link, which left us with a chain of five links, a chain of eight links and two strips of paper.

Starting at the end of the chain of eight links, we counted out a chain of four links. Then we cut the fifth link, which left us with a chain of four links, a chain of three links, the original chain of five links, and three strips of paper.

We taped the strips to make a chain of two links and a chain of one link. And we're done! Did you come up with a different way to do it?

Walk Through Paper (page 271)

This is the folded side.

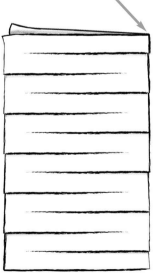

First, fold your paper in half. Put the paper down in front of you with the fold side toward you. Place your scissors about 1 inch in from the edge of the paper. Now cut the paper, stopping about 1 inch from the non-folded side. (Do not cut all the way up!). Then, turn the paper around so the fold is facing away from you. Make a cut $1/2$ inch away from your last cut. Again, cut up, stopping about 1 inch from the folded side. Turn the paper around again so the fold is toward you. Move over $1/2$ inch and cut, stopping about 1 inch from the top. Turn the paper around, cut again $1/2$ inch away from the last cut and stop short of the top. Repeat the pattern of turning, cutting, and stopping. Keep doing this until you reach the other side of the paper. Your paper will look something like the picture at left. You will see you have a folded piece of paper with alternating strips.

There's one last cut to make. Cut through the fold in the middle — just the middle portion, not the two strips on either end. We repeat: Do not cut through the fold on the two outer strips!

Shake your paper out and see what you've got.

You have replaced your original sheet of paper with a big paper circle — big enough to walk through.

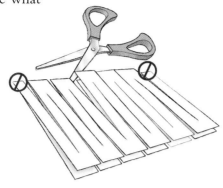

Chapter 17 Optical Illusions

Want to Buy a Rock? (page 274)

We asked you to choose which rock you wanted to carry away. Are you surprised at the size of the rock you chose?

Chapter 18 Light

Looking Through Lenses (page 290)

Tools for Exploration

Here's what we did to figure out how much bigger the lines looked through the magnifying glass. We used a ruler to measure the space between the lines viewed through the magnifying glass. Then we measured the space between the lines without the magnifying glass. When we compared the two numbers, we discovered that the distance between the lines viewed through the magnifying glass was four times the distance between the lines without the magnifying glass. So the magnifying glass is making the lines look four times bigger.

Chapter 20 Electricity & Magnetism

Floating Magnets (page 324)

To make the magnets float, you need to arrange them so that similar poles of the magnets are facing each other. To learn about magnetic poles, try the "Magnetic Poles" experiment on page 321.

If you try to push two magnets on this stack together, they'll push apart, and it will feel like there's an invisible magnetic spring between the two magnets. Similar poles push each other away or repel each other. This keeps the magnets apart.

Complete Circuit (page 330)

At left is one way to make your flashlight bulb light up.

Chapter 21 Exploring Sound

Talk to a Wok (page 350)

Tools for Exploration

Did you try talking to the back of your wok? What did you notice about the sound?

When the bowl of the wok is facing you, the curve of the bowl reflects sound waves back at your head. The bowl of the wok focuses the sound. But when you turned the wok around, the waves bounced off the bottom and spread out in all directions.

Contributors

Written by Pat Murphy, Ellen Macaulay, and the staff of the Exploratorium

Jason Gorski, illustrator
Amy Snyder, photographer
Lily Rodriguez, photographer
Paul Doherty, science advisor
Laura Jacoby, photo wrangler
Melissa Thomas, editorial assistant

Acknowledgments

At the Exploratorium, no one works alone. Whether we are sharing the work side by side or building upon what others before us have created, we are privileged to exist in a great community of people who love science and who enjoy sharing their knowledge and skills. *Exploratopia* would not have been possible without the help of individuals both inside and outside the museum, and we gratefully acknowledge their contributions.

Among those who helped us bring the Exploratopia concept into reality were our editor, the ever-pleasant and patient Amy Hsu; our literary agent, Chris Tomasino; our budget guru, Kurt Feichtmeir; our unflappable graphics advisor, Gary Crounse; our hard-working copyeditor, Kerry Johnson; and our amazing designers, Jackie and Billy Kelly at YAY! Design. Thanks also to Colin, Elyse, Kirsten, and Greg Macaulay, who managed to survive without Ellen while she was deep in manuscript pages, and to Dave Wright, recipient of many phone calls from Pat saying she would be "just a little bit late" getting home. And a special thank-you goes to Thomas Carlson, who coined the one word that we felt perfectly described our book-to-be: Exploratopia.

Activities were developed and refined by staff throughout the Exploratorium, but we would specifically like to thank Vivian Altmann of the Children's Educational Outreach, Ken Finn of the Summer Camp Program, Fred Stein of the Institute for Inquiry, the folks in our Field Trip program, and everyone in the Teacher Institute.

Another book could be written about the countless ways in which many others helped to smooth the long and rocky path to publication, doing everything from authoring articles that inspired us to explaining the intricacies of pixels and dots per inch. We thank all you wonderful folks: Larry Antila, Angela Armendariz, David Barker, Maurice Bazin, Jamie Bell, Tory Brady, Iris Brooks, Ruth Brown, Diane Burk, Meg Bury, Charles Carlson, Sitara Cave, Micah Garb, Anne Gardiner, Susan Gordon, Amy Hacker, Ron Hipschman, Brenda Hutchinson, Anne Akers Johnson, Karen Kalumuck, Walter Kanat, Ellen Klages, Klutz Press, Lori Lambertson, Peggy Law, Ellen Lieber, Alisa Lowden, Karen Mendelow, Mary Miller, Eric Muller, Mark Nichol, Pauline Oliveros, Deborah O. Raphael, Don Rathjen, Lowell Robinson, Barbra Rodriguez, R. Murray Schafer, Susan Schwartzenberg, Linda Shore, Paul Stephahin, Modesto Tamez, Norman Ten, Pearl Tesler, Jeffrey T. Toy, Noah Wittman, John Wilkes, Sue Wilson, Barbara Ziegenhals, and everyone at the Exploratorium.

We would also like to acknowledge others—both human and not—who held meringue over their heads, painted their tongues blue, donned the dreaded money glasses, or simply stood still for our photographers: Cameron BaSaing, Ashish Bohringer,

Savannah Burke, Maria Cardosa, Ralph Carney, Seraphina Cobeen, Dooney Duckworth, Richard Elmore, Malcolm Fooks, Erica Gersowitz, Steve Gingrich, Rebecca Hertz, Katie Hillenga, Eva Ho, Mary Ellen Hunt, Chiare Hwang, Rachel Jackson, Sadie Jacoby, Amy Johnson, Bernie Jungle, Janet Lam, Poppy Lambertson, Tyler Langenbrunner, Alina Larson, Dora Lee, Laura Likhmer, Maya Loutfi, Greg Macaulay, Emaline Mann-Sanchez, Cory McCroy, Maya Monico-Klein Minnick, Michael Mohammed, Nick Muller, Ruben Negrete, Tom Noddy, Andres Ocampo, Sebastian Ocampo, Trevor Paine, Bobby Pore, Robert Pritikin, Ben Rayikanti, Taffy Reighley, Sarah Reiwitch, Adriana Sanchez, Spencer Snook, Amy Snyder, Daphne Snyder, Jarod Sport, Ping Theberge, Melissa Thomas, Roger Upton, Adrian Van Allen, Elena C. Wagoner, Greg Ward, Charlie Wilkes, Edward O. Wilson, Nancy Wilson, Benjamin Zheng.

Last, but far from least, we thank Goéry Delacôte and Rob Semper for providing the institutional support necessary to transform a vision into a reality.

Credits

Illustration Credits

Unless otherwise noted, all illustrations are by Jason Gorski. (Position code: t = top, b = bottom, l = left, r = right, c = center)

25, 28: Melissa Thomas; **50**: Courtesy of San Francisco Zoo; **53**: David Barker; **73tr**: Gary Crounse/Alisa Lowden; **190**: Copyright © 1983 Exploratorium; **192tl**: Gary Crounse; **197**: Randy Comer; **202**: X-MEN TM and copyright © 2004 Marvel Characters, Inc. Used with permission. **209**: Marine Corps logo courtesy of www.edwards.af.mil/archive; **227tr**: Gary Crounse; **247**: Dollar bill ring based on Dollar Bill Ring from *The Buck Book*, by Anne Akers Johnson. Reprinted with permission. Copyright © 1993 Klutz; **279**: Exploratorium staff; **280c**: Copyright © Exploratorium, illusion discovered by Dr. Richard Gregory; **281b**: "Pintos," Copyright © 2005 Bev Doolittle; **282**: (saxophone/woman) "Sara Nader/Serenader," illustration from *Mind Sights* by Roger Shepard ©1990 by Roger Shepard. Reprinted by permission of Henry Holt and Company, LLC; (vases/face) Gary Crounse; (rabbit/duck) Gary Crounse, based on an image by Joseph Jastrow; (man/mouse) Irvin Rock; **300, 302**: Exploratorium staff; **304**: Gary Crounse; **359c**: Randy Comer

Photography Credits

Unless otherwise noted, all photographs are by Amy Snyder. (Position code: t = top, b = bottom, l = left, r = right, c = center)

v, vi: Susan Schwartzenberg; **xi**: (eye, red eyes) Lily Rodriguez; (brain, hand shadow) Susan Schwartzenberg; (hand x-ray) courtesy of Ellen Lieber; **1, 2**: Lily Rodriguez; **4**: (gecko) Copyright © Jim Merli / Visuals Unlimited; (flour bug) Courtesy of Almut Vollmer; (moth) Paul Doherty; (crab) Courtesy of Nazeri Abghani; (human eye) Courtesy of George W. Hartwell; **5**: Animals Animals / Copyright © Michael Dick; **6**: (gecko) Copyright © Jim Merli / Visuals Unlimited; (flour bug) Courtesy of Almut Vollmer; (moth) Paul Doherty; (crab) Courtesy of Nazeri Abghani; (human eye) Courtesy of George W. Hartwell; **7b**: John Moran; **8, 10t, 13, 16cl, 18c**: Lily Rodriguez; **22**: Copyright © Exploratorium; **27**: Courtesy of the Smithsonian Institution; **31b**: Zoological Society of San Diego; **40**: Michael W. Davidson at Florida State University; **44**: Gary Crounse; **53tl**: Courtesy of Ellen Lieber; **55l**: anonymous; **55r**: United States Department of Justice, Federal Bureau of Investigation; **56, 65, 66, 68, 69**: Susan Schwartzenberg; **70tl**: Charles Carlson; **70tr, br**: Thomas Deerinck and Mark Ellisman, the National Center for Microscopy and Imaging Research, University of California at San Diego (UCSD); **71, 72**: David Barker; **77**: Pat Murphy; **83**: (Ferris wheel) Copyright © Cedar Point; (water strider) David Hu, Brian Chan, John Bush; (monarch butterfly) Larvalbug.com; (rocket launch) Courtesy of Chuck Johnson; (wave) Lily Rodriguez;

Index

laws of nature, 143, 158

lenses, 4, 11, 288, 290–299
    camera, 10, 290, 294
    concave, 292, 295
    convex, 292–297
    focal length of, 296

light; *see also* electricity, lightbulbs
    bending of, 4, 11, 135, 187, 285–299
    mirrors and, 104
    vision and, 2, 4–12
    waves of, 311–313

lightbulbs, 329–331

lighthouses, 293

lightning, 183, 319, 320, 351

limbic system, 35

linguistics, 192, 194, 203; *see also* language

loci method, 76

M

Madagascar Solitaire, 229–232

magic tricks, 233–237

magnets, 172–173, 251, 283, 320–324, 326, 332–333, 336
    poles of, 321–323, 336

magnifying glasses, *see* lenses

maglev train, 324

margin of error, 151

marine biology, 185

"Marine Corps Hymn," 208, 209

"Mary Had a Little Lamb," 221

math, 223–237, 270; *see also* exponents
    games and, 227–232
    magic and, 233–237

memory, 67, 71, 73–77
    loci method and, 76
    retrieval cues and, 74
    smells and, 35–37

meringue, 85, 88–91

meteors, 135, 283

microscopes, 40, 70, 125

mirages, 289

mirrors, 104–106, 276

Mobius, August Ferdinand, 270

Mobius band, 269–271

mold, 93, 99

molecules, 43, 101, 109, 112, 113, 309
    smell receptors and, 37, 39–40

momentum, 164

Mondegreens, 30

money, 239–253
    as medium of exchange, 253
    bills, 239–248
    coins, 73, 249–252, 279
    counterfeit, 240, 242–245, 251
    folding, 246–248

monosodium glutamate (MSG), 44

moon, 8, 131–134, 184, 277, 309

mosquitoes, 131, 135

motors, 334–337
    troubleshooting, 337

Muller, Eric, 352

mummification, 97–99

music, 23, 29, 205–221, 266, 345–346
    scale, 217

mussels, 185

"My Darling Clementine," 208

Mystery Spot, 283

N

Napier, John, 53

Navajo code talkers, 199

neon, 309, 324

neurons, 70

neutrons, 319, 326

Newton, Isaac, 160–161, 162, 163, 306, 307

Newton's laws of motion, 160–161, 162, 167

Nick the Dog, 351–352

noses, 33–40
    animals and, 38
    pheromones and, 38, 121
    smell receptors in, 37, 39–40
    taste and, 39–40

nudibranchs, 185

O

oceans, 177–179, 180, 182, 184, 185

Oddball, 227–228

Oersted, Hans Christian, 333

onomatopoeia, 27, 202–203

owls, 6

oxygen, 87, 109, 127, 173, 252

P

palindromes, 106

paper, 255–271
    building with, 255, 263–264
    folding, 265–266
    handmade, 256–262

parrot fish, 116

Paulsrud, Pamela, 256

pendulum, 137

peripheral vision, 13

periwinkles, 174, 185

pheromones, 38, 121

phosphors, 329

Pig Latin, 199–200

pigments, 309, 314–315, 317

pillbugs, 126

pipes, 216, 220–221

plants, 127–130, 185, 262

pollen, 128, 129, 305

poop, 115–117, 259

potential energy, 139, 158, 166

prisms, 160, 306

protons, 319, 326

pulse, 210–211

pupil, 2, 3, 5, 6, 7, 11, 12

puzzles, 78–81

R

rainbows, 160, 187, 303, 306–308, 309, 311, 317

rattlesnakes, 40

red-eye effect, 10

refraction, 306–308

retina, 11, 295

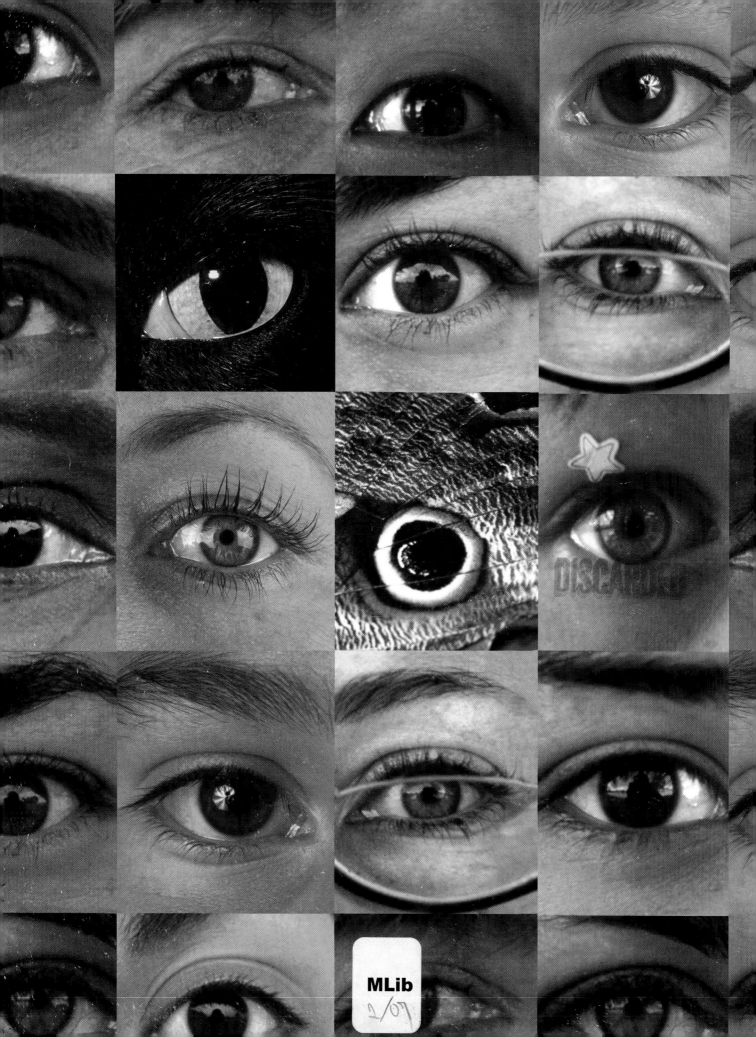